Education and Empowered Citizenship in Mali

Education and Empowered Citizenship in Mali

JAIMIE BLECK

Johns Hopkins University Press

Baltimore

This book has been brought to publication with the generous assistance of the Institute for Scholarship in the Liberal Arts, College of Arts and Letters, University of Notre Dame.

2 4 6 8 9 7 5 3

Johns Hopkins University Press
2715 North Charles Street
Baltimore, Maryland 21218-4363
www.press.jhu.edu

Library of Congress Cataloging-in-Publication Data

Bleck, Jaimie, 1980–
Education and empowered citizenship in Mali / Jaimie Bleck.
pages cm
Includes bibliographical references and index.
ISBN 978-1-4214-1781-3 (paperback) — ISBN 978-1-4214-1782-0
(electronic) — ISBN 1-4214-1781-2 (paperback) — ISBN 1-4214-1782-0
(electronic)   1. Democracy and education—Mali.   2. Education and state—
Mali.   3. Citizenship—Mali.   I. Title.
LC95.M42B54 2015
379.6623—dc23   2014049711

A catalog record for this book is available from the British Library.

Special discounts are available for bulk purchases of this book.
For more information, please contact Special Sales at 410-516-6936 or
specialsales@press.jhu.edu.

Johns Hopkins University Press uses environmentally friendly book materials, including recycled text paper that is composed of at least 30 percent post-consumer waste, whenever possible.

In September 2006, Oumar Diakite and more than 25 other youth activists were killed in a bus accident while returning from a political rally in Gao. I dedicate this book to Oumar—truly a model citizen for the world.

The feasibility of democracy in Africa will depend crucially on how it relates to the social experience of Africans and how far it serves their social needs.

—Claude Ake, *The Feasibility of Democracy in Africa*

CONTENTS

ADEMA	Alliance for Democracy in Mali
AQIM	Al Qaeda in the Islamic Maghreb
ATT	Amadou Toumani Touré
BA	Banconi, Bamako
BC	Bamako Coura, Bamako
F	Faladie, Bamako
HCI	High Council of Islam
IBK	Ibrahim Boubacar Keita
K	Kayes Rive Gauche
KV	Kayes Rive Droite
M	Mopti
MNLA	National Movement for the Liberation of Azawad
NGO	nongovernmental organization
S	Sikasso
SR	Sikasso II
SV	Sévaré
T	Timbuktu
U	university student interview
USAID	US Agency for International Development

I selected education as the lens through which to explore contemporary African politics while working on the USAID-funded African Education Initiative (AEI). From 2004 to 2006, I worked as a program assistant for a project
charged with distributing more than 20,000 primary school scholarships in
15 countries in central and southern Africa. My employer, Winrock International, worked with 20 African NGOs to identify bright, vulnerable girls and
to provide them with uniquely tailored scholarship packages. The scholarships
consisted of whatever it took to keep a girl in school: school fees, pencils, a
uniform, or sometimes a kerosene lamp so she could study at night.

The best part of my job was visiting scholarship recipients and their families. These young women exuded a fearlessness and determination that was
infectious. They were hungry to make the most of their scholarship, to get
an education, and to forge a future for themselves. Many of the girls were
orphans, many of their lives had been touched by HIV/AIDS, and all of them
came from the poorest households in their communities. They were all smart
and driven. I couldn't help but daydream about how a few of these girls might
someday change the future of African governments.

During the three years I worked on the project, I was exposed to a range of
political systems in flux. A decade after third-wave transitions to democracy,
countries and institutions were evolving at different rates: despite regular
elections in Gabon, Omar Bongo still ruled the country as his personal fief-
dom, while other countries, like Mozambique and Namibia, were experiencing their first turnovers in executive power. However, at the village level—in
the context of poverty and local governments' bureaucracy—the distinction
between elected democracies and closed regimes was far less pronounced.

Conversations about social service provision, aggressive tax authorities,
and unaccountable government institutions forced me to reflect on how de-

mocracy and governance actually translate on the quotidian level. How are emerging opportunities for political participation perceived and actualized by citizens? In most of these hybrid regimes, there was a sense that institutions were shifting in the direction of democracy, and citizens were negotiating their own opportunities for political involvement. Village chiefs, former educators, taxi drivers, and homemakers prompted me to think long and hard about what "democracy" means to African citizens. These conversations and my experience with the scholarship program underscored the role of welfare provision in the democratization process.

In all of these countries, I was dumbfounded by the ability of a small public school scholarship to change the trajectory of a girl's life. Parents cared deeply about educational opportunities as a key to both social mobility and empowered citizenship. To many parents and grandparents, the African state seemed far out of reach—an alien institution reserved for the privileged, educated elite. Their hopes and dreams for their daughters and granddaughters culminated in their ability to get an education and, subsequently, navigate and profit from state institutions. The girls, many proudly speaking a bureaucratic language that was unintelligible to their families, radiated a hope that through education anything was possible.

This book and the research it is based on were spurred directly by my experiences talking with young students, their parents, school officials, and government administrators. I highlight how education might contribute to empowered citizenship in democratizing regimes in Africa, and I examine the impact of government efforts and donor initiatives, like AEI, to expand access to citizenship in nascent African democracies.

ACKNOWLEDGMENTS

I am indebted to a large group of individuals who have shared their knowledge and support to make this book possible. First, I thank the hundreds of Malians who took the time to share their wisdom, concerns, and reflections with me. Second, nothing would have been possible without my research team: Amadou Guindo, Seydou Niambele, Djenebou Sogodogo, Elcaid Youba Ould Khalifa, and our stylish driver, Solo Togola. I thank each of you for your unique contributions: Guindo, for your intellectual curiosity and willingness to challenge me; Seydou, for your dedication, precision, and attention to detail; Djenebou, for your fearlessness, inspiration, and poise; and Youba, for your sense of humor, flexibility, and commitment to the team.

Many others made the project possible, including the So family in Kayes, the Ministry of Education, the Territorial Administration, the National Election Commission, Amadou Samake, Mody Boubacar Guindo, Moumouni Soumano, and all of the educators who spoke with me. I also thank my broader network of support in Mali, including my Malian parents, Haoua Cisse and Moussa Sissoko; my in-laws, Sala and Salimata Sidibe; my brothers- and sisters-in-law; Cheblen "Jah" Samake; the Kalabancoura Sports Club; Bintou Traoré; Lala Walet; and my mentor and friend Bara Kassambara. I also want to thank the other expats whose love of Bamako inflamed my own and kept me sane in the 115° heat: Brandon County, Paul Davis, Marie Venner, Jessica Chervin, Owen and Hilary Swearengen, Spencer Orey, David Wong, and Devon Golaszewski.

I also acknowledge a diverse group of mentors and friends on the other side of the Atlantic, who lent their expertise and support to the project. I thank Will Reno and Lee Seymour for teaching me that political scientists are cool. I am forever grateful to my former boss Martha Saldinger for her encouragement and guidance. I benefited from an extremely supportive faculty at Cornell, including David Patel, Peter Enns, Tom Pepinsky, Richard Bensel, and Peter Katzenstein. The non-Africanist members of my dissertation committee, Ken Roberts and Valerie Bunce, improved this book significantly by forcing me to think comparatively. Devra Moehler has been a true role model for me; her consistent guidance throughout all stages of this project was indispensable. Finally, I thank my outstanding mentor, Nicolas van de Walle, who believed in me and my research from the very start. With humor, humility, and wisdom, he has guided my transformation into a political scientist.

At Cornell I had the most supportive grad school cohort one could ever imagine. I give particular thanks to Julie Ajinkya, Phil Ayoub, Benjamin Brake, Simon Cotton, Janice Gallagher, Simon Gilhooley, Onur Ulas Ince, Desmond Jagamond, Don Leonard, Igor Logvinenko, Michael Miller, Danielle Resnick, Deondra Rose, Tariq Thachil, Pablo Yanguas, and Chris Zepeda. I thank the American Political Science Association (APSA) and the participants at the APSA Africa Conference, the Contemporary African Political Economy Research Seminar, and the African Studies Association conferences as well as the faculty at the Kellogg Institute at Notre Dame and Cornell's Institute for African Development for valuable feedback. I must single out Kristin Michelitch, Keith Weghorst, Kevin Fridy, El Hassen Ould Ahmed, Dan Smith, Emeka Okerere, AbdoulKarim Saidou, Staffan Lindberg, Leonardo Villalón, Peter VonDoepp, Jessica Gottlieb, Adam Auerbach, Abdoulaye Dembele, and David Stasavage for their constructive comments. Finally, I thank my colleagues at Notre Dame for feedback on the manuscript: Nara Pavao, Guillermo Trejo, Sarah Daly, Scott Mainwaring, and Sean McGraw. I also thank Jessica Peck, Liana Cramer, and Jae Won Kim for their excellent research assistance.

This book was made possible with the generous support of a Boren Fellowship, the Institute for Social Sciences, and the Judith Reppy Institute for Peace and Conflict Studies at Cornell University, as well as the Institute for Scholarship in the Liberal Arts, the Helen Kellogg Institute for International Studies, and the College of Arts and Letters at the University of Notre Dame. Chapter 3 draws on materials from a 2013 article co-authored with Boubacar Mody Guindo, "Education for All, Education for Whom, Education for What? Lessons from Mali," *Development in Practice* 23(8):1004–1017. Portions of Chapter 5 were previously published in 2013 as "Do Francophone and Islamic Schooling Communities Participate Differently: Disaggregating Parents' Political Behaviour in Mali," *Journal of Modern African Studies* 51(3):377–408.

To my rock star brother, Zander, and our parents, Tom and Doreen, thanks for encouraging me to do what I thought was interesting, for tolerating and appreciating my adventures, for supporting me unconditionally, and for always pushing me to be better. Last, to my *che*, Idrissa: thank you for challenging me to be a stronger, smarter, and more empathetic person every day. I am excited to be your *apprendike* as our journey continues.

Education and Empowered Citizenship in Mali

CHAPTER ONE

Introduction

The transitions to democracy that enveloped sub-Saharan Africa in the 1990s have been accompanied by dramatic increases in school enrollment. Since then, newly elected governments have expanded access to primary education at historically unprecedented rates. Elections afforded African citizens a new political space in which to voice their own policy priorities. Many African constituencies seized these democratic opportunities to demand greater access to education for their children. Elected leaders responded with the elimination of school fees and the construction of new schools (Harding and Stasavage 2014; Stasavage 2005). School expansion, particularly at the primary level, is arguably the most powerful domestic policy change in the majority of African countries since the transitions to democracy began.

African gross primary school enrollment increased by 48% between 2000 and 2008; pre-primary, secondary, and tertiary enrollment increased by more than 60% in the same period (UNESCO Institute of Statistics 2011). Fueled by the Millennium Development Goals and the Education for All campaign, donor aid to education in Africa doubled between 2000 and 2004, rising from US$1.8 billion to US$3.4 billion (*Education for All* 2007:2). In order to reach enrollment targets, governments allocated scarce resources to public education. Most African countries averaged 6% increases in education spending every year during the first decade of the twenty-first century (UNESCO Institute of Statistics 2011). Governments liberalized education sectors and partnered with private schools, including Islamic schools, as an additional strategy to increase the number of students counted toward gross enrollment (Rose 2006; Rose and Akyeampong 2005; Villalón, Idrissa, and Bodian 2012). Many governments slashed primary school fees; they capitalized on debt relief to further fund basic education.

While the quality of schooling during this expansion has been critiqued and debated, the implications of these policy changes for democratic citizenship are striking. An unprecedented number of African children are now able to attend school. They sit in classrooms with peers from other ethnic groups, pledge allegiance to a common flag, and learn the bureaucratic language of the state. Equally important, many parents are receiving a tangible service from the state for the first time. Most African countries and international donors did not articulate educational expansion as a strategy to improve democratic citizenship, but rather as a way to improve human development. However, the rich theoretical literature on education and democratization suggests that this policy could generate positive results for democracy and citizenship.

Despite these sweeping societal changes, scholars have not yet explored their implication for citizenship in Africa. This book aims to fill that analytical void by bridging the comparative literature on schooling and citizenship with the literature on the political economy of development and social welfare provision. Existing scholarship suggests that education can play an important role in generating knowledge and participation among students, but it also fosters parents' engagement by exposing them to a state-sponsored welfare service through a policy feedback effect. What impact does education have on students' knowledge of and engagement with politics in the multiparty era? How does the receipt of schooling for a child affect parents' participation in politics? The liberalization of the education sector presents additional questions about the effects of different types of schooling: public, private, secular, and religious. Do all types of school generate the same levels of political knowledge and engagement?

In this book I examine the relationship between schooling provision, political knowledge, and political participation in Mali. The educational expansion there is emblematic of the wider continental trend, but the increases in enrollment in Mali were among the highest in Africa. Twenty years after the first democratic transition in 1991, the Malian primary school gross enrollment rate had jumped from 26% to over 82%. Additionally, Mali is a Muslim-majority country, and education providers are diverse. As a strategy to increase enrollment, the Malian government opened up its education sector to for-profit providers, including NGO-run community schools, Christian schools, secular Francophone schools, and madrassas[1]—modern, Arabic-language, religious education providers. During the 2006–2007 school year, approximately 38% of Malian primary students attended non-public schools. The increase in enrollment and the variety of citizens' educational experiences—secular, Islamic, public, and private—provide fertile ground to test the effects of education on citizenship in nascent African democracies with liberalized education sectors.

In this book I ask two sets of questions to explore the impact of the educational expansion. The first series of questions concerns the effect of education on students. *How does attending school shape citizens' capacity and willingness to engage in politics?* Given the diversity of educational providers in sub-Saharan Africa, a related question asks if different schooling trajectories generate similar types of knowledge and engagement. *Do all schooling experiences shape students' political knowledge and engagement in the same way?* Second, I examine schooling provision's effect on parents. Education is important not only as an instructional experience for the pupil; it is also representative of the broader welfare capacity of the state. *What is the impact of a child's education on parents' political engagement? How does exposure to different types of schooling communities affect parents' political behavior?*

Traditionally, education has been an important tool for regimes to socialize citizens and build nation-state allegiance. As African states seek to consolidate power and gain relevance in citizens' lives, state schooling offers a way to reorient citizens' identities and actions away from traditional or religious leaders and toward bureaucratic and elected authorities. In the wake of the founding elections that marked the transitions to democracy, the experience of schooling has become doubly important because it can provide individual citizens with the skills to evaluate political information and to engage with the state. Political science literature typically assumes that these skills enable citizens to engage with both elected and bureaucratic institutions.

However, in emerging democracies, citizens are often confronted by weak, underfinanced, and poorly performing states. It is possible that in environments of fragile or imperfect institutions, educated, empowered citizens might be more critical of regimes than their uneducated peers are. One might observe that in environments of extreme institutional underperformance, rather than fostering engagement, education could promote a withdrawal from electoral politics. There is an additional threat that education might disrupt productive, traditional channels of political mobilization. Western education might awaken in pupils an individualist spirit, which could conflict with the communitarian organization of the larger society.[2] With sights on their own personal mobility, students might be less invested in associational or group membership and therefore be less willing to participate in traditional channels of mobilization for group grievances. Education could fragment traditional venues of interest aggregation.

It is also important to examine diverse schooling providers—public, private, secular, and religious—and ask if all types of schooling affect citizenship equally. Education is not a monolithic force. Its ability to shape citizens is related to its content, the political authority behind the provision, and its distribution across society. Citizens obtain varying levels of education, which could generate distinct citizenship outcomes. A primary education and a university education are different in terms of the skills that they provide to students, the comparative advantage they generate vis-à-vis other citizens, and also the time spent socializing in and out of classrooms. A university-educated Malian student is ostensibly fluent in French, has spent time in the capital city where the University of Bamako is located, and has interacted with peers from all over the country. A citizen who completed sixth grade in a rural public school in Sikasso has probably not achieved the same fluency in the bureaucratic language nor had the opportunity to interact with such a diverse group of Malian citizens.

Similarly, we might not expect an education in public, Francophone, secular schools to generate the same political behavior as Arabic language instruction in Islamic schools. Education providers in the same country can use different languages of instruction and can vary on whether they contain religious content, which might affect the skills students acquire and the communities to which they are connected. Non-state providers, by bolstering weak state capacity, might contribute to an overall increase in human capital, empower citizens, and incite engagement with the state. Conversely, citizens' involvement with non-state providers might have political ramifications that pull them away from engagement with the state (Cammett and MacLean 2011, 2014). The tenuous circumstances of Islamic schooling communities—which have often been suppressed, co-opted, or marginalized by colonial and post-independence governments in many Muslim-majority African states—raise specific questions about the effects of Islamic schooling on student behavior when compared to the effects of secular schooling on citizens who associate with other educational tracks.

The second set of questions examines the impact of schooling on parents. An older political science literature chronicles colonial and postcolonial regimes' chronic underperformance as service providers, which undercuts their legitimacy in the eyes of most citizens (see Ake 1996, 2000; Ekeh 1972; Mamdani 1996). However, given the state's efforts to provide a larger community of citizens with opportunities for schooling, the policy feedback literature suggests that the expansion of access to education could foster citizens' engagement with the state. Increases in state welfare provision could also generate legitimacy and relevance for governments.

The liberalization of the education sector and a widespread belief in the poor quality of public education complicate the expectation that state provision will automatically stimulate political participation. If public education is evaluated as inferior to private education, citizens may make harsh comparative judgments, and this could cultivate negative assessments of the state. Additionally, different providers are connected to the diverse loci of traditional, religious, and non-state authorities. Historically, states are not the only actors to use education for state-building. Religious, rebel, and political actors have also proved their ability to harness legitimacy and allegiance through social service provision. Non-state schooling might draw citizens into political engagement mediated by non-state forms of authority rather than by elected or bureaucratic authorities.

Mali's turbulent political trajectory has increased the urgency of understanding the relationships among education, citizenship, and political authority. In 2012, junior officers staged a coup d'état in response to the state's mismanagement of a burgeoning rebellion in the north of the country. It removed Mali's democratically elected president, Amadou Toumani Touré, only one month prior to what would have been Mali's fifth presidential election and third executive turnover. Shortly thereafter, the political uncertainty in Bamako allowed rebel groups to seize the three northern regions of the country. After a year and a half of political uncertainty and the state's near-collapse, the country held a presidential election to usher Mali back into an era of "democracy."

The data presented in this book were collected during President Touré's second term—in the summer after he was first reelected in 2007—and over the course of 2009, approximately three years before the rebellion and the coup d'état removed him from office. The research provides insight into how Malians were experiencing democracy during the years prior to the coup. I draw on a diverse body of evidence, including an original "immersive" survey of 1,000 Malian citizens in the Bamako, Kayes, Sikasso, Timbuktu, and Mopti regions; interviews with more than 50 education professionals; and an exit poll of 450 people during the municipal elections in Bamako.

It remains to be seen how the tremors of political crisis will affect Malian democracy moving forward. While the arguments of this book are based on research conducted prior to the coup, the themes and trends inform Mali's current situation. How can the current government close the democratic

deficit that existed in Mali prior to the coup? How can government actors foster allegiance and channel participation toward the state? Do some Muslim
actors continue to feel marginalized from democratic participation? What
role can education play in building citizenship? In this book I offer evidence
of the relationship between citizens and the state as seen by Malians. I also
demonstrate the ways that education provision, one primary channel of state
policy making, might slowly improve citizenship and consolidate democratic
governance over time.

Why Citizenship Matters for Democracy

More than 20 years after the third wave of democracy swept over the continent, the vast majority of sub-Saharan African states hold regular elections,
but democratic progress has been inconsistent. The quality of democracy and
governance in most countries is still hotly debated. While some countries
have witnessed an expansion of civil freedoms and watched sitting presidents
step down, others have slid back into cycles of violence and extrajudicial
power grabs. As the case of Mali highlights, 20 years of electoral experience
does not ensure that democratic institutions consolidate and become more
responsive to citizen demands.

In this book I focus away from this political turbulence to look at citizens' relationship to the state.[3] I problematize two aspects of citizenship that
plague contemporary procedural democracies. First, I emphasize the importance of empowered democratic agents as a necessary condition for democracy. Following Amartya Sen (1999), I define *empowered democratic agents*
as citizens who are knowledgeable about the political system, the range of
potential political choices, and the avenues for expression in democratic institutions.[4] Second, I discuss the challenge of orienting citizens' engagement
toward the state rather than toward competing forms of authority. These distinct concepts—empowerment and engagement with the state—need not be
linked. Empowered engagement can be directed toward traditional leaders,
religious authorities, or regional brokers. In weak states where democracy
is not consolidated, non-state authorities are often more responsive and accountable than the state is. However, from the perspective of state-building
or democratic accountability, citizen engagement is critical for institutional
growth and democratic consolidation.

Since I seek to move past minimalist definitions of democracy and to evaluate "participatory" or "egalitarian" democracies (Coppedge et al. 2010), I

must investigate whether ordinary citizens participate in politics and the range and scope of citizens' participation in government channels. The strength of citizens' engagement with state institutions is a central determinant of the accountable and responsive governance that characterizes consolidated democracies (Bunce and Wolchik 2007; Ippolito-O'Donnell 2006; O'Donnell 2010).[5] In the words of Albert Hirschman (1970), this expression of citizen "voice" is necessary in order to keep states from "falling into cycles of slack."[6] This participation can take a multitude of forms, varying from political participation—such as voting, contact with representatives, or running for office oneself—to involvement in contentious politics, such as protests, strikes, and boycotts. The question of citizens' relationship with the state is important not only to understanding more equitable and inclusive representation, but also to understanding the very nature of democratic governance and institutions.

Many African democracies and semi-democracies lack dialogue between citizens and democratic institutions. In his seminal study of African political economies, van de Walle (2001) concludes that weak governments are allowed to underperform precisely because of the lack of pressure from citizens and civil society on these institutions. In the absence of a strong state, citizens develop mechanisms of self-reliance, including kinship and familial networks, religious communities, affiliation with patrons, and other types of associations. As Claude Ake (2000:47) describes it, associational (non-state) life can be understood as "booming from the vanishing legitimacy of the state, and the withdrawal of identity and loyalty, fear and suspicion and even hostility." Rather than imagining a de facto loyalty to the state, an allegiance to and engagement with the African state needs to be constructed.

While state illegitimacy threatens any constellation of governance, the consequences are particularly dire for fledgling democracies. In his depiction of minority communities in the United States, Sen (1999:155) warns that non-participation or non-engagement with the state can lead to a lack of representation:

> Democracy has to be seen as creating a set of opportunities, and the use of these opportunities calls for the analysis of a different kind, dealing with the practice of democratic and political rights. In this respect, the low percentage of voting in American elections, especially by African Americans, and other signs of apathy and alienation, cannot be ignored. Democracy does not serve as an automatic remedy of ailments as quinine works to remedy malaria. The opportunity it opens up has to be positively grabbed in order to achieve the desired effect.

Passive exit threatens the representativeness of democracy for those communities that disengage. If passive exit happens on a large scale, and the majority of citizens withdraw from politics, it threatens the very nature of the nascent democratic institution.

Obstacles to Democratic Agency

African states continue to populate 27 of the 30 lowest rankings on the United Nations' Human Development Index.[7] In many countries, the limited bureaucratic capacity of the state and the tremendous daily challenges facing citizens beg for an exploration of how human development affects opportunities for political expression. Since many African democracies have low levels of development that might constrain citizens' rights and capabilities, the autonomy and freedom of political action cannot be assumed. The distinction between meaningful, informed participation and mobilized or coerced participation becomes critical. Even though informed participation might not be sufficient to reform stubborn or nonresponsive institutions, it is a necessary condition for change to take place. Throughout democratic history, education has been a systematic tool for states to increase citizens' capabilities to evaluate and engage with institutions. While nascent regimes may be uninterested or unable to endow citizens with the skills or information they need for political engagement, the educational expansion, pushed by donors and parents alike, might make these transformations more likely.

As outlined by Dahl in the first pages of *Polyarchy* (1971:2), democratic institutions will only be responsive to citizens' needs and desires if citizens "formulate their preferences" and "signify their preferences to their fellow citizens and the government by individual and collective action." However, all political acts do not automatically translate into the expression of political voice. Perverse incentives for political engagement in procedural democracy complicate the meaning of participation in many democratic countries in sub-Saharan Africa. While the magnitude of these imperfections in African elections is debated, most researchers acknowledge the widespread role of short-term incentives on election day. The ubiquitous presence of political brokers, who distribute cash or gifts in exchange for a vote, problematizes the conceptualization of all political behavior as constructive for democratic institutions.

Campaign swag in Africa surpasses pens, stickers, and buttons; many voters expect T-shirts or, in rural areas, salt or sugar as a prerequisite for party visits to villages. In some instances, these types of gift are merely part of appropriate protocol. A candidate cannot come to a village to plead his case without offering some gesture of his benevolence, but accepting a gift does not constrain a citizen's ability to vote based on alternative programmatic criteria (Lindberg 2013). The distribution becomes symbolic of a candidate's generosity and his awareness of rural-dwellers' plight (Jourde 2005). However, in other instances, gifts and favors for voting are directly or indirectly tied to a candidate's performance at the ballot box. Whether vote monitoring, coercion, or convincing the population that they are being monitored, short-term incentives disconnect the political act from the policy outcome (Collier and Vicente 2012).

In this environment, some citizens who are observed to be participating might not actually have the capabilities or rights necessary for autonomous political engagement (O'Donnell 2004:27). Before turning to the question of participation, we therefore must understand citizens' transformation into democratic agents. Even though their behavior might look identical, those citizens with knowledge of the political terrain who have their own political preferences are qualitatively different from those citizens who vote because of a political broker's request. Democratic agents must have a level of awareness that "motivates their desire to acquire and process information" (Mattes and Shenga 2007:20). We can distinguish between democratic agents and those who express "allegiant" participation (Shingles 1981)—due to unreflective trust of authority, in an attempt to "show loyalty to more powerful actors"—or citizens who are co-opted or coerced into particular forms of participation.

In addition, many democratic societies are hierarchical and characterized by vertical networks of civil society where politicians are dependent on patrons or brokers to reach voting blocs (Beck 2008; Koter 2013; Villalón 1995). If citizens cast their vote as instructed by a patron, family member, or electoral entrepreneur, or if they claim allegiance to a party without knowing the competing candidates or the consequences of their vote, then one cannot claim that these citizens are imprinting their own preferences on the state through the exercise of political voice. In many instances, mediators or brokers can be constructive conduits that link citizens to institutions and welfare programs or offer heuristics in an environment of scarce information (Baldwin 2013; Krishna 2002; Lerner 1958). While this type of assistance aids citizens in expressing their political voice in the short term, it is problematic because it obstructs the personal link between citizens and democratic institutions. When brokers mediate the relationships between citizens and the state, they keep citizens an arm's length from institutions. Rather than gaining familiarity with the electoral process during their own experience with it, those citizens who rely on mediators might remain alienated and afraid of state institutions. Further, those mediators, including political parties and other brokers, might capitalize on state welfare provision to entrench their own political power (Fox 1994).

Another concern is that one cannot be sure that this kind of interest aggregation captures citizens' true preferences. Unlike horizontal institutions, brokerage relationships are by nature hierarchical and sometimes fused by traditional or family bonds, which can be unquestioned and embraced reflexively (Hydén 2006). While any interest group claiming to speak for all members risks marginalizing or suppressing individual voices, those organizations claiming to represent the "authentic voice" consistently hide or misrepresent the preferences of some for the continuity of the group narrative (Benhabib 2002; Young 2012).

Empirically, it is very difficult to determine which citizens are empowered and which are passively mobilized. One key and measurable attribute of democratic agents is their political knowledge. Knowledge creates the foundation for all participation. Knowledge need not entail memorization of party manifestos or the electoral codebook. In systems where the informal rules weigh as heavily as what is inscribed in legal texts, the memorization of idiosyncratic constitutional regulations may be irrelevant. In these contexts, the significant knowledge could include the ability to use proxies to make guesses about the political system. At a minimum, democratic agents should know the basic rules of the game and the basic actors involved: who is running, who is in power, and what the limitations are to power within the electoral system.

By measuring citizens' knowledge one can arrive at a proxy for their level of political empowerment. But knowledge is insufficient for political empowerment, which might also require increased internal efficacy. Following Pollock (1983), I define *internal efficacy* as citizens' assessment of their own competence as political actors. While counting politically knowledgeable citizens as empowered democratic agents risks overstating their level of political empowerment, one can use the assessment of knowledge to get at the initial variation between citizens who are mobilized into political action and those who interact with politics in a measured, knowledgeable way.

In this book I use four measures to assess citizens' knowledge. Three questions measure citizens' ability to name different actors and parties (the mayor, the president of the National Assembly, and the majority party in the National Assembly). The fourth measure is a rules-of-the-game question: do citizens know the executive term limits? This question was particularly relevant in Mali in 2009 because the sitting president was completing his second and final term in power and because President Mamadou Tandja, in neighboring Niger, had just attempted to alter term limits.

Efficacy, Participation, and Underperforming Regimes

Afrobarometer data show that 62% of Africans feel that their voices are not heard between election cycles (Logan 2010:25). The problem of short-term incentives is compounded by widespread belief that the state will do little to respond to citizens. The perception is that as soon as the votes are cast, government officials recede back into their comfortable government offices with little concern for their constituencies' needs. When this perception of low external efficacy is widespread, citizens are less sure that their participation will count. I use Pollock's (1983:403) definition of *low external efficacy* as a system of governance that individuals perceive as unresponsive to popular demands. These environments may foster feelings of helplessness or apathy. Citizens may become disillusioned or uninterested in trying to link political behavior to policy outcomes. Decades of poor state performance could make many citizens question the utility of the state (Bratton 1989). Citizens could withdraw to the protection of local barons, religious authorities, or extended family networks without making further demands on the state. This exit from institutional channels is emblematic of the problem of orienting citizens' engagement toward the state.

Literature on US politics suggests that high levels of internal efficacy can buoy specific types of participation even in environments of extreme skepticism about institutional responsiveness (see Craig 1980; Craig and Maggiotto 1982; Fraser 1970). These increases in internal efficacy will not uniformly stimulate political participation, however. Confident citizens in these contexts are more likely to engage in high-initiative or contentious behavior (Pollock 1983). *High-initiative participation*—synonymous with what Nie and colleagues (1996) refer to as "difficult" participation—includes acts such as campaigning, running for office, and contacting a government official, which require greater skill regardless of the incentives offered. Contentious behavior includes protests, boycotts, and other non-institutional forms of participation aimed at influencing government policy.[8] In contrast, high levels of internal efficacy are not typically associated with "easy political behavior," such as voting or identifying with a party.

In environments where citizens are skeptical about state responsiveness, varying levels of internal efficacy can generate distinct and nonlinear patterns of political participation. In other words, not all political acts will be correlated. Some actors might eschew mass forms of participation, which are viewed as less efficient or plagued by corrupt processes, for more intimate exchanges with state officials. Conversely, some actors might be willing to leave their thumbprint at the polls, but they are intimidated to approach state authority directly. As mentioned above, imperfect institutional conditions tend to incentivize certain types of participation among empowered citizens, including high-initiative and contentious behavior, over more institutional, formal ways of engaging, such as voting or joining a party.

Possibilities for Empowered Engagement with the State

There are many channels through which citizens could gain information to prepare for informed engagement. Rather than predicting which channel will be the most effective in transforming subjects into informed citizens, I focus exclusively on the role of education. How does education affect empowered democratic citizenship and engagement? In doing so, I do not claim that education is a panacea for political empowerment, nor do I question the utility of other forms of outreach and empowerment. Basing my work on an extensive literature in the field of US politics and an emerging literature in comparative politics, I seek to understand the relationship between education and informed, participatory citizenship.

I do not claim that education is the only pathway to informed citizenship. Membership in an organization or association could help direct citizens toward political information that is relevant to their interest group. Political parties, for instance, are conduits of information about the electoral process as well as information, albeit biased, about the field of competitors. In his study of Tanzania in the 1960s, Göran Hydén (2006) finds that many remote villagers were extremely well informed about the political processes and players because of tremendous party outreach. Party outreach and competition also generate information about electoral processes or democratic institutions more generally.

Citizens could also gather information through other associational channels. For instance, in Mozambique Mattes and Shenga (2007) find that those citizens who most frequently seek out religious leaders to help them solve important problems are more likely to support democracy, to demand democracy, and to be critical of political performance. Labor organizations in countries like Zambia have played a tremendous role in backing political parties, but also in protesting political parties' positions. In Uganda, evangelical churches have been active in championing anti-gay legislation (Grossman 2015).

Additionally, the expansion of mass media—including radio and television liberalization—has made information about electoral processes more widely available (see, for example, Moehler and Singh 2011). Many Malians rely on community or private radio and participate in lively debates on local call-in shows (Tower 2008). Studies have shown that exposure to mass media is positively correlated with political knowledge (e.g., Mattes and Shenga 2007). Internet and cell phone availability, which has grown dramatically in the twenty first century, enables connected users to crowd-source information. As demonstrated by the Arab Spring of 2011, but also through African-born innovations, such as the Ushahidi platform, this technology has a dramatic potential to shape political participation and electoral accountability (Mäkinen and Wangu Kuira 2008).

As early modernization theorists argued, migration to urban zones is also expected to expose citizens to more political information (Lipset 1959; Deutsch 1961; Deutsch and Foltz 1966). In the capital city, citizens are closer to the central government, and it is cheaper for candidates and parties to contact them. Furthermore, in urban zones citizens are more likely to join multiple associations and networks. Greater population density ensures that citizens are in contact with people of varying perspectives and with different nodes of information. Similarly, travel can often serve to expand the range of actions and situations that citizens are exposed to. Through travel, citizens can expand their linguistic repertoire and their comparative vantage point to analyze the politics of different regions, villages, and towns.[9]

Participation in the political process itself can also generate informed citizenship. Lindberg (2006) argues that elections are conduits of information, and participation in them sensitizes citizens to the goals of the democratic system. Moehler (2008) notes that citizens who participated in Uganda's constitutional reform became more discerning democratic consumers and tended to be more critical of the performance of local government.

As these examples demonstrate, there are many transformative pathways through which citizens could gain knowledge, which in turn prepares them for informed participation. However, given the theorized importance of education in cross-national studies of participation and the fact that education policy offers the state a tool to systematically empower citizens, in the rest of the book I focus exclusively on the relationship between education and citizenship in African democracies.

Education Fostering Knowledge and Participation in Nascent Democracies: Limits and Possibilities

An extensive literature on US politics explains that education is key to creating loyal, democratic citizens. Twentieth-century theorists of democracy understand school to be a critical tool for socializing future citizens and teaching them how to participate in democracy. In *The Civic Culture*, Almond and Verba (1963:317–318) provide a long list of practical reasons that educated citizens are better democratic consumers. Educated citizens consume and disseminate political education to and from a broader range of sources, they are more aware of politics, they have greater internal and external efficacy, they are more likely to be members of organizations, and they are more confident in their social environment. Education is thought to play a constitutive role in transforming "subjects into critical citizens" through the process of democratic enlightenment (Nie, Junn, and Stehlik-Barry 1996, Norris 1999). It is almost undisputed that education fosters political participation in the Western context. Scholars of US democracy show that higher levels of education are consistently associated with higher levels of political participation even when the researchers control for other socioeconomic factors (Converse 1972; Rosenstone and Hansen 1993; Verba, Schlozman, and Brady 1995).

However, educational expansion in recent African democracies challenges some of the assumptions that these scholars make about the relationship between education and engaged citizenship. First, the current expansion of access to education has brought with it questions about state school quality and the content of what is being taught. Since the 1990s, regimes have been typically more concerned with building schools and eliminating barriers to enrollment than with reforming curriculum or pedagogy. Ideally, democratic regimes would transmit civic content inside the classroom. This content might include an explicit civics curriculum (Campbell 2006; Finkel and Smith 2011) or the transmission of liberal democratic values (Dahl 1967), or it might work indirectly through history and geography courses that expose students to the structure and importance of government (Weber 1976). However, if African regimes do not invest in this type of content or are plagued by a weak execution of this curriculum, one cannot be certain that citizens will be socialized appropriately.

Second, as mentioned earlier, citizens often operate in an environment of underperforming institutions. One cannot be sure that higher education will automatically spur appreciation of or participation in the regime. Although educated citizens might be more supportive of the theoretical idea of democracy, it is not evident that they would provide "specific support" to poorly functioning institutions.[10] It would be naïve to assume that educated citizens would reward underperforming institutions with loyalty or unqualified support. Previous analyses of Afrobarometer data do not demonstrate a clear, direct relationship between education and political participation.[11] Other evidence suggests that uneducated citizens might be more likely to succumb to vote buying (Kramon 2010), more likely to be coerced into support for the ruling regime, and less likely to offer criticism of the government (McCauley and Gyimah-Boadi 2009). Political entrepreneurs may be less likely to target those in highly educated neighborhoods for mobilization (Isaksson, Kotsadam, and Nerman 2014). The relationship between education and voting in systems characterized by vote buying, mobilized turnout, or short-term incentives for participation could actually be negatively correlated.[12]

However, certain mechanisms that link education and citizenship in the US context hold, and are even magnified, in nascent democracies in sub-Saharan Africa. Education can impart general skills, distinct from any specific curriculum, such as bolstering citizens' verbal cognitive capacity, increasing citizens' ability to harness more information from the outside world, and lowering the informational costs associated with political action (Dalton 2007, Nie, Junn, and Stehlik-Barry 1996; Neuman, Just, and Crigler 1992). These skills aid citizens in obtaining objective information from multiple sources and expressing preferences. Access to diverse sources of information enables citizens to fact-check with multiple sources and makes them less vulnerable to threats and incentives offered by political entrepreneurs. Given the lower levels of political information and the higher political uncertainty in the African context, these skills could prove even more important than they do in an information-saturated political context.

There is evidence that education is associated with greater political knowledge. Mattes and Mughogho (2009) draw on cross-national Afrobarometer data to demonstrate that better educated citizens make greater use of available media and are more informed. In her study of slum-dwellers in Senegal, Resnick (2010:64) finds that attending school is positively and significantly correlated to a respondent's ability to describe the opposition's development plan, Assises Nationales. Robert Mattes and Carlos Shenga (2007) argue that better educated citizens as well as those who use news media more frequently are more likely to offer political opinions in Mozambique.

In many countries in Africa, education has an accelerated effect on verbal cognitive proficiency because it eliminates an obstacle that plagues most citizens: the government speaks a language that is not their own. At independence most African states adopted the language of their former colonizers (Albaugh 2007; Laitin 1992). Even today, successful politicians generally have to demonstrate dexterity in the former colonial language (Bleck and van de Walle 2011; Ekeh 1975). For instance, in the Sahel, where politics is associated with a French-speaking, secular elite (Villalón 2010), those with French-language skills have a comparative advantage because of their ability to understand and interpret the workings of politics and government. For the general public, literacy in the colonial language enables citizens to listen to the nightly news broadcast or televised debates and communicate with members of different linguistic groups (Laitin 1998).

Education demystifies the new forms of bureaucratic authority and gives citizens the skills to understand and participate in this new arena of power. Schooling provides these skills to entire families; literature from the United States demonstrates how children of recent immigrants that learn the state language at school are able to mediate interactions and engagements between their parents, siblings, neighbors, and the state (see Bloemraad and Trost 2008; Weisskirch and Alva 2002). This phenomenon stretches beyond Africa into much of the postcolonial world in countries where a large percentage of the population is not fluent in the language of the bureaucracy. For example, Krishna's (2002) study of educated brokers in Indian villages highlights their investment in learning bureaucratic procedures and understanding government as a way to secure an income from less educated peers.

The comparative value of a degree is also higher in contexts where the mean rate of schooling is comparably low. Attending a university or secondary school distinguishes learners from the majority of the population in countries like Mali, where the mean school attendance is only two years. Nie and colleagues (1996) argue that education inserts citizens into politically relevant centralized networks, which enables them to participate in more "difficult" political activities, such as contacting representatives, campaigning, and participating in community organization. Networks of African elites, who were educated in the same primary schools, illustrate the role of education in building connections across a distinct political class (Sabatier 1978:266). Education endows citizens with connections and resources to invest in politics as well as the credentials to be "heard." These skills and connections bolster citizens' own sense of internal efficacy (i.e., citizens' belief in their own competence as political actors).

While education and participation do not appear to constitute a linear relationship, there is evidence that education can spur some forms of participation, particularly in the difficult or contentious channels. Dalton (2008) argues that as educated citizens transition to "engaged" citizenship from partisan, "duty-based citizenship," they are more likely to take part in these direct, contentious forms of participation. Education increases internal efficacy, which in turn fosters high-initiative or contentious participation in environments of low external efficacy (Craig 1980; Fraser 1970; Shingles 1981). These theories challenge expectations that education will uniformly increase political participation.

Consistent with the theorized relationship between education and different types of participation, analyses of cross-national Afrobarometer data show that education has no discernible effect on voting, but it has a large and significant positive effect on participation between electoral cycles, such as attending a community meeting, contacting an official, or joining an association (Isaksson 2013; MacLean 2011; Mattes and Mughogho 2009). The same data demonstrate that educated citizens also are more critical of political authorities, are more likely to offer opinions, are able to define democracy, and can provide political preferences (Mattes and Mughogho 2009). These findings suggest that education generates informed, empowered citizens rather than nonreflective, allegiant participation. There is some evidence that suggests even informal education can shape empowered engagement. Michelle Kuenzi (2006:5) demonstrates that in rural Senegal experience with informal education—literacy and numeracy classes—has a strong positive impact on political participation and community participation by increasing citizens' self-esteem, civic skills, and community solidarity.

The Impact of Education on Political Engagement through Broader Welfare Effects

Education plays a pivotal role in creating loyalty and credibility for the government, which bonds citizens to formal channels of political expression. While governing regimes in established democracies do not compete with alternative hierarchical authorities, nascent democracies are charged with a simultaneous task of state-building. In Europe, education provision played a vital role in the early years of state-building by establishing legitimacy, encouraging citizen support, and fostering civic virtue and nationalism (Anderson 1983; Gellner 1983; Hobsbawm 1990; Laitin 1977, 1998; Weber 1976). Eric Hobsbawm writes in *Nations and Nationalism Since 1780*: "Naturally states would use the increasingly powerful machinery for communicating with their inhabitants, above all the primary schools, to spread the image and heritage of 'nation' and to inculcate attachment to it and to attach all to country and flag, often 'inventing traditions' or even nations for this purpose" (1990:92). Many countries in Africa are still working to pave roads; provide electricity, water, and sanitation services; and build schools and health centers that reach rural populations or slum-dwellers in urban zones. In this context, the goal of allegiance building is particularly important since the provision of primary school education, along with other verifiable outputs, such as health services and infrastructure, represent a way for governments to connect with voters in rural areas (Harding and Stasavage 2014). If citizens are without tangible evidence of their governments, it is more difficult for them to recognize the government's capabilities. In weak or low infrastructure states in sub-Saharan Africa, public education spreads a sense of national unity for learners, but education provision also gives the government credibility and an increased ability to monitor populations. Politicians can use education, as well as other types of social services, to flaunt their authority.

In the US context, studies have shown that social service programs have the ability to shape political behavior through a policy feedback mechanism. For instance, Campbell (2003) has demonstrated how the government's provision of Social Security has shaped an active constituency of "über-citizens" out of the nation's once marginalized senior citizens. Mettler (2005) shows that the GI Bill similarly created more politically active citizens who felt capable and empowered. Fox (1994) chronicles Mexican president Carlos Salinas's use of decentralized service provision to reestablish the nation's credibility and to build direct support for the central government instead of local party bosses. More recent work in Brazil and Mexico highlights how conditional cash transfer programs have raised voter turnout and support of the incumbent (De La O 2013; Zucco 2011). While these studies focus on the role of welfare in increasing support for a specific regime or candidate, an emerging literature suggests that radical changes in welfare policy could impact citizens' identity as well as their perception of the legitimacy of the state (Cammett and MacLean 2011, 2014).

Given scant government services in many rural areas in sub-Saharan Africa, the provision of welfare services, such as schooling, is likely to be very visible to citizens. A brand-new public school in a village might be rural-dwellers' first real introduction to positive citizenship rights provided by the state. In the only study to look at policy feedback effects in sub-Saharan Africa, Lauren MacLean (2011) demonstrates that citizens in Ghana and Côte d'Ivoire who have contact with either public schools or public health clinics are more likely than citizens who did not have this contact to vote, contact political leaders, attend community meetings, join with others to make their voices heard, and protest. Those citizens who had no experience with public schools or clinics used non-state channels of representation more frequently (ibid.:25). These findings suggest that politicians could build credibility for the state and also induce citizens who receive services to engage with them. This includes not only children who attend schools, but also the parents who benefit from their children's education.

The Question of Non-State Educational Providers

The liberalization of the education market raises additional questions about the distinct effects of different types of schooling on political knowledge and political engagement. We do not yet understand the role and impact of non-state providers on democratic participation, especially in the context of relatively weak states. Non-state education providers include different content than what is offered in public schools, and some schools use a language of pedagogy different from that of the bureaucracy; in other words, non-state schools might develop different skills for learners. Non-state schools are also often tied to different types of political authority, which might compete with the state. In a worst-case scenario, non-state schools could divide citizens, foster parochial attitudes, undermine state legitimacy, and remove one of—if not the only—sources of citizen contact with the state, thus decreasing political knowledge and participation.

Non-state provision through either a secular or religious provider could pull people away from the public sphere by making the performance of the state less relevant to their lives. Scholars have documented an emerging class stratification by school type as the middle classes are increasingly leaving public schools in Africa because of a perceived decline in public school quality (Boyle 1999; MacLean 2011). In his study of Kenya, Congo, and Cameroon, Patrick Boyle (1999) highlights the exodus of wealthy citizens from public to private schools in what he calls the era of *sauve qui peut*, or every man for himself. There has been a significant growth of low-cost, for-profit providers in urban and semi-urban areas in Africa (Rose and Akyeampong 2005). The demand for low-cost private schools suggests a shift of middle-class parents away from public schools. A study of school fee abolition in Africa reveals that the poorest households are the most likely to benefit from the elimination of school fees, which implies that wealthier actors are obtaining education for their children elsewhere (Harding and Stasavage 2014). The exit from public education makes government institutions less relevant for middle-class citizens, thus perhaps decreasing their incentive to provide political feedback to the government.

Historically, non-state entities have used service provision to build support. During the colonial period, Christian missionaries in Africa built schools as entry points to communities where they wanted to build churches (Abernethy 1968). The Muslim Brotherhood and Hamas have used social service provision as a foundation for their successful political movements (Wickham 2002). Political parties in India and Lebanon have used social service provision to recruit voters outside of their traditional base of support (Cammett and Issar 2010; Thachil 2011). Rebel groups have also used service provision and indoctrination through education to build legitimacy for their movements (Keister 2011; Weinstein 2007). By liberalizing the education sector, African governments may be not only forfeiting the allegiance building that can be reaped from public goods provision, but passing them on to other entities.

The threat that a non-state provider poses to state legitimacy is partially a function of the sponsoring institution's past relationship with the ruling regime. In the Sahel, madrassas and Quranic schools are tied to a specific history of contestation with the secular state. In contrast, in much of Africa, the Catholic Church received subsidies and support from colonial authorities and post-independence regimes. Islamic schools faced either isolation from the state, in the case of the British administration, or elimination and resistance, in the case of French colonial authorities. The French government struggled to establish rule in many territories with predominantly Muslim populations and sought to co-opt or eliminate Quranic education. French officials feared "Islamic fanaticism" and saw it as a significant challenge to their *mission civilisatrice*.[13] They closed many schools and led campaigns against Muslim leaders. In some of the French-held colonial territory, the campaign against Islam, as well as the colonialists' aggressive forced-labor recruitment practices, reduced the number of students in Quranic schools.[14] This tension between the secular state and Islamic schooling plagued independence transitions since many postcolonial states continued to exclude Islamic schools from government aid or accreditation.

Given the tumultuous relationship between the government and Islamic education, fear and distrust might linger despite recent pacts and partnerships (Gandolfi 2003). It therefore is particularly important to investigate the role of Islamic education in shaping political knowledge and political participation. It is possible that by attending and supporting a madrassa, students and their parents could become integrated into an alternative community that values concentration on their personal moral improvement and relationship with God. These communities might encourage civic engagement exclusively through actions mediated by their mosque or religious leaders, as well as distrust and opposition to the state and its formal channels of participation.

Finally, the content offered at non-state schools could differ from the state education that is associated with citizen-making. There is an active policy debate about the role of madrassas and state authority in Muslim societies (Hefner and Zaman 2007). Non-state providers, particularly ideologically charged Islamic schools, could pose a challenge to liberal democracy. It is unclear if madrassas and Quranic schools will instill the liberal-democratic ethos and support for the ruling regime that Dahl (1967) deems crucial for democratic citizenship. Furthermore, apart from ideology, Quranic schools and madrassas use Arabic and indigenous languages as their languages of pedagogy and therefore provide a different skill set than what is offered by Francophone schools. Students who attend these schools do not have access to the same linguistic currency, which is needed to interact with the state bureaucracy.

Structure of the Book

In this introduction, I have discussed the reasons that education should matter for democratic citizenship and why it is likely that different schools have different effects on political knowledge and participation. I have emphasized the importance of empowered and engaged citizens and suggested ways in which education may contribute to greater political knowledge and participation. In chapter 2, I explore the methodological approach I used to capture Malian perspectives on the relationship between education, citizenship, and democracy. I describe the subnational research design and methods of data collection, including the strategy of an immersive survey.

In chapter 3, I examine the political culture in Mali, revealing mass skepticism toward formal, electoral politics. I suggest ways in which educated and empowered citizenship might overcome these low levels of external efficacy. In chapter 4, I describe the dramatic expansion of schooling after the transition to democracy in the early 1990s and the diversity of education providers in the context of liberalization. I detail the demand side for education and discuss parents' motivations for selecting different schooling options in Mali.

I assess the impact of different types of schooling on respondents' political knowledge and participation in chapter 5. I find that education in any school type empowers citizens to learn more about politics. Even citizens with a Quranic education or only literacy training were, on average, better informed about politics than their peers with no education. Citizens' political knowledge increases with each subsequent level of education, but there is no significant difference across those in different types of primary schools. Further, citizens with primary education from any school type are more likely to vote and campaign than are those with no schooling at all. I did not find differences in the political engagement of students who attended Islamic schools, public schools, or Francophone private schools. However, the relationship between education and participation is not linear. Evidence suggests that students who obtain higher education often gain French fluency, which increases their level of internal efficacy but does not automatically translate into greater electoral participation. Consistent with the literature from other environments where citizens are skeptical of state responsiveness to their demands (i.e., low external efficacy), secondary and university education are only associated with significant increases in difficult forms of participation: campaigning, contacting a government official, and expressing willingness to run for office (Craig 1980; Craig and Maggiotto 1982; Fraser 1970). Those with secondary or university education are no more likely to vote or campaign than are their peers with no education. Education builds the skills to engage the state, but citizens ultimately decide how to best allocate these skills.

In chapter 6 I turn to parents' experiences with two different education providers: public schools and madrassas. I reveal that public education, as a welfare service, can foster connections between parents and the state. Holding all other factors constant, parents who enroll their children in public schools are significantly more likely to vote and have a voter ID card than those parents who do not enroll their children in public schools and those citizens who do not have school-age children. Conversely, parents who send their children to madrassas claim that they vote less often when compared to a reference category of parents who do not enroll their children in school and citizens without school-age children. There are not comparable differences in participation among parents who send their children to Quranic schools. Nor are there significant differences between parents who send their children to madrassas and those who send their children to public schools in terms of non-electoral channels of participation.

In chapter 7 I discuss the implications of the findings of this book for the future of democracy in Mali and for the study of political behavior in Africa. I recommend that greater attention be afforded to the impact of educational experiences on the expansion of citizens' capabilities and to the role of education, and other welfare services, in establishing a connection between citizens and state authority.

CHAPTER TWO

Research Design and Methodological Approach

Political science is increasingly demanding greater transparency in scholars' research design and data collection processes (see, for example, Elman, Kapiszewski, and Vinuela 2010; Kapiszewski, MacLean, and Read 2015). Here, I discuss my theoretical motivations and offer an honest assessment of my pragmatic considerations. I outline the various methodologies employed in data collection, the motivation for my case selection, and the sampling strategies. I describe the context in which our research team conducted the survey, exit polls, and interviews to give readers a sense of the research environment. Since many political science theories, as well as research methodologies, are adapted from work in American politics, this contextual information is particularly important in understanding how (and if) these theories and techniques can travel to dramatically different research environments, such as Mali.

In this chapter, I also highlight some research innovations of the study—particularly the recording of behavioral observations and qualitative justifications to complement the standard survey responses. The research team was trained to code responses but also to include information about the participants' justifications, their candor, any common phrasing, and ethnographic details that could further enrich our interpretation of their responses. The team's familiarity with the project and our commitment to the research goals enabled us to capture rich qualitative data while conducting a survey of more than 1,000 citizens.

Case Selection

In order to understand the grassroots underpinnings of citizens' knowledge of and engagement with the state, it is essential to ask citizens themselves.

The goal of my study was to see how education affected students' and parents' political knowledge and participation. I chose to run my study in Mali—a country I had been visiting since 2002. Before the 2012 coup, Mali, a poor, Muslim-majority country, had been an unlikely democratic star due to its procedural progress; it had held four presidential elections, experienced two alternations of power, and boasted the second freest press in Africa. Compared to other countries that had made third-wave transitions in Africa, Mali had been lauded as one of the highest-ranking democracies. However, Mali's democracy was full of complexities and contradictions. It boasted one of the freest presses in Africa, yet also one of the highest illiteracy rates in the bureaucratic language of the state.[1]

I adopted a subnational research design instead of using a cross-national research design, for three reasons as outlined by Snyder (2001): the ability to generate many observations but control for context; better coding and inferential accuracy; and the opportunity to explore regional and geographic differences. A subnational design enabled me to control for many institutional factors that would typically mediate the relationship between schooling and citizenship behavior: systems of governance, the Malian educational system, and the value of different levels of education compared to the rest of society. The continental adult literacy rate is 62% (http://www.unesco.org/new/en/dakar/education/literacy), while it is a mere 33% in Mali, so schooling in Mali is likely to have a different comparative value than it does in other African countries. In addition, Mali's recent educational expansion and the liberalization of the education sector provided adequate variation to test the impact of different types of schooling experiences—public, private, secular, and religious—on citizen knowledge and participation; there also was a large reference category of citizens with no schooling at all.

The focus on Mali also allowed me to cultivate and capitalize on my specialized area knowledge and Bambara language proficiency—thus increasing the accuracy of my coding and interpretation of causal inferences (Adcock and Collier 2001). Language and country knowledge are useful in dissecting and translating citizens' understanding of democratic concepts borrowed from the Western context (Schaffer 2000). I conducted my dissertation research after already having spent almost a year living with Malian host families between college and graduate school. This time in Mali allowed me to develop the language competency needed to conduct an analysis of regular citizens' opinions and behavior in a country where most meaningful conversations happen in local languages. My residency in Mali also provided me with a political primer on the country's vast web of historical social and political relations, which enabled me to contextualize responses and interpret double meanings.

Mali's multiethnic political heritage and decentralized political tradition are so strong that they affect day-to-day logistics. In order to successfully make purchases, travel, and follow appropriate protocol, one must embed oneself in social categories from Mali's rich history by adopting a Malian last name or, in Bambara, *jamu*, which enables a foreigner to integrate into society. For instance, my business card and my research permits include my Malian name, Madame Sidibe Yama Coulibaly. While I clearly have no genetic relation to Bitòn Coulibaly, a ruthless Bambara ruler of Ségou in the 1600s, my assumed position as his kin is taken seriously when I am in Mali. Rarely does anyone ask my "real name." My *jamu* enables me to connect to others across ethnic groups in Mali by referencing the historical interactions of our ancestors through Mali's system of *sanankuya*, or joking cousins.[2]

I embarked on "immersive survey research." Rather than sourcing enumerators and logisticians from a local firm, I trained and managed a team of five enumerator-coders, including myself. My language skills enabled me to participate in the actual survey process since nearly 80% of the surveys were coded in Bambara. I was present and personally coded responses for 190 surveys in seven school districts in Bamako, Kayes, and Sikasso. By listening to and observing nearly 200 survey respondents, I was able to better assess the quality of the questions and the responses and to make observations about Malian households, transport systems, and power relations. To assess Malians' perspectives on politics, the government, and education, our research team walked through cities and villages in Mali. We sat in compounds and talked to respondents as they washed clothes, played cards, nursed babies, chopped wood, pounded millet, cooked, collected well water, and tinkered with broken appliances. After 11 months, we had amassed a survey of 1,000 citizens in 10 school districts.

By comparing residents in school districts thousands of kilometers apart, I was able to investigate important spatial variation in political phenomena while again controlling for the institutional and educational environment. Mali is one of the largest and most diverse countries in Africa. Covering more than 478,767 square miles, it contains dense forest regions, a vast savanna, and uninhabitable desert. My original strategy was to select two districts from each of a geographically diverse five regions: Bamako, Kayes, Sikasso, Timbuktu, and Mopti. Due to insecurity in the north of Mali, however, we

were only able to conduct surveys in one school district in Timbuktu. Therefore, we included three districts in Bamako to compensate for the political
tension in Timbuktu.

Methodology
Immersive Survey Research

In this book I leverage qualitative and quantitative data to test observable implications of hypothesized relationships between schooling, political knowledge, and political participation. I draw primarily from an immersive survey
of 1,000 citizens in 10 school districts in five regions in Mali. I define an
immersive survey as a researcher-led survey in which the researcher works
alongside a small team of enumerators and sits in on interviews (and may
code responses) over the course of the study. This enables the researcher to
assess the quality of the data through every stage of the process. A researcher-
led survey team is in no way a methodological innovation,[3] but I introduce
this term to distinguish this approach from the stereotype of survey research
in which a principal investigator's role consists of a week-long training with
enumerators and outsourcing to local firms.

Over the course of the year of research, my discussions, debates, and negotiations with Malian stakeholders forced me to reexamine and critically
engage with the stereotypes and assumptions that I brought to the study from
my literature review and my own experience in the US educational system. I
conducted the survey with the help of four research assistants: Guindo, Seydou, Youba, and Djenebou. As recent graduates of the University of Bamako,
my team members provided the language support I needed to translate and
interpret findings and also furnished intimate, personal knowledge of the
Malian education sector. The primary members of the team participated in
a month-long training in which we covered relevant political science theories and research methodology. During the same period, my team members
provided me with intensive Bambara tutoring, which helped me to join in
debates about translation. After much discussion over phrasing, cultural ap-
propriateness, and measurement, the survey instrument was translated into
French, Bambara, and Songhrai.[4]

I have high confidence in the data that my team members collected without me because I have an intimate knowledge of their capacity, and I know
that they were committed to the research project. The experience of living
and working together over the course of 11 months built solidarity, trust, and

intellectual interest in the project among our five team members. We were able to obtain the survey data despite stifling 115° heat in Bamako, extensive mechanical problems with our car, bouts of malaria, snakes that invaded our concrete bedrooms in Sikasso, commutes in wooden *pinasses* during bridge outages, and an Al Qaeda in the Islamic Maghreb (AQIM) travel warning that prevented me from accompanying my team to the north of the country.[5] Each team member was integral to the development of this book, and the research would not have been possible without their involvement.

The majority of surveys were conducted by a team of two—one coder and one who posed the questions—so that the coder was able to capture the participant's qualitative justifications for closed-ended responses.[6] In this way, the surveys often became more like interviews: coders could simultaneously capture any qualitative data inserted by respondents despite using a standard survey script. While the use of two enumerators is ultimately more costly, it yields greater coding accuracy, a better ability to assess the honesty of responses, and a way to capture qualitative descriptions of the logic and context of political decision making. The inclusion of qualitative data aided in my interpretation of causal mechanisms, but also served a practical role in helping me to evaluate the measurement validity of the questions. In instances where the qualitative justifications repeatedly had contradictory relationships to the closed-ended coding, that variable was rated as poor quality and excluded from my analysis. In other instances, citizens' similar use of language to rephrase the question alerted us to the ways that the question was being understood. The vast majority of surveys were conducted without interpretation—enabling respondents to express themselves freely in their own language.

Additional Data

Before conducting the survey, I took an initial trip to Bamako in the summer of 2007 to obtain information about the educational and political landscape. I obtained subnational data from the Ministry of Education, the Territorial Administration, the National Archives of Mali, and the National Assembly. I also spoke with educators and school directors who narrated the historical trajectory of education and politics in Mali. These descriptive data allowed me to better understand the current and historic educational opportunities in Mali, the country's rapidly evolving experience with democracy, and variations and trends across the variables of interest.

In 2009, I returned to Mali to conduct the survey and to collect other forms of complementary data, including more than 50 interviews with educators, government officials, and members of civil society; a survey of 200 university students; elected officials' education profiles; and an exit poll of 450 voters during the municipal elections in Bamako. These data provided a further test of the implications of the mechanisms driving correlations generated through the survey work by providing insight into observed voting behavior and descriptions of educational differences between citizens and elected leaders, which also allowed us to compare respondents to an "elite" group of university students.

Measures and Variables

The survey generated education profiles for parents and their children, which allowed me to analyze the impact of length of education and type of schooling on respondents' political knowledge, trust, and participation. The best existing data on African citizenship and education are found in the Afrobarometer survey, but this survey is limited in its ability to capture complete educational profiles. It includes each respondent's level of education, but fails to disaggregate educational profiles by school type. My study's focus on education brings greater precision to the measurement of each respondent's education history by including school type as well as the length of their schooling experience.

The research team placed additional emphasis on eliciting comprehensive responses about education in all school types. For instance, in pretesting the survey, we found that the French and Bambara words for school, école and *kalanso*, carried an association with formal Western education. When asked about their education history, citizens who had attended Islamic schools or participated in informal literacy trainings would often claim that they never went to school. Our team learned that it was necessary to make a secondary prompt that probed into specific types of informal or Islamic education in order for respondents to reveal that they did in fact go to a school. Without the second prompt, Islamic schooling would have been underreported.[7]

My research project added another dimension to the Afrobarometer data by coding if and where parents sent their children to school. These data help us to understand how parents' relationship with the state as a welfare provider might impact their relationship with the government and their relationships to other citizens. The survey included a series of questions about parents' enrollment strategies and justifications for school choice. The expansion of education in Africa represents the largest government effort to increase the social well-being of everyday citizens. In the wake of this monumental policy change, it is critical that we better understand the effects of provision on social service consumers.

Sampling

My survey uses stratified, area probability sampling from 10 school districts (Fowler 2009:29). I selected school districts using Ministry of Education national data on education provision by type of school. I chose districts based on three factors: to maximize variation on the key independent variable (schooling type); to facilitate logistics; and to achieve regional variation. In order to maximize variation on my independent variable, type of school, I selected school districts that had disproportionately high levels of enrollment in each type—public, private, madrassa, and community—to increase the probability that respondents would have attended or sent their children to a diverse set of schools.[8]

In each school district, we used randomized cluster sampling. First, we obtained neighborhood maps from the municipal authorities or Mali's Geographic Institute.[9] Once we received the map of a school district, we drew equal quadrants directly onto the map. In the case of rural areas, we worked with knowledgeable informants (e.g., teachers, doctors) to create a list of "accessible villages" in the school district. Accessibility to rural zones was primarily determined by the proximity to our starting point and whether roads were accessible or if there was alternative transportation (boat, moto taxi, donkey cart). After determining the universe of accessible zones or villages within the school district, we selected four to five quadrants (or villages from a list) by using an online randomizer (http://www.randomizer.org).

In urban areas, two teams started in the middle of the quadrant and then proceeded in opposite directions, surveying every fifth household. Individual respondents in households were selected randomly among household members who were present and at least 18 years of age by using playing cards. Surveys were conducted on weekdays and weekends at varying times in order to ensure that we reached all population types.[10] In villages, when possible, teams began at the *dugutigi's* (chief's) home and then proceeded in opposite directions, stopping at intervals of five or three houses, depending on village size. In certain instances, especially in the rural school districts in Sikasso and Sévaré, some chiefs insisted on calling respondents into their compounds to be interviewed.[11] Interviewers recorded GPS coordinates for approximately 40% of all respondents' homes as well as neighboring schools to ensure that the research teams were operating in the correct zones.

Because I sought variation on schooling type and excluded areas with low school enrollment, the sample reflects an urban bias. Additionally, due to budget and time constraints, I focused primarily on urban and peri-urban zones because travel to the rural zones is costly, difficult, and time-consuming. Only two of the ten school districts were completely rural, and thus my project has a bias toward a population with a greater choice of educational options. Respondents' educational levels from the survey are slightly higher than national averages, which also reflects the urban bias of the sample. In 2006 the combined primary, secondary, and tertiary gross enrollment rate in Mali was 36.7% while 53% of all respondents had primary, secondary, or tertiary schooling in my survey sample (Thunnissen 2009).

I did include two rural school districts in Sikasso and Sévaré to try to capture the specific challenges facing rural communities. However, this book should be read as largely a reflection of how citizens in urban and peri-urban zones in the capital city and in regional capitals of Mali interact with the contemporary educational and political situation. While this focus on peri-urban and urban zones may be limiting, the results do offer comparative insight into school districts thousands of kilometers away from each other. Future research should build on the formative work of Étienne Gérard (1992, 1993, 1997b) in order to understand the dynamics between schooling and participation in the more isolated parts of the country.

Table 2.1 summarizes the characteristics of each school district and compares them to national averages. I highlight the variation that I hoped to capture with each district's inclusion. Significant departures from the national average are shown in bold. Because most learners, especially historically, attended public schools, it was important to identify districts with high non-state enrollment in order to generate enough variation in school type to compare different educational trajectories. For instance, Faladie was selected because 44% percent of children there attend private schools (compared to the national average of only 10%), and thus it helped us to achieve an oversample of private schools to enable a better comparison across school types. Similarly, Banconi was selected because of the high rate of students attending madrassas (20% as compared to the national average of 12%) to ensure

TABLE 2.1.
Selected school districts

School district	Region	Gross enrollment rate (%)	Public (%)	Community (%)	Private (%)	Madrassa (%)	Rural or urban	Poverty index (2001)[1] (%)
	National	78	62	17	10	12	NA	68
Faladie	Bamako	119	37	7	**44**	12	U	29
Bamako Coura	Bamako	112	**81**	0	16	4	U	29
Banconi	Bamako	126	38	11	**31**	**20**	U	29
Kayes Rive Droite	Kayes	92	65	3	1	**32**	U, R	68
Kayes Rive Gauche	Kayes	103	**73**	6	5	**16**	U, R	68
Sikasso I	Sikasso	83	**71**	11	7	11	U	82
Sikasso II	Sikasso	**48**	59	**29**	2	10	R	82
Mopti	Mopti	80	**83**	2	8	6	U	79
Sévaré	Mopti	46	79	6	0	**15**	R	79
Timbuktu	Timbuktu	**148**	67	**18**	1	12	U	54

Source: Annuaire National 2006–2007

Notes: Boldface indicates a significant departure from the national average; NA = non-applicable
[1] Percentage of the regional population calculated to be living in poverty.

that there would be enough respondents who attended madrassas or whose children attended madrassas to facilitate a comparison with public schools. Districts in the four other regions were also chosen to maximize variation in the type of schools that students were attending.[12]

Schooling in Mali consists of nine years of basic or primary education, followed by three years at a formal lycée or a two- or four-year course at a vocational school. The primary schooling is divided into a first and second cycle. After students complete six years of primary school, they must pass an exam to enter the second cycle of primary school. After they complete three additional years, they take an entrance exam that determines if they can place into a lycée.

In the 2006–2007 school year, 62% of first-cycle primary school children attended public schools, 12% attended madrassas, 17% attended decentralized community schools, and 10% attended private secular or Christian schools in Mali (Annuaire National 2006–2007; note that this report does not include Quranic school enrollment). My sample reflects both current and past educational trends and captures Quranic education and literacy centers, which are not included in the Ministry of Education statistics: 44% of respondents attended public schools, 31% attended Quranic schools, 10% attended madrassas, 12% attended private secular or Christian schools, and 3% attended community schools or literacy centers. Since community school programs are relatively recent and I targeted respondents over 18 years of age and did not include a representative sample of citizens from rural zones, I was not able to sufficiently capture students who had attended community schools in my survey sample. I was able to include some recipients of government-sponsored literacy training, who are coded as having received "informal education." I also treat Quranic instruction, regardless of length of tutelage, as informal education.

Timeline

I conducted my first pilot trip to Mali to gather data on educational institutions and variation in enrollment in the summer of 2007. Amadou Toumani Touré had just been elected to his second term in office. People were still wearing presidential campaign T-shirts, and Bamako was littered with political posters. Touré, who ran as an independent with the backing of a 42-party coalition including Mali's strongest party, Alliance for Democracy in Mali (ADEMA), won a majority of votes in only one round against Ibrahim

Boubacar Keita (IBK)—his future successor. The coalition backing Touré's candidacy won all but 34 of 147 seats in the concurrent election for the National Assembly. The country was already beginning to display a democratic malaise; turnout was less than 40%, reflecting many Malians' belief that there was no real choice in the presidential election. Afrobarometer data indicate that Malians' dissatisfaction with democracy increased during ATT's second term (Coulibaly and Bratton 2013).

I spent a little over a month interviewing teachers at different school types, talking to former administrators, and visiting the Ministry of Education to obtain the enrollment statistics that I would use to select school districts for inclusion in my study. The pilot trip laid the foundation for my major period of data collection and reduced the start-up time for my larger study. For instance, I was able to select the school districts before arriving in Bamako, so I knew what linguistic skills my research assistants needed to have, and I was able to start scouting out host families for us to stay with as soon as I arrived in Bamako.

The major period of data collection was January 2009–December 2009. This was approximately three years before the 2012 coup that would remove Touré a month prior to what would have been Mali's fifth election and third executive turnover. Bamako was developing at a rapid pace. New hair salons, private universities, personal cars, and Chinese-built infrastructure projects indicated the rise of a consumption class. However, by 2009, the security situation in the north of the country already had vastly deteriorated. Mali was embroiled in its third northern insurgency; Tuareg rebels had taken up arms again and were attacking government and military installations. Al Qaeda in the Islamic Maghreb regularly plucked hostages from neighboring Mauritania and Niger and brought them into northern Mali to negotiate their release for ransom. During the summer of 2009, a prominent military officer was killed inside Timbuktu's city limits, foreshadowing the instability that was to come.

In the first quarter of 2009, I continued to collect descriptive data on the educational landscape of Mali. I also recruited and trained my research assistants, secured housing, and bought the 1984 Mercedes D-190 that would take us across the country. I took advantage of the municipal elections in February 2009 and conducted a short exit poll. We piloted and refined the survey instrument that month. Finally, we launched the survey in March and continued gathering data through November 2009; we began in Bamako, then proceeded to Kayes, Sikasso, and finally to Mopti and Timbuktu. After my data analysis, I made two short follow-up visits to collect data with which to evaluate mechanisms in the spring and fall of 2011.

Malian Geography

During my previous travels in Mali and in researching the survey locations, I have been fortunate to experience the diversity of Mali's eight regions. While I cannot hope to re-create the colorful and vibrant Malian landscape, I take a cue from Lauren MacLean's (2010) rich depiction of village life in Ghana and Côte d'Ivoire and offer a brief description of the 10 school districts where we administered the survey: Faladie, Banconi, and Bamako Coura (all in Bamako), Kayes Rive Droite and Kayes Rive Gauche, Sikasso I and II, Mopti, Sévaré, and Timbuktu.

Bamako

Bamako is a dusty, sprawling city with an estimated population of 1 million or 3 million, depending on whom you ask. The population is diverse and includes most of the country's more than 60 ethnic groups. As the national capital, Bamako has always had the most schooling options and is home to the national university, which attracts learners from all regions of the country. In 2009, Bamako's roads were paved only in the most trafficked areas, while the other roads were still red dirt. Architecture in the capital city ranges from large cement three-story houses that hold extended families to more modest mud or cement one-story homes. Bamako's "skyscrapers," which in 2009 could be counted on two hands, include awkward government ministries, banks, and newly constructed Libyan-Chinese hotels. With few landmarks or street signs, the city's plan eludes all but the most seasoned public transport drivers. Music blares from all angles and seems to intensify Bamako's frenzied pace. Since 2001, donkey carts and *sotramas*[13] have given way to air-conditioned Indian taxis and flashy SUVs. Cell phones and plastic motorbikes called *jakartas* have become commonplace in most Bamakoise households.

Today many members of the younger generations have abandoned more traditional Malian boubous and pagnes for cosmopolitan Western prêt-à-porter styles. Simultaneously more and more women are wearing burqas, niqabs, and ostentatiously embroidered abayas imported from Dubai. The streets of the capital are now littered with multistory buildings that did not exist five years ago, and paved roads now integrate many peripheral villages into the city's maze of streets. On Sundays and Thursdays, women in wedding parties still wear matching *complets* in the most creative color combinations: tie-dyes, batiks, and neons with elaborate embroidery and tailoring. Malian music continues to dominate the world music scene and local nightlife. Mali has expanded its repertoire to hip-hop—a genre that is home to some of the country's most politically outspoken artists.

Bamako's most prominent feature is the Niger River, which divides the city into two distinct sides: Rive Droite and Rive Gauche. Two bridges, referred to as the "new" and the "old" bridge, strain to cope with the steady flow of cars, motos, and bicycles between the residential neighborhoods in Rive Droite and the commercial centers in Rive Gauche. In 2010, the Chinese built a third, state-of-the-art bridge, which connects the growing peripheral neighborhoods on both sides of the river. The oldest neighborhoods in Bamako, as well as the most famous markets, are located in Rive Gauche. Rive Droite, settled in the 1950s when residents could still purchase land using kola nuts, is home to the Bamako airport. The educational landscape of each side of the river reflects their historical legacies. The older neighborhoods in Rive Gauche have greater rates of public school provision per capita, while the recent private school boom is most apparent in Rive Droite.

Public schools on the newer side of the Niger have been overwhelmed by demographic growth. Teachers struggle with more than 100 students in a classroom. One sixth-grade teacher explained, "Technically, we are only supposed to allow a maximum of 75 learners in the class, but often you face more than 100 pupils in your class. What are you going to do—turn those kids away?" (interview with public school teacher, Niamakoro, July 2007). Overenrollment and overcrowding in public schools have diverted many learners to private schools. A school director in Bamako explained, "There has been a certain demographic growth that makes it difficult to satisfy the demand for education. There are a lot of students who cannot get into public school, so they are forced to go to private school" (interview with private school director, Niamakoro, February 2009). Lower poverty rates and lesser reliance on agricultural labor in Bamako have created conditions for higher student enrollment than in any other region of the country. Public school crowding has created an insatiable demand for cheap, private education. As a result, some school districts in newly settled sections of Bamako have private school enrollment rates of over 40%—more than four times the national average. My sample includes one district in Rive Droite: Faladie. Faladie is one of Bamako's newest communities and stretches from the northern perimeter of the city toward the airport and includes the peri-urban village of Senou, which was not yet electrified at the time of my survey.

The other two districts that I surveyed—Bamako Coura and Banconi—are in the more established Rive Gauche. Bamako Coura lies at the heart of downtown Bamako. Although its name means New Bamako, its faded sidewalks and European-style parks are reminiscent of another era. Banconi lies farther along the railroad line toward Koulikoro. It is home to Haidara, one of a new breed of charismatic religious leaders (see Soares 2005, 2012). One of the most popular figures in Mali and the head of the largest religious organization in the country, Haidara is among the handful of Malian leaders who can consistently fill a soccer stadium for a speech or sermon. During the northern occupation, he was outspoken in his critique of Islamists groups, including Ansar Dine, which used the same name as his own religious association. His presence is felt not only through the merchandise adorned with his image, which is sold on street corners in Banconi, but in the high rate of enrollment in madrassas in this school district.

Bamako has a strong market for Islamic education. Some of the first madrassas were built in Bamako in the 1950s, including the École Coranique Supérieure, a madrassa founded by university-educated Malians who returned from studies in Egypt and felt deceived and disappointed by the lack of job opportunities despite their prestigious diplomas (Brenner 2001:56). As in other regions, many madrassas find their base constituencies in trading communities—particularly Soninke traders—and among those Malians who subscribe to a "reformist" version of Islam.[14] Some wealthy members of these communities constitute a differentiated market for Islamic education. They choose to enroll their children in religious schools despite the variety of Francophone education providers that exist in Bamako.

Kayes

Kayes is the final railroad stop in Mali before the Senegalese border. The culture and legacy of the railroad resonates throughout the city. Kayes, the former colonial capital, was home to the first French schools in Mali and is one of the few places in the country where you can see remnants of colonial architecture, including the railroad station. Kayes is one of the hottest cities in the world, and many of the villages in the region become flooded and are inaccessible during the rainy season. The majority of citizens in Kayes are Kassonke, Peul, Malinke, and Soninke.

Kayes, like Bamako, is divided by a river—the Senegal. The bus from Bamako first reaches the urban part of Kayes Rive Gauche, which is part of a large
school district encompassing a vast network of villages in the region—before
crossing the Senegal River to the smaller, more compact Kayes Rive Droite.
Residents complain that life in Kayes is expensive. There is no public transit
in the city; taxi rides in Kayes cost a fixed rate of 1,000 CFA (US$2), which,
relative to the distance covered, would be considered exorbitant in Bamako.
The price reflects the poor quality of the roads, which are nearly impassable
when muddy. Kayes boasts a very high emigration rate per capita. Juxtaposed
against the dirty landscape of the city are extravagant villas that were built
with remittances from Malian expatriates.

Kayes's education profile also reflects the disjuncture between the French
legacy and expatriate remittance flows. The first French schools in Mali were
built in Kayes in the late 1800s. However, two ethnic groups, the Soninke and
Peul, have historically opted to send their children to Islamic schools. In one
of the two school districts in Kayes, which includes many of its surrounding
villages, more than 30% of all primary learners go to madrassas. Unfortunately, the Ministry of Education data do not capture enrollment in Quranic
schools, but in our survey, Kayes had the largest number of respondents who
sent their children exclusively to Quranic schools.

The Soninke have dominated the trade that stretched across the Sahel since
before the Middle Ages and now constitute a sizable migrant community in
France (see Manchuelle 1997 for a comprehensive study of Soninke trade and
migration). Like all trading communities, the Soninke have had a contentious
relationship with government regimes, which seek to restrict movement and
collect taxes. Known for their religious fervor, Soninke traditionally refused
to send their children to French "Christian" schools (ibid.:204). The tension
continues as Soninke emigrants in France send remittances back to Mali to
build new madrassas instead of helping to fund the public schools in their
villages. Teachers and doctors working in rural Kayes reported that Soninke
expatriates in France and the United States send remittances to build osten-
tatious houses and private health centers in villages throughout the region
(interviews with doctor, teachers, and school director working in rural Kayes,
August 2009). A public school director who works in a village in the region
of Kayes with a predominantly Soninke population described his frustration
with the parallel systems of service provision: the poorly funded state services
and the well-funded private providers funded by remittance flows. Soninke
expatriates in France fund a state-of-the-art madrassa in the same small vil-

lage where his public school is. He wrote a letter to the men in France and appealed to them to send some funding for his underfinanced public school, but he was unsuccessful (interview with school director, August 2009).

Soninke emigration from the region is so pronounced that the absence of Soninke men was obvious during our survey work. We encountered many households headed by women, who would respond to our questionnaires clutching smartphones sent to them by their husbands and brothers in France.

The Fulani, or Peul, communities in this region, while less affluent, also tend to favor Islamic education, particularly Quranic schools. Many members of the Peul community in the Kayes region prefer Quranic education because it is tied to their religious heritage and membership in the Sufi brotherhoods. In our survey, 64% of respondents who enrolled children in Quranic schools claimed to speak Pulaar at home.

Sikasso

Sikasso is an agricultural region in southern Mali bordering Burkina Faso, Côte d'Ivoire, and Guinea. Sikasso produces the majority of the country's cotton—Mali's primary export—and weak world cotton prices have hurt producers. Referred to as the "Sikasso paradox," the rich agricultural region has Mali's second highest poverty rate and lowest regional school enrollment (Delarue et al. 2009). Because it is an agricultural region, many families rely on their children's labor to run the family farms. The city of Sikasso's population is predominantly Senoufo, Mianka, and Bambara. However, immigration into the region by a number of different ethnic groups is common, given its position on the roads to neighboring countries. In comparison to Kayes, Sikasso's shady, tree-lined streets lack energy and cosmopolitan accoutrements. The Sikasso region was home to some of the strongest colonial resistance movements, including those of Samory Touré and the rulers of Kénédougou. In the sheep market in the center of the city, you can still spot the crumbling remains of a wall built by Babemba Traoré, the king of Kénédougou in the late 1800s, which protected the city from French invaders until his kingdom's ultimate defeat.

Sikasso has traditionally had the lowest rate of school enrollment in the country, but has benefited greatly from NGO-funded community school programs. Now, close to 30% of all primary school learners in Sikasso attend community schools. As in the other regions, initially madrassas in Sikasso were populated by the children of the Malian trading community (Amselle

1985). Teachers reported that urban Sikasso has a growing market for Islamic education among the broader population (interviews with school director and Arabic teacher, Sikasso, October 2009).

We conducted surveys both in Sikasso city and in villages in the rural school district Sikasso II, which were located 20–40 miles northwest of the city. Most of the community schools in our sample are in such rural villages. The villages selected for our study in Sikasso II were predominantly Senoufo, and most residents worked as farmers on the lush green landscape. Survey work in these zones required preliminary meetings with a village leader (*dugutigi*) and, in the larger villages, the mayor as well as the nationally appointed *commandant*.

Mopti/Sévaré

Mopti and Sévaré are twin cities in the middle of Mali, found along the country's "best road," which stretches from Bamako to Douentza to Gao. The gateway to the northern part of Mali, the Mopti and Sévaré school districts are a blend of southern and northern cultures. This fault line has intensified since the 2012 occupation, when Mopti/Sévaré became the dividing line between the rebel-occupied north and the government-controlled south of the country. Before the conflict, these towns' central location on the roads to Douentza, Bamako, Dogon Country, and Koutiala made them a popular stop for tourists and NGOs. Sévaré sits a couple of kilometers inland from Mopti. It is littered with NGO offices and hotels.

A small, crowded city, Mopti exports fish to the other regions of Mali. Mopti sits along a narrow peninsula surrounded by the Niger and Bani Rivers. Referred to as the Venice of Africa, Mopti's ports welcome large, colorful *pinasses* that ferry people, livestock, and commerce from villages along the river into the vibrant market. Like other historic cities in the region, including Djenné, Mopti has a long history of Islamic education.

We conducted surveys in Mopti's urban school district and in the villages in the greater Mopti region (Sévaré school district). The Sévaré school district includes villages up and down the roads between San and Douentza. During the rebel incursion, some of these villages sat at the border of rebel and state-controlled territory. The villages are ethnically diverse: Peul, Bozo, Soninke, Songhrai, and Dogon. Mopti has high public school enrollment: more than 80% of all enrolled primary students attend public school. Madrassa education is also popular in the villages of the Sévaré region; according to Ministry of Education statistics, 15% of all primary students in the school district attend madrassas, and many others attend Quranic schools.

Timbuktu

In today's international media, Timbuktu's instability is likely to outshine its prestigious academic past. Muammar Gaddafi, the former Libyan president, often visited Timbuktu to distribute aid and to visit allies.[15] His fall from power heightened regional insecurity as former mercenaries and light arms flooded the Sahel. In November 2011, three tourists were abducted and one was killed by Al Qaeda in the Islamic Maghreb while they were dining at a restaurant in downtown Timbuktu. Later that month, there were reports that rebels had commandeered the vehicles of high-ranking government officials. Despite these developments, U2's Bono and throngs of defiant music lovers traveled to Timbuktu in early 2012 to attend the Annual Festival in the Desert. Less than two weeks later, a northern secessionist group led by former mercenaries returning from Libya launched its first attacks in Mali.

From the end of March 2012 until January 2013, Timbuktu was under the control of Ansar Dine. Upon capturing Timbuktu, the group implemented a sharia law that required women to cover their heads, forbade dancing and cigarette smoking, and instituted severe forms of corporal punishment. In addition, the group tried to destroy ancient tombs, manuscripts, and mausoleums that they viewed as being incommensurate with their vision of Islam. However, it also subsidized electricity and provided fertilizer to farmers in an attempt to win supporters in the city. The occupation disrupted education systems in the north as teachers fled and the schools in the Timbuktu region were no longer under direct government control. Students living in the northern regions traveled to Mopti to take their high school entrance exams in the fall of 2012. The women students took their exams wearing burqas.

Timbuktu has long been a leading center of Islamic and scientific thought and has been home to some of the oldest and most prestigious universities in the world. By the sixteenth century, under the Askia dynasty, Timbuktu boasted 150 Quranic schools (Saad 1983:23). Approximately 15,000–20,000 students attended the famed University of Sankore and surrounding independent colleges and schools (Sanankoua 1985:359, citing Cissoko 1975:205).[16] A full degree took approximately 10 years and required mastering Arabic as well as memorization of the Quran. During this period, Timbuktu had one of the highest literacy rates in the world.

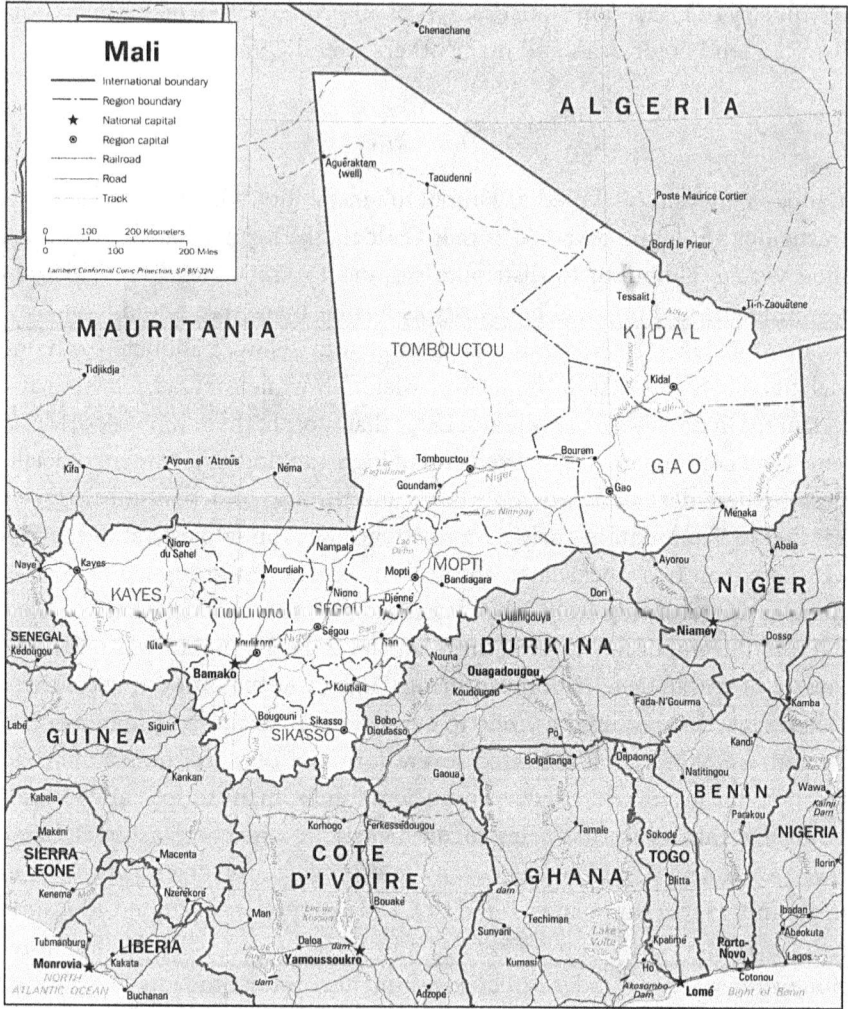

Figure 2.1. Mali. Source: www.mapcruzin.com

At the time of my study in 2009, Timbuktu was still governed by the Malian state despite not being connected to the rest of Mali by any paved roads. Timbuktu sits on the Niger—a half day's drive up the dirt road from Douentza. The tree-lined entrance to the city is reminiscent of Mopti, but the sandy landscape quickly reminds visitors that they are on the edge of the desert. Side streets, covered with sand, are impassable for all but 4x4s and solid Peugeot motorcycles. The city's unique architecture and meticulously adorned wooden doors exude its rich heritage. Like the other regions in the north of Mali, Kidal and Gao, Timbuktu looks distinct from the rest of Mali—as Bambara gives way to Songhrai as the prominent market language. Timbuktu's diverse population includes Tuareg, Songhrai, Arabs, Bella, and Peuls. Respondents to our survey included those living in permanent houses and those who live in makeshift huts nestled in openings along the city streets.

According to one of my research assistants, who grew up in Timbuktu, almost all public school learners also attend Quranic schools. He explained, "I remember getting up early to do my lessons at Quranic school, then we would all go to public school, and then after public school, we would return to Quranic school." Our surveys in Timbuktu confirmed this pattern of public school parents simultaneously enrolling their children in Quranic schools for supplementary religious instruction.

The recent occupation of the north is linked to a longer history of instability over the last 20 years. The uprisings of the 1990s, aimed in part at improving access to social services for the north of the country, and the subsequent violence destroyed many schools and disrupted education provision in the region. Despite peace accords signed in the 1990s, insecurity began to plague Timbuktu and the rest of northern Mali again with the introduction of rebel and intra-community fighting between 2006 and 2009. Tension between the central government and the north remained as the northerners felt marginalized: they had fewer job opportunities and less access to state resources, including education. The 2012–2013 conflict displaced more than 400,000 people from northern Mali, and many civil servants, including teachers, fled the region. Many former residents of the Timbuktu region remain abroad, fearful that if they return they will be targeted in an atmosphere of heightened ethnic tension. Beginning in late 2013, some residents started to trickle back to face the tremendous challenges of rebuilding their home city. However, insecurity in much of the region continues, and the future of education provision in Timbuktu remains to be seen.

CHAPTER THREE

Politiki ni Fanga Mali la /
Power and Politics in Mali

Understanding the relationship between education, knowledge, and political participation requires an exploration of Malians' opinions and attitudes toward the
government. Citizens' perceptions of democratic institutions shape their subsequent engagement with these institutions. In the introductory chapter I theorized
that active, informed citizenship was critical for democratic consolidation and
discussed the ways that education could generate knowledge and participation.
I also underscored the importance of challenging assumptions of institutional
responsiveness and regime legitimacy when exploring the relationship between
education, knowledge, and participation in nascent African democracies. Participation often takes place in a context where citizens are not completely convinced
of the competency or the utility of the state. In these environments other actors—
including religious and traditional authorities—often play a more prominent role
in providing solutions to citizens' demands. Citizens must be convinced to engage with the state rather than seeking other audiences or solutions.

In this chapter I demonstrate these dynamics by probing Malian political
culture almost 20 years after the democratic transition (three years before the
2012 coup). Understanding citizens' perceptions of the electoral context helps
us to better anticipate the relationship between education and democracy. I
discuss the pervasive view of politics as bad (*politiki man ɲi*), which persisted
even in the context of increasing education expansion and routine elections. I
then identify seven factors that contribute to a widespread skepticism about
the responsiveness of elected officials and bureaucratic institutions in Mali:
Mali's weak judiciary; partisan politics that challenge traditional deliberative
democratic procedures; co-opted participation; the linguistic barriers in Malian bureaucracy; the dominance of an educated elite minority in politics; the
weakness of political parties; the strength of non-electoral authorities; and
the lack of Islamic actors in the electoral sphere. I then introduce descriptive

statistics on Malians' political knowledge and participation as well as data from exit polls conducted during the municipal election in 2009 to describe Malians' views of democracy in the pre-coup era.

Politiki man ɲi: Popular Skepticism about Malian Democracy

When I embarked on my preliminary research in Mali in the summer of 2007, directly in the wake of the presidential election, I was eager to delve into popular political opinions. I would ask friends, neighbors, family members, and shopkeepers what they thought about the current state of Malian democracy. To my surprise, I was confronted by citizens' reluctance to discuss politics. Malians, even some of the people I admired most, would respond with a standard phrase: *politiki man ɲi*, "politics are bad."[1] I had anticipated criticism of specific leaders, parties, or institutions, but the blanket response after nearly 20 years of multiparty elections startled me. I was frustrated by what I initially perceived as Malians' disinterest in my topic.

I was convinced, however, that the intersection of education, an expanding and diversified sector, and politics was a fruitful research area, and I continued with my interviews. Eventually, the repetition of *politiki man ɲi* forced me to reflect on what multiparty democracy actually meant to most citizens. Their skepticism contrasted with Mali's heralded position as a democratic star relative to other African countries.[2] The pervasive pessimism stirring under Mali's democratic façade, especially given its recent democratic breakdown, merits deeper consideration.

The majority of Malians view electoral democracy and its related institutions as a foreign system, which does little to provide for their own needs. The mistrust breeds a characterization of politics as dishonest or impure. The following quotes demonstrate other ways that citizens tried to explain *politiki man ɲi*:[3]

> Everything that is related to politics in Mali is dishonest. It's to fill pockets and get out.
> > —Mamadou, 20, high school graduate, Sikasso (S11)

> I have no trust in *politiki mogo* [political candidates].
> > —Salimatou, attended some secondary school,
> > mother of three children, Banconi (BA7)

> I don't like politics; it's nothing more than pure lies.
> > —Aminata, Bella, 50s, Quranic education, Mopti (M40)

> I don't discuss politics at all. To discuss politics is a bad thing. *Politiki man ɲi.*
> > —Ami, 25, left her village to seek work in Bamako; her child lives
> > with an aunt and attends school in the village (F81)

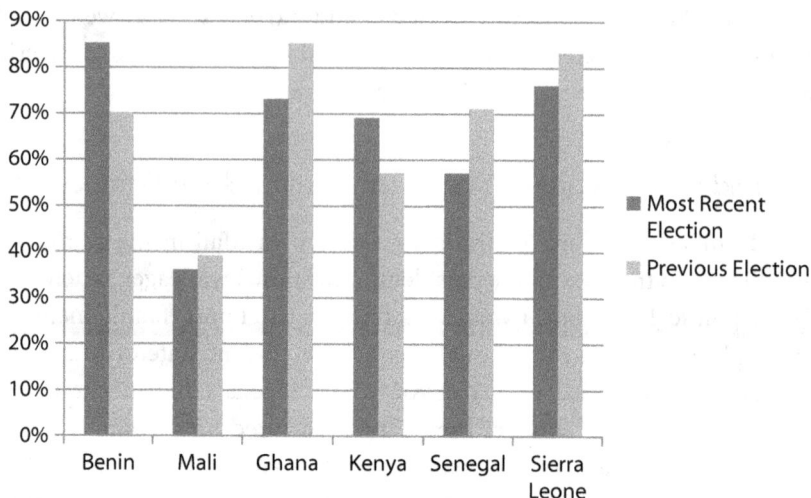

Figure 3.1. Percentage of registered voters who voted in presidential elections, 2002–2008. Source: Institute for Democracy and Electoral Assistance, www.idea.int

The [political] authorities do not do anything but trick us. We do not get anything from their behalf.
—Amadou, 45, Quranic education, Sévaré region (SV84)

It is evident from these quotes that most Malians are dissatisfied with politicians, whom they view as dishonest and exploitative. In her analysis of Afrobarometer data collected in a 2008 survey, Carolyn Logan (2010:25) shows that 70% of Malians feel that their voices are not heard between election cycles, a number that is above the African mean of 62% who felt the same way. This skepticism is manifested in Mali's low voter turnout. National turnout in the 2002 and 2007 presidential elections was less than 40% of all voters. The 2009 municipal elections registered 45% turnout, but this is still far below other countries on the continent.[4] Figure 3.1 compares the turnout in presidential elections in Mali with those of other democratic regimes in Africa. It shows that voting rates are much lower in Mali than in other countries in Africa.

Weak Judiciary

Malians' mistrust of government extends past electoral politics to the Malian state bureaucracy. In a 2008 Afrobarometer survey of 18 countries, Malians were the most dissatisfied with their country's judiciary; 54% of Malian respondents thought that most or all of the judiciary was involved in corruption (Little and Logan 2008). In contrast to the view of religious and traditional authorities, the judiciary and the police are generally seen as corrupt and predatory. "Money has ruined everything," complained Sidiki, who is from a rural village about 50 kilometers from Sikasso (SR11). In a 2010 survey, 65% of all Malians were dissatisfied or highly dissatisfied with the police and gendarmes, and 66% were dissatisfied with the justice system (CATEK 2010). For those without the monetary means or personal connections, attempts to successfully navigate the justice system will be futile. However, even Bamako's elites recognize the corruption of the judicial system as a pressing problem. Alassane, a doctor from Bamako who sends his children to school in Algeria, said: "All the judges and lawyers are corrupt" (BC60). Some Malian scholars have voiced concerns about a culture of impunity for those in power (e.g., Dougnon 2013). For instance, Mali started to produce reports on corruption scandals under Amadou Toumani Touré, but the regime was extremely reluctant to prosecute anyone on the list. When the public sees repeated scandals that are unpunished or accepted, this further reduces the credibility of the judicial system.

When asked about a hypothetical scenario—if they would contact the police in case of a dispute—fewer than 10% of respondents said that they would even "possibly" contact the authorities.[5] More than 90% replied with an authoritative "no." The few respondents, like Sadio in Kayes, who gave affirmative responses often qualified their answers by saying that they only felt the police should be contacted in cases of murder (K34). This overwhelming avoidance of the justice system reflects Malians' preference for disputes to be settled among families with the help of traditional authorities or religious figures instead of representatives of the state. When we posed the question about contacting the police, many respondents countered that they preferred to speak with traditional authorities than involve the law (S69, SR47). As Babah, a Tuareg man in his early 20s, explained, "We always settle things ourselves; we prefer not to involve the authorities" (T54). Contacting the police was treated as a last resort; involving the authorities is a less honorable alternative than problem solving within the community. Fode from the village of Diare explained, "Muslims shouldn't contact political authorities; it's a bad idea" (K45). Lassina from Timbuktu said, "We Muslims who have problems—we accept them. . . . If you make your name heard, it will be dirtied" (T6). The population's reluctance to contact the police or judiciary not only reflects greater trust in traditional and religious institutions, but also suggests the state institutions' inability to grow and improve. If Malian citizens do not use these institutional channels, it is unlikely that they will adapt or conform to citizens' needs or become more accountable to their demands.

Partisan versus Consensus Conceptions of Democracy

As noted in the seminal work of Frederic Schaffer (2000), in order to understand the obstacles to Malian citizens' engagement with democracy, it is important to interrogate their conception of *politiki*. The fact that the Bambara language borrows the French word *politique* to describe the current system reveals the Malian conception of *politiki* as something alien to their traditional understanding of governance. The appropriation of the French term is particularly striking because the Bambara language is brimming with a rich vocabulary related to governance, stemming from centuries of experience with decentralized rule. Malians have adapted aspects of this vast political vocabulary to describe other parts of the current system of governance.

Malians' comprehension of *politiki* is directly tied to their understanding of multiparty democracy. *Politiki* is conceived by citizens as a narrow range of partisan politics and not as related to public policy or broader subjects related to politics. For instance, the phrase *politiki ton*, which literally means "politics group," describes political parties rather than civil servants or policy makers. In the minds of most Malians, politics is not a means for voicing their preferences or creating policy change—it is an isolated realm of competition for electoral power.

Conversations with citizens revealed the perception of politics' narrow scope. In Kayes, we talked to Ahmed, an artisan who left his native village of Sofara in the Mopti region to look for employment in Kayes. During our survey, he was busy making aluminum cooking spoons, but he took time to respond to each of our questions thoughtfully. He spoke eloquently about the problems facing the residents of Sofara, but when we asked if he would ever run for office (and participate in *politiki*) in the future, he replied, "I would run [only] if the development of my commune [Sofara] was linked to my candidacy . . . if politics could affect development" (KV38). Ahmed talked about development and politics as if the two were fundamentally disconnected.

Studies of political culture in Senegal find a similar negative characterization of electoral politics in the Wolof word *politig*. Schaffer's (2000:77) study of democracy in Senegal traces the negative associations of *politig* back to

TABLE 3.1.
Bamana political vocabulary

fanga	Power or force. Someone who has power or is in charge would be referred to as a *fangatigi* (lit., the one with power). *Fanga ton* is a group of people in power.
faso	Homeland, native land.
jamana	Collective grouping, country. The president is often referred to as the *jamanatigi*.
malidenw, jamanadenw	Citizens (lit., children of Mali).
nyogon-deme	Civic spirit, a willingness to help one another.

Note: For a discussion of the historical roots and appropriation of Bambara political vocabulary, see County and Skinner 2008; Bagayoko 1989. For a discussion of distinctions between *jamana* and *faso*, see Skinner 2012.

colonial times: "For Wolofones, then, the 'French' meaning of *politig* carries a range of positive connotations; the 'Wolof' meaning, in contrast, is strongly pejorative and indicates a variety of dishonest or deceitful behaviors. Many Senegalese associate this Wolof meaning of *politig* with the self-serving lies politicians tend to tell in search of votes and support." Schaffer contrasts *politig* with the Wolof word *demokaraasi*, which has also been borrowed from the French language but is used to describe the tenets of consensual democracy, such as mutual understanding, equality, consensus, and deliberation (ibid.:58). Another scholar of Senegal, Sheldon Gellar (2005:12), explains *demokaraasi*: "The concept of *demokaraasi* is particularly prevalent in villages and local communities where people prefer to come to a consensus on the candidate or party of their choice in order to reinforce local solidarity. . . . The communitarian values inherent in the Wolof notion of *demokaraasi* also work to promote reconciliation after conflict and reduce the likelihood of these conflicts ending in violence."

As these depictions of Senegalese political culture reveal, one problematic aspect of *politiki*, or pluralist democracy, is that its partisan nature contradicts almost a thousand years of rule through consensual democracy in the West African region. Consensual democracy is similar to the idea of deliberative democracy, where citizens are free to express their concerns and they discuss multiple perspectives until all group members agree on a final solution. This practice dates back to the thirteenth century when Sundiata Keita, the founder of the Mali Empire, ruled indirectly over decentralized kingdoms by consulting regularly with the leaders from conquered areas. The tradition of consultation continued with the Kulubali *ton fanga* in the seventeenth century and Cheikhou Amadou's consultative *madjilis* in the nineteenth century (Baudais and Chauzal 2006; Gellar 2005; Sears 2007).

In contrast, the concepts of "opposition" and minority versus majority were not introduced until colonial times and most recently were reintroduced during the transition to multiparty democracy. These dramatic changes to established systems of power and authority were unsettling to many citizens. As a high-ranking member of the National Independent Electoral Commission explained: "Starting in 1992, the guiding principle—one man, one vote—this was a huge change in the way that Malians perceived participation. At the village level all decision making was done in consensus style—discussions might take forever, but everyone needed to be convinced. [Elections] introduced this aspect of individualism, the ability to dissent. We had to learn about a majority and a minority that opposed it" (interview, May 18, 2009).[6]

Data from the 2002–2003 Afrobarometer survey support this thesis. In response to a question that asked respondents whether "in order to make decisions in our community, we should talk until everyone agrees," or whether "since we will never agree on everything, we must learn to accept differences of opinion within our community," 66% of Malians said they prefer the consensus style, compared to an African mean of 50% (Logan 2008:9). The reluctance to embrace the concept of opposition is certainly not just a Malian, or even African, phenomenon. Adam Przeworski (2008:12) shows that the US founding fathers were extremely hesitant to welcome opposition politics, fearing violence and division, and that their initial understanding of representation was closer to the deliberation and consensus valued by Malians. The acceptance of the utility of parties as representing different constituents' interests happened over time as leaders saw that consensual governance was not feasible on a large scale.

Jonathan Sears (2007:172) argues that Mali's history of consensus democracy impedes a full transition to pluralist democracy because citizens are wary of the opposition. This creates an environment where there is little real political competition. In her analysis of election results and public goods provision in Mali, Jessica Gottlieb (2015) demonstrates how damaging the lack of credible opposition is. She finds that when all parties win seats on municipal governing councils, they are more likely to collude and provide fewer public goods than in instances where at least one party does not win a seat.

This is not to say that the implementation of multiparty democracy has prevented Mali's political culture and political institutions from benefiting from elements of its consensual democratic heritage (Pringle 2005). The Malian government has attempted to harness some of this tradition in the form of institutional innovations. Shortly after deposing dictator Moussa Traoré, the transitional governing committee convened a national conference in July 1991 with members of the military, political parties, labor unions, and human rights associations and other representatives of civil society in what many regard as the most inclusive forum to take place on the continent. The conference shaped the elements that would enter the new constitution. After the founding election, the new president, Alpha Oumar Konaré, introduced the Question and Answer Assembly (Espace d'interpellation démocratique), an annual opportunity for citizens to present their grievances to a national audience in the deliberative tradition (Wing 2008:125).

Villages continue to uphold the tradition of consensual democracy. Aggrieved citizens have the right to present their perspectives to a traditional leader in a specified meeting place. There is some evidence that municipal officials have internalized the need to receive constituents and listen to their concerns. Compared to 19 other African countries, Mali ranks second best, behind Burkina Faso, in terms of citizens' perception that municipal officials listen to their grievances—consistent with the tenets of consensual democracy (Logan 2010:25). Malian municipal officials also fall above the African median in terms of citizens' perception of their ability to "handle" complaints (ibid.). Citizens' interactions with mayoral offices are critical. If citizens incorporate their traditions of airing grievances, deliberation, and group problem solving into the way that they engage with local bureaucratic politics, this exercise of voice could eventually make elected officials more relevant and accountable. Citizens will have firsthand experience with politicians and bureaucrats, which will enable them to evaluate and reward or sanction their performance. Without this engagement, mayors and their staffs can operate without being accountable to constituents, and those offices will stagnate or become self-serving.

Co-opted Participation

Many Malians are skeptical of electoral processes because they have witnessed vote buying or other types of material rewards or sanctions for participation. The short-term calculus that motivates this type of participation crowds out citizens' true expression of political voice. While some entrepreneurial Malians rightly recognize *kalata wati* (the campaign period) as a rare opportunity to extract resources from the state, this type of distribution does not have a productive impact on broader political institutions. Rather than collecting information about the interests of their constituents or formulating policy platforms to meet citizens' needs, Malian politicians engage in what the local vernacular describes as "fishing." A village leader from the Koulikoro region explained, "We are nothing but fish to them [political parties]. They come to our village during the campaigns and cast their nets. Once they reel in their catch—their work is done" (interview, October 2011).

Interviews in Mali confirmed that incentivized or co-opted participation during election time was rampant. An environment of imperfect electoral processes complicates the assumption that participation is the active expression of political preferences, while abstention is indicative of apathy or ignorance. Two respondents from Timbuktu illustrate how internal efficacy and participation are not always positively related. Saouda, a Tuareg woman living in a makeshift shack on one of the sand streets in Timbuktu, ranked in the lowest economic quintile of our survey respondents. She could not afford the fees to send any of her five children to any school. She could not explain executive term limits nor name the president of the National Assembly, her mayor, or the majority party, but she claimed to identify with that majority party: ADEMA (T25). Although Saouda expressed a partisan identity as a member of ADEMA, she lacked many of the attributes required for full democratic agency.

I contrast Saouda with Boubacar, a Songhai respondent from a nearby neighborhood in Timbuktu. In describing his experience leading up to the 2009 municipal elections, Boubacar highlighted the role of the conditional monetary aid provided by electoral entrepreneurs. Boubacar explained how foreign aid is often appropriated as a political resource. He described his refusal to trade his vote for aid: "The neighborhood received some aid from abroad, so I went to the *chef du quartier* to get my allotment, but he refused to give it to me. This was unjust as I'm very poor with a lot of children to feed. Not long after, when the election campaigns started, I saw him coming around with electoral cards. He told me to vote for a certain party, but I refused. I never got any aid. The relationship between power and politics happens like that" (T39). This description of collusion between traditional authorities and a dominant party in the context of extreme poverty problematizes understanding of Saouda's political agency. Despite her low level of information and income, she may be very aware of how her party allegiance can earn greater access to resources, which can finance some meat for the family's dinner pot. This, however, cannot be characterized as constructive democratic participation.

On the contrary, Boubacar's refusal to trade his vote for aid money is an empowered act of defiance against a rigged system. Boubacar is in a much better economic and social position than Saouda. Thirteen of Boubacar's children attended public school and three went on to university—a feat less than 3% of the population manages to attain. Now in his 60s, perhaps Boubacar feels that he can rely on his children's support and is less desperate for politicized assistance. His protest cost him access to economic resources, but reflected his commitment to the integrity of democratic politics. Boubacar is not unlike skeptical democratic consumers in other contexts with weak democratic institutions, such as Krishna's (2002) despondent citizens in India or Moehler's (2008) distrusting democrats in Uganda. The problem is that if mistrust breeds non-participation, then institutions will not have to face the pressure from citizen demands that is generated during citizen engagement. When Boubacar chooses not to vote out of further protest, his preferences are never captured at the ballot box. This dynamic complicates the notion of participation as an expression of voice. Boubacar's story also captures the role of local power brokers as mediating citizens' participation in the electoral process.

Language Barriers

The state bureaucracy in Mali operates in the former colonial language (French), which most Malians do not speak in their own homes. During its colonial rule, France did little to provide education or infrastructure resources for most of Mali; literacy in French was less than 7% at independence. However, the Malian government, like most other African independence regimes, adopted French as the official and functional language of the bureaucracy (Albaugh 2007). Despite initial attempts by Mali's first president, Modibo Keita, to build support and resources for local language media, there was no significant government policy to integrate local languages into governance structures.

The alien nature of bureaucratic institutions, emblematic of the former colonial power, is tangible to anyone who spends time in the Malian world outside of air-conditioned donors' offices or government ministries. Citizens conduct economic transactions in local languages, gossip with friends and relatives in local languages, and handle most other everyday interactions in local languages. In Mali, French is primarily spoken on school campuses, between university students, in government buildings, and in NGO or private sector offices. This linguistic separation is a constant reminder of the cleavage between the educated minority and the uneducated majority. For instance,

Nana was fortunate among her peers to have attended primary school for a few years as a young girl living in Kayes in the 1950s. However, she was not in school long enough to be able to achieve French literacy. She feels that this directly impedes her ability to interact with the government: "Since I can't write [in French], I can't get much from the government" (K39).

The democratic era of politics is still linked to the foreign tongue of the colonizers, which more than 70% of Malians do not speak. The disjuncture between the regional languages of trade—Bambara and Songhai—and the French-speaking bureaucracy weakens citizens' connection to the state in three ways. First, when bureaucratic institutions that are linked to service delivery, governance, or justice operate in a foreign tongue, it decreases their transparency and accessibility to many Malians. Those citizens who do not speak French rely on brokers who speak French or have intimate local knowledge of the system to mediate their interactions with state institutions. The inability to communicate with the bureaucracy may dampen citizens' willingness to engage with these institutions or prompt them to pursue other more intelligible and efficacious solutions if there are other options. For instance, why would non-French-speaking citizens pursue formal court rulings if they can turn to a traditional leader who operates under more transparent guidelines in an accessible language? Second, if citizens cannot read the formal laws on the books, it becomes difficult to anticipate, expose, or address injustice. If citizens do not know the formal laws that exist, it reduces their bargaining power with bureaucratic authorities. Finally, astute citizens know that local judicial institutions may pursue rulings that favor the most powerful citizens rather than strictly adhering to what is written on paper. Idrissa, a resident of Mopti, explained his cynical take on the justice system by using a Bambara proverb: "Even if it is easy to judge a poor person, it is very difficult to judge a rich person" (M36). In other words, the powerful are protected and exempt from the law. This bifurcated class system further reduces ordinary citizens' sense of external efficacy.

The Dominant Francophone Elite

Those Malians who managed to obtain a colonial education benefited from their comparative language advantage in the post-independence era. Scholars of Mali have described the colonial authorities' introduction of French-language bureaucracy and schooling as a violent assault on local traditions of societal organization. A small group of individuals who attained French literacy became a fabricated new class, and this social elite was able to dominate the rest of the population with their linguistic skills (Brenner 2001; Gérard 1992). Since the colonial era, fluency in the official language of the Malian state has translated into political power. This new political power of education has been so strong that Shaka Bagayoko (1987:103) compares the post-independence ascendance of educated elites to the Malian folk tradition of a dominant leader reordering chaos with a simultaneous mastery of force, knowledge, and wealth.

At independence, the illiterate aristocracy and the rich bourgeoisie were marginalized from the political process (Meillassoux 1970:98). Ironically, due to their reluctance to attend colonial schools, the Malian aristocracy inadvertently allowed poorer and lower-caste citizens to profit from Western education (ibid.:102). In the first decades of independence, education created strong economic dividends; a college diploma guaranteed a salaried civil service job (Ba 2009).

In the multiparty context, the Malian political landscape remains dominated by a secular, Francophone-educated elite despite the country's majority-Muslim population. While French-language schooling no longer assures government employment, it remains a necessary condition for a position in government, international institutions, or international NGOs. Malian political leaders, especially at the national level, are a highly educated elite in contrast with the vastly preliterate society. Figure 3.2 compares the education levels of Malian legislators in office in 2009 and Malian respondents from the Afrobarometer survey. While the political elites are generally more educated than the masses that they represent in most African countries, the education gap in Mali is particularly pronounced. More than 45% of legislators have a university degree as compared to 2% of the Malian population. The same is true for ministry officials. In 2009, all but 2 of Mali's 30 ministers had university degrees, and those 2 went to Mali's prestigious military academy.

It is logical that Malians observe the differences between the people who run the government and themselves. However, unlike domination by caste, gender, or birthright, educational barriers can be overcome and degrees can be earned. Malian citizens, the vast majority of whom speak indigenous languages at home, have learned that French schooling is a key to political power and increased economic opportunities. Theoretically, Malian citizens or their children can gain the qualifications to fully engage with their system. This gives parents hope that their children might reach the top of this social hierarchy. Unfortunately, in recent years, burgeoning university enrollment and declining civil service opportunities have resulted in a growing number of

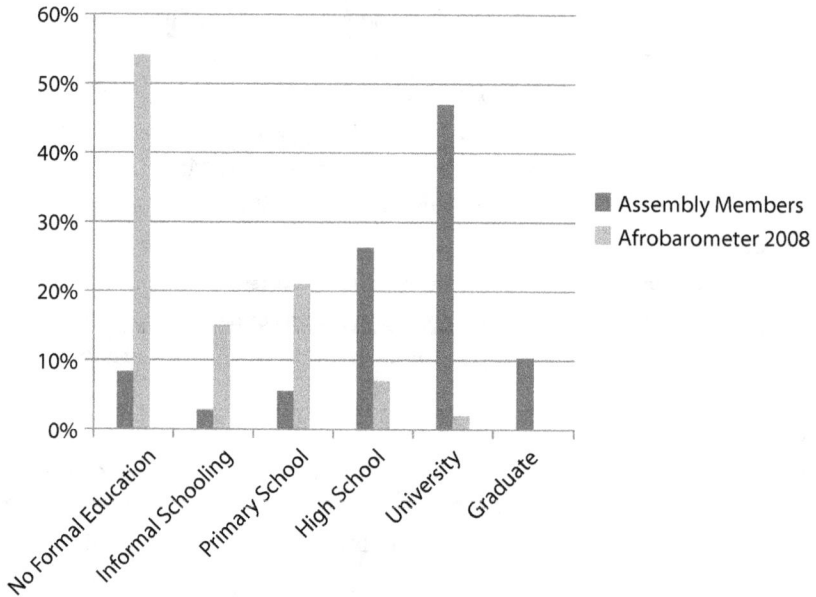

Figure 3.2. Comparison of assembly members' education levels to the Malian population. Sources: Elected leaders' education levels from *L'Assemblée nationale du Mali
sous la Troisieme Republique: Un guide à l'usage des élus, des citoyens et des partenaires extérieurs* (Bamako, Mali: Fourth Legislature, 2007–2012); national education
averages from www.afrobarometer.org, Round 4

unemployed university graduates and fewer opportunities for upward mobility through the state bureaucracy. Some parents have become extremely
skeptical about the economic returns from education.

Party Weakness

Malian parties are weak compared to those in other countries in sub-Saharan
Africa; most parties in pre-coup Mali lacked political legitimacy. Citizens
characterized their relationships with elected official and candidates as tem-
poral and inconsistent, and contrasted them with traditional or religious
leaders whose lives are entwined with their constituents in a more permanent way. Many respondents noted the divergence between the behavior of
elected officials before and after the electoral cycle: "Officials only come to
visit during elections" (K52). In contrast, traditional or religious leaders are
typically seen as more accountable. Djeneba said, "You can count more on
them [religious leaders] to help you resolve your problems" as opposed to the

president and other elected officials, where "the situation never changes, they are comfortable" (K52). In addition, parties are perceived as contrived and potentially disruptive. Kadiatou in Kayes explained why she isn't close to a political party, "We have tried a lot of different paths in vain" (K55). When asked if they were close to any political party, other respondents said *a be kele*—it is all the same.

Parties have not successfully introduced ideologically infused platforms and have neglected to engage with some of the most pressing societal issues (Bleck and van de Walle 2011). When respondents claim that "parties are all the same," they are accurately describing the political terrain. In national-level races, Malian parties are handicapped because they generally operate without ethnic bases of support and thus do not have clearly demarcated constituencies. Malians are at a disadvantage because ethnic or regional party affiliation might offer citizens cognitive shortcuts about which parties will best support their interests (Fridy 2007). If party leaders used similar heuristics, they could also easily identify their constituents and those constituencies' preferences.

While Malians still may be more likely to vote for a co-ethnic, or a "cousin,"[7] and parties might run candidates with greater relationships to the demographic groups of a particularly constituency (Dunning and Harrison 2010), these interest groups, since they are not courted systematically, do not affect party platforms or ideology. Most parties continue to rely on group mobilization and seek out patrons or leaders who can organize constituencies of clients, but this is a more decentralized effort than in other countries; recruitment and allegiance are determined at a very localized level (Koter 2013). It is not uncommon in rural areas to find one village voting for one party and, right down the road, partisan supporters of another party. At the local level, ethnic groups might vote along different party lines, but this does not apply at the national level.

The dearth of ethnic organizing is most likely a factor that contributes to Mali's low voter turnout. In other countries, strict ethnic or regional mobilization serves as a palliative for skepticism about the political system. Even though citizens might be guessing about a co-ethnic's ability to legislate more favorable policy, this mobilization still draws citizens into the political process. If participation in the electoral process breeds support for democracy and internal efficacy, this engagement is ultimately productive for democracy (Lindberg 2006). In Mali, the absence of consistent party platforms, stereotyped party membership, or other heuristics means that prospective voters have few clues to distinguish between different parties and candidates. Subsequently, they are less engaged in the political process.

Former president Touré leveraged the public's distaste for partisanship by running as an independent in the 2002 and 2007 presidential elections. ATT capitalized on his reputation as a military hero and national unifier by running on a "consensus" platform, which explicitly referenced Mali's tradition of consensual democracy. Once in office, he appointed members of all different parties and used his apolitical association, Mouvement Citoyen (Citizen Movement), as a tactic to gain their allegiance, thus eliminating any viable opposition (Baudais and Chauzal 2006). In the 2007 election, Touré was backed by a super-alliance of 43 parties, including Mali's strongest party—the Alliance for Democracy in Mali (ADEMA). ATT's actions and ADEMA's willingness to align with him blocked the threat of a credible opposition and significantly weakened the party system. ATT's nonpartisan strategy has been copied by candidates in legislative and municipal elections; since 2002, there has been an increase in independent candidates and independent victories in Mali. In his tenure as an independent, Touré contributed to the erosion of a Malian opposition. During his second election campaign, all but two parties joined the president's coalition.

Institutional Alternatives: Civil Society, Religious Leadership, and Traditional Authorities

In contrast to the gradual weakening of political parties in the wake of the democratic transition, other types of political representation, including civil society and religious associations, have flourished. These groups often fulfill functions that the state or elected officials cannot or choose not to do. They provide Malians with alternative pathways to achieve their day-to-day goals. Mali boasts an active civil society due in part to the democratic opening of the public sphere, but also due to a historic need for self-reliance. The Bambara saying "putting our hands together gives power to everyone" pre-dates the democratic era. Many Malians are members of groups or associations called *tonw* (the plural form of *ton*). These associations exemplify the consensual tradition and provide members with the strength in numbers to protect their rights and aggregate their interests. *Ton* is a popular and expansively utilized term. For instance, in Bambara, the European Union translates to Toubabouw Ton (European Group) and *fanga ton* (power group) refers to the ruling elites at the center of all political power. Many Malians also engage in less formalized structures of exchange and support called *grinw*. Typically, a group of Malians will sit around, drink tea, and discuss politics and other topics, but these groups can also help provide moral and financial support and provide public goods for their communities. The different indigenous organizations provide a range of services, including access to credit and social support networks, but they also provide members with vehicles to address their grievances. Malian citizens feel more comfortable approaching bureaucratic or traditional authorities as part of a group.

The communal organization of political action is reflected in citizens' conception of participation. When we spoke to Malians about their interaction with elected officials, we asked the standard Afrobarometer question in the singular, "Have you contacted an elected official in the past year?" However, the vast majority of our respondents explained the contact in terms of group membership—what their *ton* had done. Daly, a 30-something Malian in the Lafiabougou neighborhood of Kayes, never attended school but serves as the president of a women's association. She and her fellow members had contacted the authorities multiple times in order to address the flooding problem in her neighborhood (KV53). Apparently Daly's *ton* was fairly well known in her community. Other respondents in the same neighborhood talked about the group's activism in separate interviews, noting that there was a women's association that had gone to speak with the mayor's office about the flooding issue. Another respondent was Nanette, who is Bobo—a minority ethnic group in the Sikasso region. A lifelong Catholic (and one of the few Christian participants in our survey), she attended the mission's primary school in the colonial era and is now an active member of the Catholic association in Sikasso. She often goes with her Catholic association to the mayor's office to address problems (S54).

Associational life even dictates citizens' understanding of what is possible. When asked if he had personally ever contacted a government official, Modibo from Sikasso responded by referencing the actions of an association of which he is a member. "We have a fishing association, but we didn't go see the authorities" (S42). This was completely outside of the phrasing of the question, but for Modibo, and many other respondents, visiting a government official requires a preliminary condition of associational membership. Modibo was not alone in his rephrasing of the question. My research assistants would always pose the question about visiting municipal authorities in the singular, and, consistently, respondents would reply in the plural (we) to talk about what their *ton* had or hadn't done.

While robust networks in civil society provide Malians with communal support to achieve their goals, group mobilization could also undermine the principle of one man, one vote. As Sears (2007:176) warns, just because decisions are made collectively does not require them to be made democratically. Mali is still largely stratified by age, gender, wealth, and, in some instances, caste.[8] Many Malians participate in hierarchical associations, which often include deliberative procedures and offer members a chance to voice their opinions, but ultimately many of these groups follow the authority of the strongest member or patron.

Much of rural Mali remains hierarchically organized at the family and village level. There is a head of household in the family compound, which is usually inhabited by multiple families and generations, who is called the *dutigi* (Bambara). Most villages have a *dugutigi* as well as a council of advisors (Bagayoko 1989). In addition, marabouts (Sufi religious leaders), *donzonw* (hunters also known for their mastery of traditional medicine), councils of elders, griots or *djeliw* (oral historians), and imams are all figures who can play advisory or mediatory roles related to everyday governance. Given the widespread poverty in Mali, those members of society with substantial resources can also be called upon for advice, material contributions, or brokering relationships with government figures or the bureaucracy in times of need. Communal mobilization or mobilization through brokers often takes place through hierarchical, vertical networks, in which some members' voices count more than others. For instance, it is not uncommon for women to vote with their husbands or to follow a chief's voting instructions (Bleck and Michelitch 2015a). To assure that all citizens are capable of and willing to express their own opinion of democratic authorities, these types of mobilization might be best as a complement to other types of direct engagement with the state.

Alternative Forms of Representation through Traditional and Religious Authority

The confidence that 82% of Malians place in traditional authorities, such as the chiefs mentioned above, is higher than their confidence in any other political institution (Little and Logan 2008:13). In comparison, the percentage of Malians who trust the courts, local council members, and the National Assembly is, respectively, only 43%, 59%, and 61% (ibid.). Lala in Bamako described the difference between the population's perception of the justice system and of traditional chiefs: "Everyone follows the chief—whatever he says—people really trust him," but to engage with the justice system, "you need money to make things happen" (BA60). In the Afrobarometer survey, Malians also rated traditional authorities as the least corrupt of any institution (Little and Logan 2008:14). The gap between Malians' confidence in traditional authorities and in other types of political authorities is wider than in any of the other 17 countries surveyed. As a result, most Malians, especially in rural areas, prefer to consult with traditional or religious leaders rather than contact elected officials (Coulibaly and Diarra 2004:17).

In Mali, politics is described in juxtaposition to more "legitimate" forms of political authority: religious and traditional leaders. Seventy-six percent of Afrobarometer respondents wanted their traditional leaders to have greater influence in governing the local community (Mali Summary of Results 2009:42, available at www.afrobarometer.org). Politics, frequently associated with greed and material interest, is described as "dirty" in contrast to religious or traditional leaders, who are described as pure and clean. Our interviews revealed a mental compartmentalization of the political and the religious and traditional spheres. Many respondents believed that participation in *politiki* corrupts, and they stressed the importance of separation between the political and religious spheres.

Boubacar, the same resident of Timbuktu who refused to sell his vote, complained, "Religious authorities can act like those in political power. It [religion or religious practice] should be different than politics" (T39). *Politiki* is also perceived as corrupting traditional elites.[9] The Afrobarometer Round 4 data reveal that 56% of Malian respondents preferred that traditional leaders stay out of politics (Summary of Results 2009:43).[10] This also reflects a legacy of separation between the communities of scholars and warriors; the former were distinguished by their religious devotion and by the latter's distance from them (Brenner 2001:90).

The existence of competing forms of authority in the Malian context complicates voter participation in ways that do not matter in consolidated democracies. While low American electoral participation is comparable to Mali's paltry turnout, disaffected American voters cannot turn to paramount chiefs instead of mayors. Even if they turn to religious authorities to resolve a problem, they will eventually need to work through bureaucratic channels. However, state weakness in Mali puts the relevance of the state in question. Faced with a problem or wanting to access a service, Malians have a choice to exit bureaucratic state channels and consult with a different authority figure who can find a solution. The separation of many citizens from the secular state is exacerbated by religious or traditional authorities, who willingly court those who are unsatisfied or alienated by the secular state authority.

As I discussed in the previous chapter, this is problematic for democratic institutionalization because unless these intermediary authorities apply pressure on state authorities to address authentic citizen grievances, the state will fall into a "cycle of slack" (Hirschman 1970). The exodus out of bureaucratic state channels has the simultaneous effect of reducing the relevance of the state to citizens' lives and lessening the likelihood that they will engage with it in the future. Furthermore, even when intermediary institutions make contact with the state, there is a risk that the individual voices of less powerful citizens will be lost or misrepresented in the aggregated lobby, especially when the mediating institution is hierarchical.[11] It is true that these brokers offer viable alternatives of accountability and representation. However, an overreliance on non-state intermediaries may have longer-term impacts on state capacity, perceptions of legitimacy, or citizenship (Cammett and Mac-Lean 2011).

Islam and Electoral Politics in Mali

In other parts of the Islamic world, religious authorities and associations have assisted voters' transition into the world of multiparty elections or democracy by running Islamic candidates. These candidates might appear more credible or familiar since they are linked to religious institutions present in citizens' everyday lives. For instance, Pepinsky and Welborne (2010) show that Indonesian voters perceive Islamic parties to be more credible than other parties. But Mali maintains a stark divide between religion and formal electoral politics. Religious and secular authorities live in relative harmony and govern separate spheres of societal relations. One pertains to elections and governance through the mayor's office, while the other regulates everyday events such as weddings, baptisms, and conflict resolution.

In his dissertation on the political culture in Niger, Idrissa (2008) describes this divide as "competing modernities"—one tied to the West and the other to the Muslim world. In Niger, the struggle for power and political authority between secular and Islamic elites is more contentious than in Mali, but the tension and competition between spheres of authority are relevant for understanding Mali. Idrissa writes: "they [the competing modernities] produce the

specific cultures of the 'civil society' and of the 'clerical society,' which lead . . .
to a kind of heterogeneous order irreducible to either the liberal republican
sovereign or the Islamist sovereign" (ibid.:10).

Like most other nations in Africa, Mali has strict laws banning religious
political parties (Bogaards, Basedau, and Hartmann 2010). Most political elites
are Western-educated and committed to French secularism (Bleck and van
de Walle 2011; Villalón 2010). Under the Traoré dictatorship, the AMUPI
(Association Malienne pour l'Unité et le Progrès de l'Islam) was the only recognized Islamic association. It was made up of clerics backed by the ruling
party. The dissolution of the ruling party's ban on religious groups outside of
its own AMUPI and the transition to democracy facilitated the promulgation
of religious associations and public discourse surrounding Islamic principles
and practices (Launay and Soares 1999; Soares 2005; Villalón 2010).

Democratization opened the door for the creation of a multitude of diverse
religious organizations and Islamic self-help associations. These gains have
not translated into the formal political sphere, however, since Islamic actors
remain outside it. Idrissa explains an analogous division of the secular state
sphere and Islamic actors in Niger despite the Muslim-majority population.
Francophone Muslims with no ideological orientation toward Islam tend to
"consider *laïcité*[12] as a form of practical arrangement which does not need to
be questioned as such—even though Islam necessarily influences their social
and political expectations. *Laïcité* allows them to privatize religion, in a way
analogous to how the principle of national unity calls for the privatization of
ethnicity. Religion and ethnicity are important factors in family life and social
gatherings, but are considered invalid orientations [in] the national public
space" (Idrissa 2008:240).

The secular state and governing elites maintain the distance between religious actors and electoral politics. Efforts by Islamic associations, such as the
Muslim Cultural Union, to integrate into the political sphere were thwarted
post-independence and then again under Moussa Traoré (Amselle 1985). Similarly, during the national conference held immediately after the transition to
democracy, Islamic groups attempted to create an Islamic state and to allow
the formation of Islamic political parties, but both attempts failed (Künkler
and Leininger 2009:1073). At least one Islamic party, Hizbollah, attempted to
enter the formal political arena in 1991, but it was stopped (Brenner 2001:294;
Soares 2005:282). Jonathan Sears (2007) chronicles candidate Keita's failed
attempt to run as an "Islamic" candidate during the 2002 presidential race

as well as the High Council of Islam's (HCI) failed attempt to find a political party to support its campaign agenda.

Islamic groups in Mali are also hindered by their fragmentation. There are an estimated 135–190 Islamic organizations, and their lack of centralization weakens their potential for mobilization in comparison to organizations like the Sufi brotherhoods of Senegal (Künkler and Leininger 2009:1077). Malians also are unlikely to identify with a specific brand of Islam. The Pew Survey (2012) reveals that over 90% of Malians describe themselves as "Muslim" rather than by a particular brotherhood or sect. While there is a divide between the historically powerful Sufi hierarchies and the "reformist" Salafists, many other Malians choose to blend elements of reformist and Sufi practices, and identify as part of neither specific group (Soares 2005).

Religious organizations have been most successful in demonstrating their organizational potential and political weight in the sphere of contentious politics rather than in formal political channels. Religious leaders continue to play a consultative and advisory role as well as acting as societal mediators. The High Council of Islam plays an official advisory role for the government. It has successfully vetoed legislation for the abolition of the death penalty and of family law. Months prior to the 2012 elections, the HCI once again filled the national soccer stadium with a rally that attempted to court candidates who reflected the HCI's values.

Malian Islamic groups have engaged in contentious politics and taken advocacy positions in an attempt to influence candidates' platforms. Throughout sub-Saharan Africa, there has not been the emergence of Islamic parties or Islamic candidates running as independents as in the rest of the Muslim-majority world (Bleck and Patel 2015). In Mali, Islamic associations have not traditionally provided an electoral network for presidential aspirants as has been observed among the Mourides in Senegal.[13] Islamic associations' reluctance or inability to partner with candidates has reduced the possibilities for electoral mobilization and incorporation. Given the strength and salience of religious networks in citizens' lives, Islamic associations' merger with political parties would surely have the effect of bolstering and legitimizing formal political participation. However, this political blending would likely only be credible if the candidate himself subscribed to discourse and actions consistent with the backing organizations. The popular response to religious mobilization against the 2009 Family Code demonstrated the latent populist audience that exists for religious political organizing.

The State of Political Knowledge

Twenty years after the democratic transition, Malians' political skepticism should not be misinterpreted as widespread ignorance or apathy. Despite high levels of poverty and relatively low education attainment rates, many Malians were very informed about the state of political affairs. In order to understand the type of knowledge that education could generate or improve, it is first important to explore the population's baseline: What do Malians know about their own political system? I describe the political knowledge and political behavior of Malians using data from our survey and comparative Afrobarometer data. As described in the previous chapter, the survey asked a series of Afrobarometer Round 3 questions in the form of a pop quiz to evaluate each respondent's political knowledge: Can you name your mayor? Can you name the president of the National Assembly? Can you name the majority party? Do you know the executive term limits?

Surprisingly, the survey results reveal that most Malians have internalized the rules of the new democratic game. More than 70% of Malians, most of whom are illiterate, were able to provide the executive term limits.[14] In fact, when asked about presidential term limits, the majority of Malians responded in the same way: *san duuru, siɲe fila* (five years, two times). The repetition of this phrase, using identical language, suggests that the rules that govern Malian democracy have seeped into public discourse.

Malians' knowledge may be due in part to public information campaigns about democracy that circulate through local radio as well as a past history of electoral turnover.[15] Sensitization efforts around democratic rules have been relatively widespread since the 1990s. For instance, during the 1997 presidential election, a well-known comedian ran as a publicity stunt and has since continued to raise awareness through comedy skits about the importance of voting. Prior to the 2009 municipal elections, USAID sponsored a commercial that juxtaposed the elections in two communes: a "bad" commune, where vote buying was rampant, which resulted in a dirty and unorganized neighborhood, and a "good" commune, where people voted their principles and candidates responded to their needs.

As figure 3.3 demonstrates, Malians outperform their peers in Benin and Senegal and match their peers in Nigeria in their knowledge of term limits. The data may reflect Mali's experience with executive turnover, including President Konaré's willingness to respect term limits and step down in 2002.

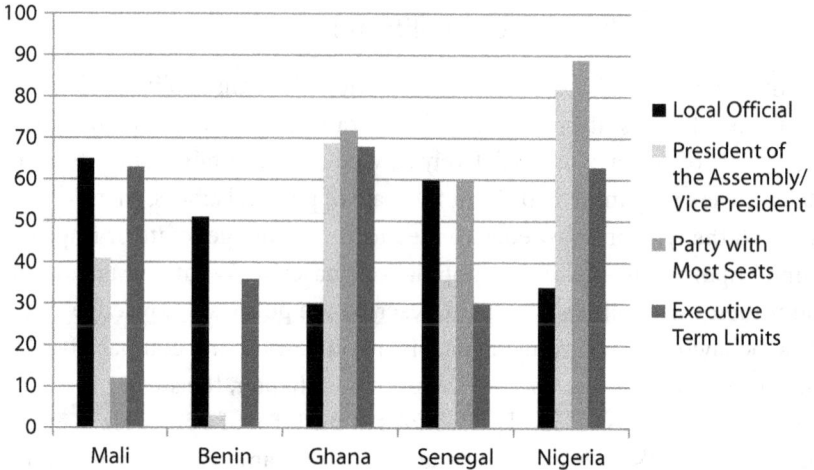

Figure 3.3. Political knowledge about the government in percentages. Note: Local officials varied according to the specific electoral system; Ghana and Nigeria poll respondents were asked about the vice president, while the Francophone countries were asked about the head of the legislature. Source: Data from "Summary of Results" 2005

In 2009, there was an active debate about ATT's obligation to step down, especially in light of President Tandja's and Blaise Compaoré's choices in neighboring Niger and Burkina.

According to the Afrobarometer survey, Malians are more likely to be able to name their local representatives than respondents in Senegal, Benin, Ghana, and Nigeria. Within the country, more Malian respondents are able to name their mayor while a lower percentage of respondents can name the president of the assembly or the party with the most seats. One factor may be that municipal elections in Mali are often described as "elections of proximity": citizens mobilize around family members or friends who are candidates. In sum, respondents reveal a higher level of familiarity with municipal authorities. This familiarity is most pronounced in the village setting, where citizens benefit from the greater visibility of candidates in their "backyard."

Citizens are also more willing to evaluate local officials. Unlike the president, who is often referred to with a statement of deference, such as "God gave him power," or political institutions like the National Independent Electoral Commission, with which citizens are largely unfamiliar, respondents speak about mayors in concrete language. Their evaluations are rooted in their own personal observation rather than abstract speculation based on third-party information. Even in instances when citizens do not interact with the candidates themselves, they are better able to monitor the success or failure of political officials. Higher electoral turnout and turnover at the municipal level also suggest that Malians are more capable and more willing to evaluate and critique members of the local government. Voting rates in the 2004 and 2009 municipal elections (43% and 45%, respectively) were higher than in the 2002 and 2007 presidential elections. There are also lower rates of incumbency wins at the local level in Mali. In the 2004 municipal elections, more than half of all mayors were voted out of office (Magassa and Meyer 2008:16). In 2009, only about 20% of incumbents were reelected (Kusch 2010).

Fewer respondents were able to provide specific information about national-level politics. Forty-one percent of Malians can name the president of the assembly while much higher percentages of Ghanaians and Nigerians can name their vice president. The inability to name the president of the National Assembly may reflect the weak visibility and power of the position. If we broaden the comparative lens, a greater percentage of Malians could name the president of their National Assembly than Americans could name the incoming Speaker of the House (Pew Survey 2010). This is striking given the comparative age of the institutions and the median education levels in the United States and serves as a reminder that greater education does not automatically translate into greater political knowledge. One explanation might be that Malian politics, like politics in many African nations, remains largely personal. Malians are able to name key political actors and locate them within Malian society. While this does not bode well for the strength of democratic institutions, it does mean that Malians tend to be fairly well informed about individual politicians.

Malians are least able to name the party with the most seats compared to their peers in neighboring countries.[16] This finding reflects the large number of Malian parties (113) and relative party weakness in Mali. While ADEMA was initially dominant in the first two presidential and legislative elections, in part due to a boycott by opposition parties in 1997, it lost its majority position in the 2002 race. This prompted the party to join the presidential coalition in 2007. Given the past history of coalitions and the fact that ADEMA did not run a presidential candidate in the 2007 elections, it is logical that Malians have the most difficulty with this question.

In Mali, it appears that education could make the greatest impact on citizens' knowledge of national politics: the name of national-level representatives other than the president and the name of the majority party. Since so many citizens, most of whom did not complete primary school, already articulate the executive term limits precisely, we would anticipate a lower likelihood that additional education would have a strong effect on this aspect of political knowledge. Education beyond primary school could have a ceiling effect on knowledge of term limits, but it might be more productive in teaching about politics on the national stage. Similarly, since more than 60% of Malians already can name their mayor, education might not add much to their ability to assess municipal politics.

The Participation Problem

It is important to understand preexisting patterns of political engagement and patterns of mobilization in order to understand the marginal changes that education could stimulate. As already mentioned, voting rates in Mali are much lower than in other countries in Africa. While voting only captures one aspect of citizens' participation, it serves as the basis for electoral democracy. Figure 3.4 shows the total levels of reported political participation of survey respondents based on six categories: if they voted in the 2007 presidential elections, if they campaigned in the 2007 presidential election, if they feel close to a party, if they have ever run for office, if they would ever consider running for office in the future, and whether they have contacted a government official in the last five years.[17]

Sixty-seven percent of respondents report voting, which is consistent with the percentage of respondents claiming to vote in the Afrobarometer data. It is important to acknowledge that responses are self-reported and therefore there is a potential for social desirability bias. The percentage of respondents claiming to have voted is more than 25 points higher than the actual national voter turnout for the 2007 presidential elections. One can assume that respondents are overreporting voting rates, and perhaps other forms of participation.[18] A little over 50% of respondents claimed to identify with a party; this is slightly lower than but consistent with the Round 1 Afrobarometer findings of 58% party identification in 2002, but much lower than the Afrobarometer Round 4 findings in 2008 of 69% party identification. Lower rates of party identification might reflect the urban bias of our survey. Rural residents often coordinate around a party through bloc voting, while urban votes are typically more malleable.

Consistent with my theoretical discussion in the previous chapter, there are lower rates of participation in "difficult" political activities (Nie, Junn, and

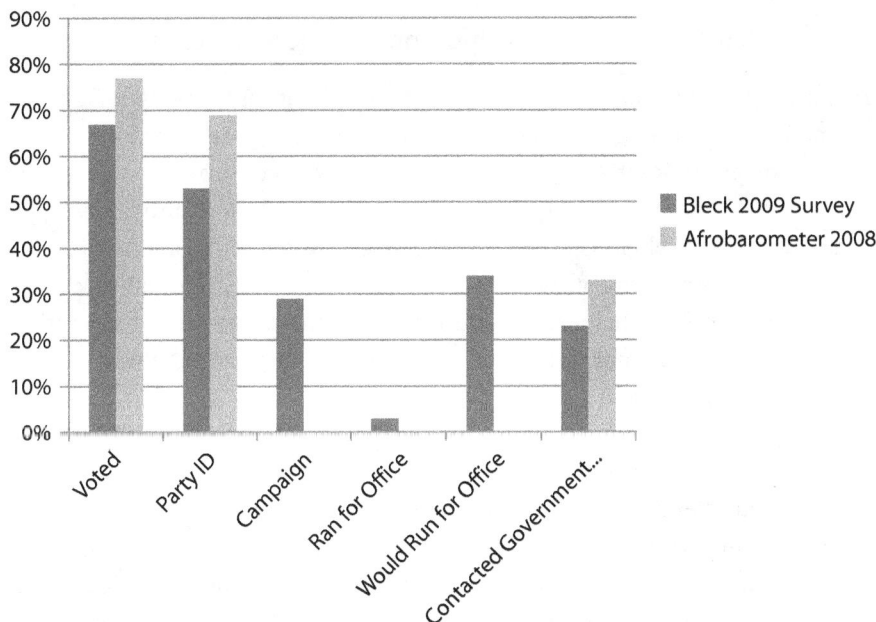

Figure 3.4. Reported participation rates. Source: Data from www.afrobarometer.org, Round 4

Stehlik-Barry 1996), which require greater amounts of internal efficacy. Low percentages of people reported a willingness to run for office (35%), participation in the 2007 presidential election campaign (29%), experience contacting a government official to address a problem or express an opinion in the last five years (23%), and past experience running for office (3%).[19] If citizens are going to campaign, they need to be able to convince others to vote for a party and thus have some knowledge about that party and the electoral race. If they ran for office or are willing to do so in the future, they need to be able to imagine themselves as competent and capable elected officials. Finally, it takes time and resources to contact a government official, who might not listen to demands or requests. This is coupled with citizens' fear of exploitation by a bureaucracy that operates in a colonial language. These factors make contacting a government official, especially without the support of an association, much more difficult. Based on the descriptive data, we can anticipate that education would have the greatest effect and make the greatest gains in more difficult forms of participation. In addition, more difficult activities should be less vulnerable to the "noise" introduced by short-term incentives, such as vote buying, because they require a threshold level of political competency.

The Obstacles to Deepening Democracy in Mali

In this chapter I have explored citizen skepticism about democracy and Francophone institutions of government to suggest the gains that education could have on democratic citizenship. The strong legacy of consensual governance, the weakness of political parties, the reliance on unelected authorities, and the reluctance of religious actors to endorse partisan politics all obstruct citizens' willingness to engage with *politiki*. While the democratic values of tolerance, trust, mutual help, and consensus that are born out of a deliberative democratic heritage may guide Malians' behavior, they do not always translate into participation in formal electoral politics.

In the following chapters, I suggest that education can empower citizens with tools and self-confidence to engage with the state and take advantage of the opportunities for self-expression offered by the new multiparty system. While existing structures of communal mobilization offer indirect opportunities for expression through group action, education could provide more individualized channels for the expression of voice. Greater engagement by individuals advocating for their own preferences could in turn stimulate more responsive institutions that would be accountable to a larger subset of the citizenry.

CHAPTER FOUR

Mali's Evolving Educational Landscape

Born in 1932, Tiemoko fought for the French army in French Indochina and later in Algeria. When he returned to Mali, he married, and he and his wife had four daughters. He supported Mali's independence movement and its first political party, the USRDA (in English, the Sudanese Union–African Democratic Rally), in its first electoral victory. He has continued to vote for the USRDA in each election since. Tiemoko never went to school, but the educational choice for his daughters was simple since there was only one school in his neighborhood of Banconi in the 1960s—the Sikoro public school. All of his daughters attended that public school. Now his neighborhood is filled with schooling options: a madrassa called Dar es Salaam; another public school, Nelson Mandela; a community school; and at least three private schools (Chez Kamikoko, Mamadou Konaté, and Jean Marie Cissé). He says, "Back then, there was only one school where we lived. Now, given the choice, I would send my children to private school" (BA51).

In Tiemoko's lifetime, Mali has not only become a sovereign nation-state, but also vastly expanded access to education and the schooling options offered to parents. In this chapter I explore the evolution of education in Mali to stress the unprecedented diversity of schooling options in the post-democratic era. I highlight the different skills and job opportunities afforded by different types of education, as well as the various sociopolitical networks and forms of authority connected to different schooling providers. I suggest that because of these different endowments, experience with public schools, madrassas, private secular schools, or community schools could shape citizenship behavior differently.

In a counterfactual world where Tiemoko could send his daughters to a private school instead of a state school, might this have changed his or their relationship to the Malian state? As a former member of the French military and supporter of the USRDA, Tiemoko's integration into Malian politics might have already been solidified and the fact that his children received a public school education might have had only a marginal impact on his relationship to the state. However, imagine one of Tiemoko's neighbors, Lassane, who recently migrated to Bamako from a village in Koulikoro that had no school. Lassane, a devout Muslim and relatively successful trader, enrolls his sons in a madrassa rather than in an overcrowded state school. How might this choice for religious, Arabic-language education shape Lassane and his sons' subsequent engagement with the state or with a religious authority? Would Lassane and his son relate to the state differently if he chose a secular, state-funded, Francophone school to educate his sons instead?

Democratization brought a dramatic expansion in primary enrollment due to three factors: liberalization, increased government resources for primary education, and greater donor support for basic education. Unlike in other contexts, where schooling and state-building were strategically reinforcing, the rapid expansion in Mali and in many other African countries focused on increasing access to education in order to bolster human development indicators. Through liberalization, the Malian public gained greater access to schools, but the Malian government simultaneously forfeited some of its control over the education sector (Lange and Diarra 1999). These policy changes resulted in large increases in enrollment and a more diverse pool of providers. In 1991, only 26% of the school-age population was enrolled in public primary schools.[1] By 2009, 82% of school-age students were enrolled in public schools, private schools, Francophone schools, madrassas, or community schools.[2] The growth of these different school types and increases in the public investment in education mean that more Malian citizens are making it into the classroom than ever before. However, these increases have precipitated a crisis of quality in Malian public schools. Many Malians lament that a primary school education or university degree mean far less, both in terms of the skills they endow the learner with and the economic opportunities they create, than they did 20 years ago. Can education foster citizenship in this context?

In this chapter I argue that different types of schooling have very different implications for students' economic and social mobility and skills for political action. I present data on parents' justifications for schooling to better understand how parents weigh various criteria when they enroll their children. Since parents' underlying values could determine both enrollment and political participation, it is important to understand these motivations if we want to understand the causal role of school consumption on parents' political behavior. The data demonstrate a diversity of enrollment strategies, but also instances where parents have been forced into school selection by constraints rather than being able to choose the school they want. This opens the possibility that the receipt of schooling itself might drive some of the differences in participation that I will discuss in chapter 6.

Schooling Options in Contemporary Mali

The educational expansion of the last 20 years has changed perceptions of quality among schooling options. For those Malians with sufficient means, public school is increasingly viewed as being of inferior quality to private school. Public schools are managed and funded by the Malian Ministry of Education, are secular, and use French as the language of instruction.[3] Most parents pay school fees, which are outlawed by law, but in practice range from 50 cents to US$10 a year per pupil. These funds were historically managed by parent-teacher associations but now by school management committees. In the past, the majority of teachers in public schools were civil servants who had obtained university degrees and the majority of private school teachers had inferior training. However, public schools are increasingly using contractual teachers who have more limited training and experience.

Since the transition to democracy in 1991, private schools mushroomed in the larger cities and now represent up to 50% of provision in some school districts in Bamako, Sikasso, and Kayes (Annuaire National 2006–2007). In these schools education is also Francophone and secular, but private schools typically offer smaller class sizes than public schools do. This is made possible through more lenient regulations about teacher qualifications and building codes. Private schools provide employment opportunities to many young diploma-holders who have not yet found work in their area of specialization.

There is a great diversity between types of private schools and also between their tuition rates. A typical private school charges between 2,000 and 2,500 CFA (US$4–$5) a month, but more elite private schools in Bamako can cost upward of US$2,000 a year. The schooling economy in Bamako is growing since many parents with sufficient means forgo public schools to enroll their children in private schools with higher graduation rates. Some public school teachers are concerned that private schooling has commoditized education and incentivized grade inflation and automatically passing students in order to improve completion rates (interviews with public school teachers in

Bamako, July 2007, and Sikasso, October 2009). Private universities have only been introduced in the past few years, but are growing in popularity in light of frequent public university strikes.

The Malian state groups Christian schools as a subset of private schools. During the colonial and post-independence periods, the government worked in exclusive collaboration with the Catholic Church as the only accredited private provider. Catholic schools received subsidies from the Malian government despite the fact that Christians make up only a small minority of the Malian population (Lange and Diarra 1999). The Catholic Church is still the dominant Christian provider in Mali; it has primary and secondary schools in many regional capitals. Some learners attend mission schools at subsidized rates, but others pay more than US$300 a year for tuition. Catholic schools are recognized for quality and are open to students of all religions. The majority of respondents in our sample who reported attending these schools were Muslim.

Decentralized community schools have existed since independence, but they flourished in the mid-1990s as a result of the USAID-funded community school program. Typically, these schools are constructed in rural areas that do not have other types of educational facilities. In 1994, community schools were formally acknowledged as "a subcategory of private schools in Mali, defined as any not-for-profit education center created and managed by a community or association, as opposed to an individual or corporations" (http://www.equip123.net/docs/e2-MaliCaseStudy.pdf). In many instances, international NGOs provide community members with training in management as well as supplementary literacy courses; the government provides monitoring and teacher training (interview with M. Coulibaly, World Education employee, March 2009). Many of the teachers are community members themselves. Some community schools use French as the language of instruction, and others use indigenous languages to transition to French instruction. Most community schools offer education only through the first cycle of primary school. Parents pay nominal fees or frequently pay with crops or other agricultural materials.

Related to community schools are community literacy centers, which offer indigenous-language literacy classes to citizens who did not receive formal education. These literacy centers were part of Konaré's campaign for "a school or community educational center . . . in each village." Classes are designed to help participants learn to read, write, and calculate in Bambara (or another relevant indigenous language), allowing them to better organize themselves and their agricultural or market activities (Gérard 1997b:75).

Madrassas are private schools that offer a modern curriculum in addition to religious instruction. Madrassas use Arabic as their primary language of instruction although the law requires them to teach French as a subject. Despite this regulation, a 2007 study of Malian madrassas revealed that the schools spent an average of only five hours a week teaching French (Moussa et al. 2007). Madrassas charge tuition rates of US$3–$5 per month, but like their peer Christian institutions, many offer subsidized tuition to some poorer students (interview with madrassa director, Niamakoro, Bamako, February 2009). Some madrassas receive external funding through remittances from the United States and Europe (interview with teachers and school directors, Kayes, July–August 2009). Foreign donors, notably Gaddafi, have also contributed money to the construction of madrassas.[4] Although more recently some madrassas have begun to offer secondary education, the majority of respondents in the sample attended madrassas exclusively at the primary level. Presently, the Malian government monitors and provides technical support to madrassas through the Center for the Promotion of the Arabic Language, which is housed in the Ministry of Education. The largest percentages of learners attending madrassas are in districts in Bamako, Sikasso, and Kayes (Annuaire National 2006–2007).

Informal Quranic education, which dates back centuries, continues to flourish in Mali today. It accommodates poorer populations who cannot afford to go to formal school or provides supplementary religious instruction for students who go to state schools (Gandolfi 2003:271). Students read texts in Arabic, but most of the instruction is in local languages until the highest levels of study. Most Quranic schools do not provide French-language education in their curriculum (Moussa et al. 2007). Education is hierarchical and personal; a teacher transfers knowledge to his student. A Quranic student is generally required to beg for alms totaling 100 CFA (20 US cents) per day to support his schooling. In some cases students live with their teachers, and this money goes toward their food and educational expenses. Other students attend Quranic schools to supplement Francophone education.

Quranic schools are the only schools, aside from adult literacy centers, that have not been accredited through integration into the government system. Many Quranic teachers feel that they have been unjustly and arbitrarily punished by the government educational system, which does not afford them subsidies or recognition. They feel that it is unfair for madrassas to receive support, while the vulnerable populations they educate are excluded from government aid. As one Quranic school director told me, "Our students— they too are *jamanadenw* [citizens]. We house them, we clothe them, and

TABLE 4.1.
Comparison of school types in Mali

School type	Language of instruction	Accredited by state	Highest level of schooling available	Primary school fees (in US currency)
Public	French or Bambara to French	yes	university	$.50–$10 per year
Private secular	French	yes	university	$4–$5 a month for most; some in Bamako up to $20–$40 a month; most prestigious over $1,000 a year
Private Christian	French	yes	high school	$10–$15 a month
Madrassa	Arabic; Franco-Arabic schools also teach in French	yes	high school	$3–$5 a month
Quranic	local language or Arabic	no	until mastery of Islamic knowledge	$1–$8 a month
Community	French or local language to French	yes	most schools only through first cycle of elementary school	sometimes goods in lieu of school fees
Literacy center	local language	no	informal only	majority are free

feed them. We should receive help from the government to accomplish these tasks" (interview with Kayes Association of Quranic Teachers, August 2009).

Table 4.1 summarizes the schooling tracks available to students in Mali. It demonstrates the variation of educational experiences among Malian students, including differences in the language of pedagogy, state oversight, and religious content. Given these differences, we might expect distinct schooling trajectories to generate different patterns of political knowledge and political participation.

State Education and Bureaucratic Mobility before the Democratic Transition

Since independence, education has facilitated political and bureaucratic mobility in most countries on the continent. In the independence era, the few Africans who managed to obtain secondary, Western schooling quickly climbed to the highest ranks of political leadership (Ekeh 1972). The Ponty School in Dakar educated the first presidents of Mali, Benin, Niger, and Côte d'Ivoire and the prime minister of Senegal (Sabatier 1978:266). Despite the potential for political and social mobility, most Malians were skeptical of French-language education. The first French-language schools in Mali confronted resistance and distrust from local populations, especially because a parallel Quranic education system was already widespread across much of the country (Ba 2009; Brenner 2001; Gérard 1997b). Many Malians, suspicious of colonial rule, refused to send their children to French schools, preferring instead to send them to Islamic schools. The French authorities courted the sons and relatives of chiefs and notables, but village chiefs would often send children of lower-caste village members to the European school, while keeping their own children far from French control (Gérard 1997b:99).

The population's suspicion of French education as well as the limited penetration of colonial infrastructure into Malian territory begot one of the lowest literacy rates of any African nation. At independence, only 7% of the Malian population was literate in the former colonial language as compared to an African average of 39%.[5] Mali's first president, Modibo Keita, campaigned on a platform to expand quality education to the masses. Under his leadership, Mali made substantive progress and increased enrollment rates to 24% in 1964.

Like many of his post-independence contemporaries, such as Julius Nyerere in Tanzania and Kwame Nkrumah in Ghana, Keita saw the educational system as part of a greater ideological revolution. The 1962 Educational Reform Law established nine years of compulsory education. There were five main principles outlined in the reform: a quality education for all; teaching that could facilitate development; teaching that respects Malian culture, but that creates diplomas that are equivalent to those in other modern states; educational content that respects not only African values and norms, but also universal values; and teaching that decolonizes the spirit and that rehabilitates Africa and its own valor (Obichere 1979:199). As these five principles reveal, Keita presented education as a tool for building human capital for the new state while simultaneously disassociating it from the former colonial power.

During Keita's tenure, the bureaucratic opportunities afforded by schooling, as well as explicit linkages between education and the regime, became more apparent. Keita enlisted students to spread the party message and his policies, and he guaranteed state employment for all graduates of secondary school, a practice that was continued until structural adjustment in the 1980s

(Brenner 2007:201). In the immediate post-independence era, even those citizens who only managed to obtain a sixth-grade diploma in the French system could qualify for a well-paying position as a civil servant.[6] Parents who enrolled their children, or at least tolerated their enrollment, began to see the financial returns of education. In the 1960s, many young, educated Malians leveraged their comparative schooling advantage to secure positions in the post-independence party.

Keita's resources ultimately proved insufficient to achieve his educational vision for Mali before he was toppled in a coup d'état in November 1968. Following the coup, the education system floundered under the Traoré dictatorship. A World Bank report estimates that gross enrollment had dropped to 20% by 1973 (Bender et al. 2007:1; Lange and Diarra 1999). In the next 15 years, gross enrollment improved a mere six percentage points.

Traoré sought tight control over the education sector: he stripped civic education from the curriculum in 1972. In the mid-1980s he made harsh changes to the education sector as a part of structural adjustment reforms. Seeking to reduce recurrent expenditures, including teachers' salaries,[7] the Traoré government reduced health and education spending from 20 billion CFA (US$40 million) in 1987 to 16 billion CFA (US$32 million) in 1991. One of the reforms was the "voluntary departure program" through which 1,000, or 12.5% of all teachers, left the education sector (Bender et al. 2007:x). These changes also dissuaded many high school graduates from joining the teaching profession. Five of eight teacher-training institutes were closed due to their inability to recruit new teachers (ibid.:15). Some school officials interviewed referred to this time as the "demobilization" period: there was not only the oppression of political life, but also limited educational opportunities. Teachers often went without payment for months at a time (interviews with educators and former ministry officials, July 2007).

Gross primary school enrollment rates remained dismally low, estimated at approximately 26%, leading up to the democratic transition in 1991. Lange and Diarra (1999:166) argue that between 1980 and 1985, parents chose not to enroll their children in school in protest against the changing socioeconomic landscape of fewer opportunities for mobility through schooling.

Islamic Schooling and State Resistance

Before 1500, thousands of students from across Africa, Europe, and the Middle East attended three universities in Timbuktu (http://www.timbuktufounda

tion.org/university.html). When the French arrived in Mali in the late nineteenth century, little of this educational infrastructure remained, but Quranic schooling was pervasive in the north of the country and the wider Sahelian region (Brenner 2001). For instance, in 1907 there were almost 3,000 Islamic schools and 18,000 students enrolled in Guinea (Johnson 1975:221). The French colonial authorities were astounded that leaders from the Fouta Djallon region of Guinea, who had a weak command of the French language, could speak fluent Arabic (ibid.).

Originally established by Muslim traders and intellectuals, Quranic schools taught students about the Islamic religion through the memorization and repetition of texts. Quranic schools were generally decentralized institutions where students worked under a specific teacher, or marabout, and slowly gained access to the more esoteric elements of Islamic knowledge (Soares 2005). These schools generally did not facilitate much social mobility, but instead reinforced hierarchical lineage structures (Brenner 2001).

Traditionally, many Malians attended Quranic schools to supplement their secular education. Louis Brenner (2007:203) describes the situation:

> Virtually all Muslim children in the past attended Qur'anic schools where most of them learned to recite at least some verses of the Qur'an and where they learned the fundamentals of their religion. A minority of these students might continue their schooling until they are able to recite the entire Qur'an, and a still smaller minority might continue their studies in *majlis*, where they would study selected texts of Muslim religious sciences. *Majlis* studies began with elementary books, usually in *tawhid* and *fiqh*, and depending on the student could continue for many years to include major Islamic texts. It was only in the *majlis* that Arabic was taught systematically.

At the most advanced levels, Quranic schools provided an opportunity to learn the Arabic language and Islamic literature, but only a minority of Quranic school students were able to reach advanced levels of study in *majlis*.

The French government feared "Islamic fanaticism and colonial authorities sought to co-opt or eliminate Quranic education. In some instances, the French campaign against Islam and the colonial authorities' aggressive forced-labor practices, which often targeted students, reduced the number of students in Quranic schools. The French built their own Franco-Arab schools in an attempt to co-opt and control local populations" (Brenner 2001:41). The French also established their own state-run madrassas in Timbuktu and Djenné as a way to appease and recruit local leaders (ibid.:200). Ironically, as the French built infrastructure, Islam and Islamic education spread rapidly through the rest of the country (Launay and Soares 1999; Soares 2004).

Against the backdrop of colonialism and government mismanagement of the primary education sector, madrassas emerged in the mid-twentieth century as educated West Africans returned from studies abroad in North Africa and the Middle East. These schools were opened by Malians with a cosmopolitan vision of a pan-Muslim community; they sought to construct modern Islamic education facilities (Brenner 2001:54). Madrassas offer a modern curriculum in addition to religious studies and use Arabic as the language of instruction. Initially, many of their founders identified with an emerging "reformist" version of Islam that aimed to align Malian religious practices with those of Muslims throughout the rest of the Islamic world. They were critical of the hierarchical Sufi networks that dominated Quranic education, and they faced resistance from Quranic school advocates (Brenner 2001:91; Brenner 2007:202; Launay and Soares 1999). However, madrassas did not belong exclusively to reformists; many Sufi leaders opened their own madrassas. For many parents, madrassas offered a modern pedagogy, which also reflected their values (Gérard 1997a; Villalón 2012).

In the past, madrassas were criticized for limiting graduates' job opportunities since they did not provide the linguistic instruction vital for participation in government channels. Many believed that graduates of madrassas could only obtain jobs as teachers in madrassas (interview with ministry monitor for madrassas, 2007; interview with madrassa teachers, 2007). Throughout the pre-democratization period, but also in the contemporary period, those who attained the highest levels of education at Quranic schools or madrassas were never offered bureaucratic opportunities comparable to the prospects of those who had received Francophone schooling. Arabic language skills and knowledge of Islamic texts do little to provide economic mobility to those who hope to find a job in the Malian civil service or in the international NGO sector.

Despite these challenges, madrassas have their own form of social power. Sanankoua and Brenner (1991:8) explain the social and political power that knowledge of Islam can wield: "But they [madrassas] also represent a strategy for creating, occupying, and controlling a defined social and political space. If madrassas have not succeeded in providing productive economic employment for the majority of their students (this is why they are often critiqued), they have certainly created a negotiable social status, and up to a certain point, a social mobility, which is not available to students of Quranic schools" (my translation). Despite the productive limitations, some parents choose religious education because they see it as morally imperative to their child's development as a Muslim. Some fear that, as Louis Brenner (2007:199) writes, "secular state schools might turn their children into 'unbelievers.'"

Since their inception, there has been considerable tension between private madrassas and government authorities (Amselle 1985; Brenner 2007; Sanankoua and Brenner 1991),[8] unlike the partnerships between the French colonial system and the Catholic Church across much of the continent; the colonial authorities were fearful of Islamic education. The French administration restricted the curriculum that these schools could legally offer by classifying them as "Quranic schools" and tried to ban them from teaching in Arabic or French (Brenner 2001:15; Brenner 2007:213). The French government also refused to grant licenses that would qualify these schools for state aid, such as that received by the Catholic schools.

The post-independence regime was similarly hostile to madrassas and Quranic education. Although Keita's Marxist government was strongly secular, in keeping with the colonial system he provided Catholic Francophone schools with state subsidies (Lange and Diarra 1999), but he nationalized one of the largest madrassas in Bamako. These schools were required to teach in French and Arabic, but were stripped of their religious curriculum. Keita planned to do the same with other madrassas in Mali before the military coup in 1968 led by Moussa Traoré (Brenner 2007:214).

Even without state assistance or recognition, madrassas have flourished, particularly during the 1970s with the influx of petro-dollars from the Middle East. Brenner (2001) estimates that enrollment in madrassas outstripped enrollment in public schools in the 1980s. Madrassas educated 6% of primary learners in 1960, but they represented 25% of all primary enrollment by the 1980s (ibid.:170, 172). Traoré reluctantly integrated madrassas into the Ministry of Education in 1985; however, many schools viewed the incorporation as an attempt at "domestication" reminiscent of French efforts to control Islamic schooling at the turn of the twentieth century (ibid.:260; Brenner 2007:215).

Madrassas represent ties to a broader Islamic community. Many students hoping to continue their studies set their sights on scholarship programs in other Islamic nations, including Algeria, Morocco, Egypt, and Saudi Arabia (Brenner 2001; Soares 2005). Many of the teachers in madrassas have spent time abroad and are perceived as having access to resources and personal connections in other countries. The Malian Annuaire National (2005–2006) reveals that there were 81 primary school teachers in madrassas with four-year college degrees, more than three times the number of primary school teachers in public schools with four-year degrees. Madrassas offer an avenue for economic and educational mobility tied to Arabic-speaking countries of North Africa and the Middle East, rather than to Mali or the Western world.

Expanding Education in the Democratic Era

When Alpha Konaré, a PhD and former educator, became Mali's first democratically elected president in 1992, he brought with him high expectations for education reform. A longtime democratic activist, he was elected with a broad base of support from networks of teachers, health workers, and students across Mali. Quickly after being elected, Konaré said that the development of the education sector was one of the democratic regime's priorities (Lange and Diarra 1999:166).

Within a year, Konaré held the National Education Forum where citizens were invited to express their opinions on the future of Malian education. For the first time, supporters of Islamic education were allowed to provide input into the government's education policy. Members of newly flourishing Muslim voluntary associations, including the Union Culturelle Musulmane and Shubban al-Muslimin—staunch advocates of the modernization of Islamic schooling—attended the conference (Brenner 2007:201). Proponents of Islamic education were very vocal and demanded more schools and government resources (Brenner 2001:281). Unlike the forced integration of the Traoré era, this conference represented a victory for Islamic interest groups in a democratic context of new possibilities.

Konaré moved quickly to write new laws to integrate private and community schools and to formalize the state's relationship with madrassas and other types of private schools. This strategy of liberalization marked a dramatic departure from Traoré's tight grip over the education sector. It also earned Konaré much-needed donor support for the education sector and got Mali closer to reaching international benchmarks since the government could now count learners in private schools, including madrassas, toward the total number of students enrolled. Madrassas, along with for-profit secular schools and NGO-run community schools, were accredited as government schools. As a result, the schools were subject to government inspections, followed government-sanctioned curricula, and issued government diplomas. By 2007, students could take the baccalaureate exams in Arabic (interview with madrassa monitoring representative for the Ministry of Education,

July 2007). The state has gradually developed a system of monitoring and standardization. Ministry of Education officials conduct school visits, oversee exam grading, and run training seminars for teachers from all different school types.

Konaré's 1998 campaign of "a school or literary center in every village" was in line with the Education for All campaign, which Mali signed in 1990, as well as the emerging Millennium Development Goals and emphasis on girls' enrollment. The government and donors poured support into the creation of teacher-training institutes and accelerated teacher-training programs to boost the number of teachers in the country. The Malian government increased the percentage of its budget going to education and built hundreds of new schools in order to accommodate new learners.

Donor support for community schools in underserved rural areas enhanced these government efforts. USAID, Norway, France, Canada, and the World Bank all financed community schools in rural areas, which often used indigenous-language instruction and local resources to reach children without access to other forms of education.[9] Designed to complement decentralization, the schools were managed and funded directly by committees of parents and community members, while NGOs took a lead in providing technical support and guidance on school management. Community school teachers were often recruited from among the local community members. Their salaries were generally paid by the local community, which often used in-kind contributions such as land, food, and crops. After debt relief and annulment, the Malian state redirected these funds to subsidize community teachers' salaries at roughly US$50 a month (Bierschenk 2007). The community schools increased the number of community school teachers from 1,106 in 1996 to 5,808 in 2003 and increased enrollment in some target regions from 35% to 62% ("USAID Meeting EFA Targets" 2006:5; Bender et al. 2007:13).

The liberalization and expansion of education was met with dramatic demand, which in turn created new employment opportunities in the public and private schools. Many unemployed university graduates opened their own private, Francophone schools to meet the heavy demand in urban centers. The number of private schools grew from 54 in 1980 to 711 in 1998 (Bender et al. 2007:21). A private school director explains his motivations for opening his own school in Niamakoro in 1992: "I already had the idea I wanted to do something for myself—that was my philosophy—I didn't really want to work for the state. It was very difficult. I was without resources, without anything. I started with 16 students, but with time, and good exam results, people talked and more people came" (interview, February 26, 2009). Indeed, the expanding private school sector provided many unemployed university graduates with work as teachers or, if they had enough financial backing, with small business opportunities as they opened their own private schools.

Expanding Access

Figure 4.1 shows the dramatic increase in primary school enrollment following democratization in 1991. With increased aid to education and the liberalization of the education sector, Malian primary school gross enrollment climbed from less than 30% before the democratic transition to 82% in the 2008–2009 school year. This growth was matched by significant government efforts to build more public infrastructure, train teachers, and commit a larger percentage of the budget to education. These efforts helped to increase equality in access to education. In doing so, the expansion had a disproportionate effect on women. In Mali, women are about 1.5 times as likely as men to be illiterate (Education for All Global Monitoring Report 2010:96). In many ways, the story of educational expansion in Mali is a story about unprecedented schooling opportunities for girls.

During the colonial period, few members of Malian society enrolled their daughters in school. In 1949, only 21% of primary school students enrolled in the French Sudan were girls (Gérard 1997b:106). In the post-independence period, little progress was made in terms of women's education. However, in the era following the transition to democracy, the campaign Education for All targeted women's enrollment. In Mali, girls' net enrollment increased from 16% before the democratic transition to almost 43% in 2004 (http://www.index mundi.com/mali/net-enrolment-ratio-in-primary-education,-girls.html).

However, many significant challenges to girls' education remain. Parents frequently pull girls out of school for early marriage or out of fear that they will become pregnant if allowed to fraternize with boys outside the home. Gérard (1997b) adds that some rural households worry that educated daughters-in-law will become too empowered and refuse arranged marriage or be able to seek administrative recourse in the case of a conflict with their husbands. Girls' primary completion rates are less than 40%, while boys' completion rates are almost 60% (World Bank 2008). The obstacles to girls' education are higher in certain ethnic groups. For instance, primary school teachers in the Kayes region explain that they face particular problems encouraging Soninke girls to stay enrolled past sixth grade despite sensitization campaigns.[10] Other

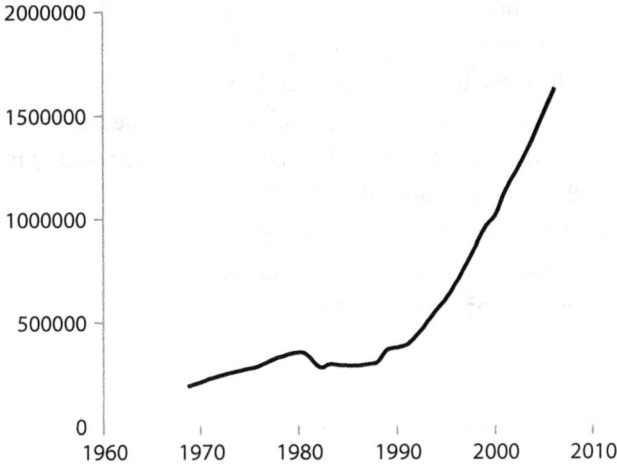

Figure 4.1. Number of children enrolled in Malian primary school, 1968–2009.
Source: Data from Malian Ministry of Education

groups, such as nomadic populations and those living in remote rural areas that do not have schooling infrastructure, continue to be marginalized despite the education expansion. Farming families, which are highly dependent on sons' and daughters' agricultural labor, have been reluctant to enroll their children in school.

There are very high attrition rates in the second cycle of primary school. Most Malians, including the majority of respondents in our survey, never make it past the first cycle. Secondary net enrollment rates were only 7% in 2006–2007, 8% and 6% for boys and girls, respectively (Pearce, Fourmy, and Kovach 2009). Many factors, including poor student performance, lack of resources to pay school fees, familial need for agricultural or domestic labor, sickness, disability, and early marriage for girls, contribute to the high attrition. The lack of secondary school infrastructure makes it particularly challenging for rural students to continue past the first cycle of primary school, since they are forced to bike or walk much longer distances to reach a school offering classes past sixth grade or to lodge with relatives in a town near adequate schooling facilities.

Even with these constraints, there has been an unprecedented increase in secondary and university enrollment, which still outpaces the public school infrastructure. The Malian government pays for the majority of its secondary students to attend private high schools rather than construct its own buildings up to the code specified for public secondary schools. Private high schools thus outnumber public providers at the secondary level. For instance, in 2007 only 4 of approximately 50 high schools in Bamako's Rive Gauche were public (interview with former member of the Ministry of Education, July 2007). Competition for secondary placement is fierce, and the government has instituted age cutoffs, which make all graduates over 17 ineligible for government scholarship to attend high school.

Despite all the challenges, more students than ever are obtaining university degrees; enrollment tripled in five years from 13,847 in 1998 to 37,000 in 2003 (Bender et al. 2007). Classrooms are overcrowded, and university professors teach hundreds of students with no teaching assistants. The academic calendar is frequently plagued by strikes.

Although there are plans to open regional educational hubs, the majority of the public university system is still based in Bamako. There is also a small, emerging private university sector. The wealthiest parents send their children abroad to Algeria, Morocco, Canada, France, the United States, and most recently China.

Uncertain Economic and Political Returns from Education

Despite these efforts, there is growing dissatisfaction with educational quality, particularly at public schools. Students in the post-democratic era face larger class sizes, fewer hours of schooling, lower requirements for teacher qualification, and frequent strikes (Bleck and Guindo 2013; Diakite 2000). Parents lament the low baccalaureate exam passage rates, which gatekeep admission into Mali's universities. In 2009, only a little over a third of students who took the general baccalaureate exam passed the test. If students cannot convert their education into a university diploma, there are no hopes of a job in the civil service or in an NGO. Many students who drop out before university turn to teacher-training programs and begin to work as contractual teachers (Bleck and Guindo 2013). Discussions of *la crise scolaire* are pervasive throughout Malian society.

According to Afrobarometer data, less than 10% of the population has attended any secondary school and less than 2% of Malians report attending university. However, despite their comparative advantage vis-à-vis the general population, young university students' diplomas do not guarantee employment in the civil service, unlike in earlier eras.[11] With a small private sector, few opportunities in the civil service, and typically no entry-level positions in NGOs, many graduates spend years in unpaid internships or end up taking jobs they could have pursued after completing nine years of primary schooling, such as working as contractual teachers or selling goods at the market. Rather than incorporating young graduates into the democratic regime, the state has largely neglected their plight. With the exception of highly politicized negotiations between student union leaders and the regime, there has been little evidence of proactive state efforts to recruit new talent or nurture future leaders. Despite increasing numbers of unemployed graduates, many parents still hold out hope for education creating greater economic opportunities.[12]

The Malian state has exerted minimal effort in spreading democratic values into schools. Initially, elected leaders employed a strong discourse around the importance of education for creating "patriotic citizens and building a democratic society" (Mali Ministry of Education 1993:2). They justified the importance of education for democracy by explaining that it helps citizens to learn and practice their obligations as "active members of democratic societies, who respect peace and [the] basic human rights of men and citizens" (ibid.). In reality, however, the Malian state did little to revise the school curriculum to reflect the democratic discourse. Civic and moral education, stripped from the Malian school curriculum during the Traoré dictatorship, was not reinstated until 2009 after teachers pleaded for its inclusion during the 2008 national education conference (interview with conference participant and university educator, March 2009).[13] The foreword to Mali's 2009 civic and moral education textbook lamented this loss:

> Moral and civic instruction, which structured our life as students in the past, [has] lost [its] force over the course of time; [its] pedagogical purpose disintegrated. It is fortunate that this new volume embodies the effort to actuate in our children, lost in the whirlwind of modernity and globalization, the reflection on what is good and what is bad, what they have the right to do and not to do. Aiming to help them to become citizens who are conscious of their duties and their rights in the community, mothers and fathers conscious of their familial and social responsibilities, is not a frivolous mission. Civic and moral education is an essential task for us as educators.[14]

The post-transition Malian governments have not capitalized on the socializing aspects of educational content beyond the proliferation of French as the national language. Through liberalization and inattention to the civic curriculum, Mali has failed to capture the unifying or nation-building benefits of education. Beyond increasing provision to a larger base of citizens, the

Malian government has not used a systematic approach to transmit messages about democracy or citizenship.

Education can indirectly support state-building and democracy by providing citizens with the ability to interact with the state, including French literacy. French-language schools give students the skills for NGO or government jobs, but also help citizens to navigate the government bureaucracy (Bergmann 1996). A 1989 survey conducted by the Ministry of Education in Mali reported parents' strong attachment to the exclusive use of French as the language of instruction despite the pedagogical challenges it poses to most Malian children, who speak other languages at home: "For them, mastering it [French] means having a better grasp of administrative procedures, and running less of a risk of being cheated by civil servants. Parents quote examples showing that the mastery of French is not only useful in Mali, but also abroad. They have not had the chance to profit from a mastery of French, but feel that their children should benefit from it" (Bergmann 1996:594).

Even if a child eventually drops out, his reading and mathematics skills are a resource for the family (Gérard 1997b:39). In rural areas, parents might enroll one child in a Francophone school just to help with "decoding and documentation" and "dealings with [the] bureaucracy" (Brenner 2001:186). In his study of a rural area near the Bougouni region of Sikasso, Étienne Gérard (1997b:187) explains how those with primary school degrees played solicited roles, assisting the village chief and his council of advisors. An educated villager does not displace the power or authority of the older elites, but his literacy enables him to work in collaboration with traditional leaders.

Francophone education, in public or private schools, helps to familiarize students and their families with the state and gives it relevance in their lives in a context where most citizens prefer to consult traditional, religious, or familial authorities. Despite the lack of a civic curriculum and the marginal economic benefit of a university degree, it is possible to observe that schooling equips citizens with skills to learn more about politics and to engage with the bureaucratic system. This endowment contrasts with the education at madrassas, which, despite their state accreditation, neither endow students with the linguistic skills to interact with the Malian bureaucracy nor bring learners closer to the state. Madrassas might instead pull students closer to alternative forms of authority in the religious sphere, such as imams, marabouts, or heads of Islamic associations. They might shape broader connections to an *umma*[15] rather than to Malian citizenship defined by sovereign national boundaries.

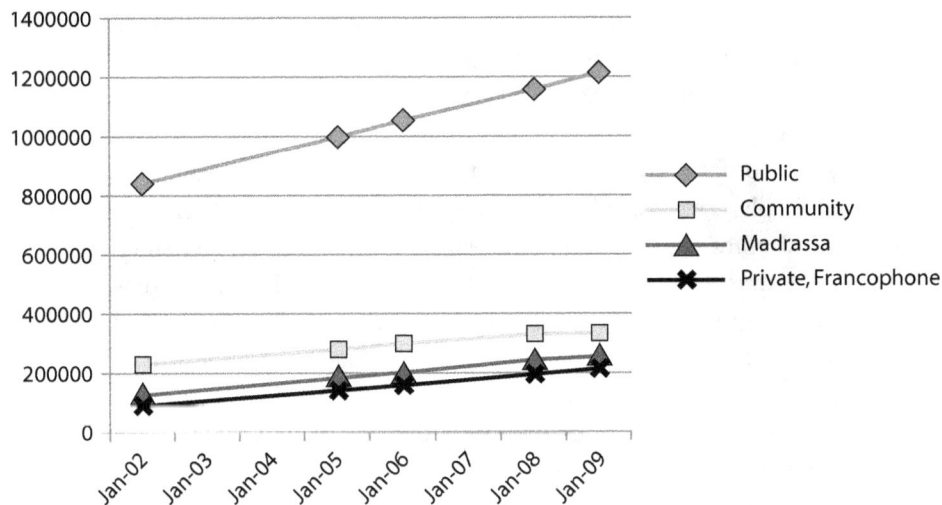

Figure 4.2. Primary enrollment over time. Source: Data from Brenner 2001; Annuaire National 2004–2005 and 2006–2007

The Growth of Madrassa Schooling

In the democratic era of greater school choice, enrollment in madrassas is growing beyond its traditional base within trading communities.[16] The state's recognition of madrassas, the rising popularity of Arabic as a language of cosmopolitan trade, increased trade with the non-Western world, and the spread of Islam has helped to ease fears that graduates of madrassas have few job options (interview with madrassa director, July 2007; interview with Ministry of Education liaison to Arabic-language schools, July 2007; interview with Arabic teacher, Sikasso, October 2009). One of the leading proponents of madrassa education, Wahhabis,[17] have created a nouveau riche class in Bamako with a cosmopolitan Muslim, rather than Western, orientation and frame of reference (Launay and Soares 1999:512). They represent a concrete material power tied to commerce networks in the Middle East. Previous tensions between Wahhabi and Sufi marabouts have largely subsided, since many Malians choose to blend and select practices they feel are appropriate to their own lives (Soares 2005). As figure 4.2 demonstrates, enrollment in madrassas has continued to grow despite the increase in the availability of French-language schooling options.

Arabic teachers in Bamako explain that there has been a substantial increase in demand for their services in the twenty-first century. Many of them teach part time at Francophone private schools that are starting to offer Arabic classes, in addition to their full-time work at madrassas (interview with focus group of four Arabic teachers at secondary madrassa, Faladie, March 2009). Initially, donors attributed the increases in enrollment to the inclusion and formal counting of madrassa students in the ministry records since many existing madrassas were brought onto the state ledger. However, statistics reveal that this growth continues. By 2009, 13% of all students in the first cycle of primary school were enrolled in madrassas. Figure 4.2 demonstrates that madrassa enrollment has been expanding at a greater rate than enrollment in private Francophone education. Quranic educators do not report a comparable increase in enrollment, which indicates that these increases are not fueled solely by parents seeking religious content, but perhaps by parents' interest in the modern, cosmopolitan associations that madrassas offer (Villalón 2012).

School Choice: Navigating Mali's Evolving Educational Landscape

If we want to understand the effects of schooling on citizenship, it is important to understand parents' decisions to select different educational tracks. Schooling choices may reflect parents' prior values, which could simultaneously influence their political behavior and their children's participation. The data reveal that schooling choices are often strategic, but sometimes they are a result of constraints or chance.

First, we must understand how schooling decisions are made. The interviews and surveys reveal that fathers or heads of household most typically make schooling decisions for the household. In some instances, women capitalized on the absence of a male family member to enroll their children in the school of their choice. In one example, a Soninke woman in Kayes explains that her family capitalized on her father's absence to enroll one of her children in a private, secular school: "In reality, our dad did not want to send the children to [Francophone] school, but only to madrassa. . . . We profited from his absence to send some of the children to French-language school" (KV55).

In many households, wives and mothers were unable to provide the names of the schools that their child attended, the child's grade level, or estimates of the cost of the school fees (field notes from interviews in Bamako, Sikasso, Mopti, and Kayes). This may reflect hierarchical decision making within the household, but could also be a product of the large gender gap in educational attainment among Malian adults. Women who have not attended school themselves may be more reluctant to talk about or less capable of describing the schooling experience of their children.

In other instances, children were sent to live with relatives who sponsored the child's education, and then the relatives were the ones who made the schooling decisions for that child.[18] These families are generally expected to pay most of the student's fees and to provide food and accommodations (informal interviews and observation of Malian households, Bamako, 2007, 2009).[19] In the majority of Malian families we spoke with, fathers selected the schools and found the resources to pay for school fees. However, it was fairly common for households to source funding from extended family members.

Clearly, school choices translate into different types of social, political, and economic mobility. The Western literature on school choice often assumes that parents pick schools in order to maximize educational quality and the family's utility (Friedman 1955). This utility can be thought of both as a consumption good, improving the well-being and personal development of their child, and as a productive good, investing in a child's future ability to bring income into the household (Bast and Walberg 2004). In developing nations, such as Mali, it is especially important to stress the productive quality of schooling: the child's future earnings can benefit the entire household and extended family (Bergmann 1996; Gérard 1997b; Glick and Sahn 2000). In Mali, it is not uncommon for educated, employed individuals to shoulder the burden of their entire extended family. It should be noted, however, that expected family returns for education are different for boys and girls. Typically, boys are expected to contribute to the household after they are married, while girls join their in-laws' family and are not required to continue to send money to their own parents. This makes the productive investment aspect of education less relevant for daughters than for sons.[20]

The vast majority of respondents stressed the importance of French-language education in a public, private, or Christian school as necessary for economic mobility, but also for interacting with the government bureaucracy. The fixation with French language attainment fuels parents' resistance to *pédagogie convergente* curricula despite the fact that this method produces better academic results (Bender et al. 2007; interviews, summer 2007). Parents with children at schools with *pédagogie convergente* would often complain about non-French instruction. I spoke with many respondents who would say, "What good is sending my child to school if she isn't learning in French? She can speak Bambara at home." We also observed parents actively drawing on their children's French skills when interacting with us. When I entered households to conduct surveys, it was common for the respondent to seek out the child in the household with the highest level of education to "assist" with the interview. Our surveys were conducted in local languages, but having the educated child there as a potential mediator seemed to put the parents at ease.

For poorer families, parents' educational preferences are constrained by the costs of schooling and the opportunity costs of forgone earnings from that child's potential labor. Parents who are unable to absorb these short-term costs are unable to enroll their children in school. In our interviews, the vast majority of respondents preferred to send their children to school, but many of the most impoverished respondents could not do so. For instance, Aminata lives in the city of Mopti with her husband and three children. They recently lost their house and all of their possessions in a fire. None of her three children are enrolled in schools. She explains, "I am too poor even to send my kids to an Islamic school" (M7). Adama, a respondent from Kayes, was only able to enroll one of his children in school: "These days, poor people can't send their kids to school like everyone else" (K23). Drahmane, a respondent in Mopti, implies that five of his six children left school early because they needed to help generate income for the family: "All the others left school because of the difficulties that our family faces every day" (M67).

A resource-based argument might explain why some parents enroll their children in inexpensive Quranic schools instead of no school at all. Students who attend Quranic schools generate their own school fees by begging for alms one to five times a week. The amount that students must generate in alms is typically less than what is charged at public schools. Salif, a 50-year-old respondent, lives in Mopti where his three children attend Quranic school. He explains his schooling choice as motivated by his limited resources: "I was in an accident 14 years ago. I don't have anything; that is why my kids are at a Quranic school" (M24). In some cases, parents send their children to live with the Quranic school teachers. The teachers become responsible for providing housing and food to subsidize what the children can earn in alms.

The rising enrollment rates in madrassas—even in the context of unprecedented Francophone schooling options—indicate that some parents place their children in madrassas as their first choice. Madrassas cost as much as most private schools and more than public school options, and the medium of instruction is Arabic, which is not a recognized language of the state bureaucracy. This is initially puzzling given the importance of French for economic mobility and interaction with the state bureaucracy. However, arguing that parents enroll children in Islamic schools as purely a second option or for economic reasons ignores the sociocultural realities and traditions of the Malian education landscape.

The respondents' sector of employment or location mediates the importance of French or the need to deal with the Malian bureaucracy. Some rural parents remain ambivalent about sending their children to school and question its practical utility.[21] One respondent in the village of Ziguena—about 75 kilometers northwest of Sikasso on the road to Koutiala—explains why his nine children are not in school: "Because [my children] are farmers. Everyone cannot be at school!" (SR50b; similar comments made by SR67, SR84). Ali in Timbuktu says that school is not a possibility for three of his four children because "we are nomadic" (T55). His son stays with a relative so he can attend the Bahadou public school in Timbuktu, while the rest of the family migrates. Hamidou, a member of a fishing caste who lives in a village outside of Sévaré, gives a similar response: "We are Bozo, our children don't do [any school]. We move too much" (SV63). Similarly, traders, who have historically formed the base of madrassa enrollment, are self-employed and less reliant on the Malian bureaucracy. Many operate in transnational networks that extend past the reach of the Malian state.

Some respondents prize social mobility within an Islamic community or personal piety over economic or bureaucratic mobility. Aboubacar, a 40-something Tuareg man in Timbuktu, explains why he sends all three of his children to Quranic school: "Many say they are Muslims, but they haven't gone to Quranic school or a madrassa or done any kind of [religious] studies. How can you declare yourself Muslim? Maybe because they pray they think that that suffices?" (T2). In his study of school choice in Mali and Burkina Faso, Étienne Gérard (1999) finds religious leaders who forbid their children to attend secular public school and others who send their children to public school while supplementing their education with Quranic studies at home. Gérard describes these different choices as two distinct strategies for dealing with the reality of the importance of French-language education and trying to preserve one's own religious authority.

Data on Parental Choice

To get to the heart of why parents send their children to different types of school, we asked them directly. Survey team members asked all respondents

TABLE 4.2.
Stated reasons for enrolling children in each school type (in percentages)

	Proximity	Affordability	Quality	Recommendation	Government placement	Religious	Other
Public	63	14	14	5	0	0	5
Private secular	38	3	52	3	3	0	1
Madrassa	25	5	0	5	0	52	11
Community	61	0	28	0	0	0	11
Quranic	15	18	0	13	0	54	0
Private Christian	0	0	71	0	0	29	0

with children if and where their children attended school. Six hundred respondents identified themselves as parents with children currently enrolled in school. We then analyzed the primary reasons that justified parents' enrollment of their children in each school type: public school, private secular school, madrassa, community school, Quranic school, and private Christian school (see table 4.2). Parents reported 983 justifications for their choices.[22]

There was significant variation in parents' stated reasons for enrolling their children in each type of school. Sixty-three percent of respondents sending their children to public school said they did so for reasons of proximity, and an additional 14% said they did so for reasons of affordability. Only 14% chose the public school for reasons of quality. Public schools present practical and affordable options to poor Malians. For instance, Issoufou, who lives in Senou, a peri-urban suburb about 10 kilometers from Bamako, has two school-age children. He used to work in the fields as a day laborer at a neighboring farm, but now that he is in his 50s and is unable to withstand the intensive labor that farming requires, he is no longer working. He enrolls one of his children in public school because "private school is too expensive" (F43). He says that he would happily enroll the other child if he had the money.

Fifty-two percent of parents claimed to enroll their children in private secular schools due to better quality, fewer strikes, and higher passage rates on exams. In urban areas, the choice between private and public schools is based on a family's economic resources and on the availability of private schools. An additional 38% of private secular school parents cited reasons of proximity. In some instances, the costs of sending students to a public school farther away from home may outweigh the school fees for less expensive private schools. Initially, private school teachers were thought of as less qualified than public school teachers. However, with the rise of contractual teachers in public schools and the increasing number of public school teachers who moonlight in private school classes, the lines have blurred (Bleck and Guindo 2013). The exception to this comes from teachers and school directors who work at public schools and see private school promoters as nothing more than entrepreneurs hoping to turn a profit. Abdrahamane, a director of a public school in the village of Fatoma in the Sévaré region, says: "Me, I would never send my child to a private school. . . . They [private schools] are [only] interested in money" (SV65).

Abou, who lives in Samé, a district on the outskirts of Bamako that borders the hill to the presidential palace, enrolled his child in a private school because "public school is sick. Plus, I know the director. It was less expensive [than the other private schools], and the teachers are capable" (BC76). Even though there is a growing class of cheap private schools, household income still limits a family's ability to enroll children in these schools. In the hypothetical scenario that a household had enough resources to pay for private education, parents said they would enroll some of their children in these schools. A Bamako respondent, Moussa, laments the poor quality of public education and the shifting loyalty of the Malian population to private providers: "It's the season to send your children to private school" (BA58). Lassana, a respondent from Kayes, gives a private school endorsement: "If you want quality education, you have to pay money for private school" (K39).

Most parents enrolled their children in community schools because their choice sets were limited. Predominantly in rural zones, 61% of parents enrolled their children in community schools because they were the closest available education providers. This is logical since the vast majority of community schools were built in places that had very little educational infrastructure. Since most parents who send their children to public or community schools justify their decisions as pragmatic, rather than ideological, this result lessens concerns that parents enrolling their children in these types of school have latent attitudes that are driving both their school choice and their political behavior.

Fifty-two percent of students attending madrassas and 54% of Quranic students were enrolled for religious reasons. When asked why he chose to enroll his children in a madrassa, Alioune, a resident in the village of Fatoma in the Sévaré region, says: "Allah is the unique creator" (SV85). In contrast, only 29% of those who send their children to Christian schools cited religious reasons. Seventy-one percent of parents with children at Christian schools reported enrolling them for reasons of quality, and the majority said they were Muslim.[23] Daouda is one of the many Muslims who choose to enroll their children in Catholic schools. He explains: "There are serious studies there. The administration has good relations with the parents. For instance, if my child isn't at school, as a parent, I am alerted immediately" (BA60).

In looking at the justifications for enrollment in private Francophone and Islamic schools, there is greater concern that underlying parental attitudes and preferences could determine both enrollment and political behavior. The risk to my analysis is that parental political preferences might determine both enrollment and political engagement; measuring the relationship between the type of school in which parents enroll their children and their political knowledge and behavior would miss the fact that the same attribute is driving both of these things. However, even within madrassa enrollment, there appear to be ample instances of parents who are forced to enroll their child not due to a first preference, but because of an outside factor. The following anecdotes describe some instances where parents enrolled their children due to constraints or happenstance.

In Sikasso, I met a marabout named Youssouf and his wife, Haoua. They used to enroll all of their children in a madrassa, but due to economic constraints on the family, they were forced to transfer their youngest son into a less expensive public school. Youssouf was pleasantly surprised by his son Mahamadou's performance. This year, Mahamadou was first in his class of more than 100 pupils. Youssouf is very satisfied with the public school's performance and rated it "very good," while only rating the madrassa his other two children attend as "okay" (S78). While Youssouf was initially committed to madrassa education, Mahamadou's experience has made him reconsider the utility of public education. Other respondents state that they prefer Islamic schooling, but do not have the resources to place their children in madrassas. Chaka from Mopti has his four girls enrolled in public school, despite the fact that he thinks "boys should go to Francophone schools and girls should go to madrassas" (M61).

In some instances, a friend or relative encourages a family, despite their preference for Islamic schooling, to enroll a child in a Francophone school. For instance, the Diallo family from the village of Soutoucoulé near Kayes Rive Gauche enrolled their son, Karim, in Quranic school but their daughter, Kadiadiatou, in public school. The Diallos are a Peul family,[24] so they didn't think twice when a relative suggested they enroll Karim in the local Quranic school where he had gone as a child. The family was very pleased with their son's education, and Karim appeared quite studious: he was busy reading his hadiths, rather conspicuously, during my interview with his father, Ibrahim. However, the Diallos decided to enroll their daughter in public school. When I asked why, Ibrahim explained that he has a friend who works in the mayor's office who thought that it would be a good idea, and they had enough resources at that time to enroll her there (K60). The Diallos were open to a suggestion from a friend and as a result have children in two very different educational trajectories.

Also in the village of Soutoucoulé, Kadiatou explains that she sends her children to Dar es Salaam, the big public school in downtown Kayes Rive Gauche approximately 3 kilometers away. However, during the rainy season the massive craters in Soutoucoulé fill with water, separating the compounds scattered along the highest peaks of the embankments like small islands. The village becomes nearly impossible to navigate except by small boat. During that period, Kadiatou sends her children to the local Quranic school in Soutoucoulé because it is too difficult to make the journey to Dar es Salaam (K13).

It is also important to note that religiosity is not perfectly correlated with Islamic schooling. Some of the most active members of Islamic associations have their children in public schools. Abdoulaye is Peul and lives in Mopti, where he is an active member of the High Council of Islam, one of the primary organizers of the protests against the Family Code. During his interview, it is clear that he is ideologically motivated, and he complains about the National Assembly passing a Family Code that is against Islam. During his youth, he received some primary schooling at a madrassa, but all of his children attend public school—a symbol of the secular state (M5). Abdoulaye claims to have enrolled his four children in public school because it is the closest school to his house. He rates his children's educational experience there as "good." This evaluation might reflect the fact that three of his children had already passed their high school exams and continued on to university.

Many parents who enroll their children in Islamic schools simultaneously enroll their children in secular, Francophone schools. Figure 4.3 shows the number of parents who enroll their children in the most popular schools— public, private, and madrassa—and the number of parents who enroll their children in multiple school types. Fewer than half of all respondents (45%) who send their children to madrassas enroll their children exclusively at these Islamic schools; the majority of these parents employ a mixed strategy.

In his study of the education sector in southern Mali, Étienne Gérard

Public School

330

Private,
Francophone
School

117

62

42

Madrassa

41

8

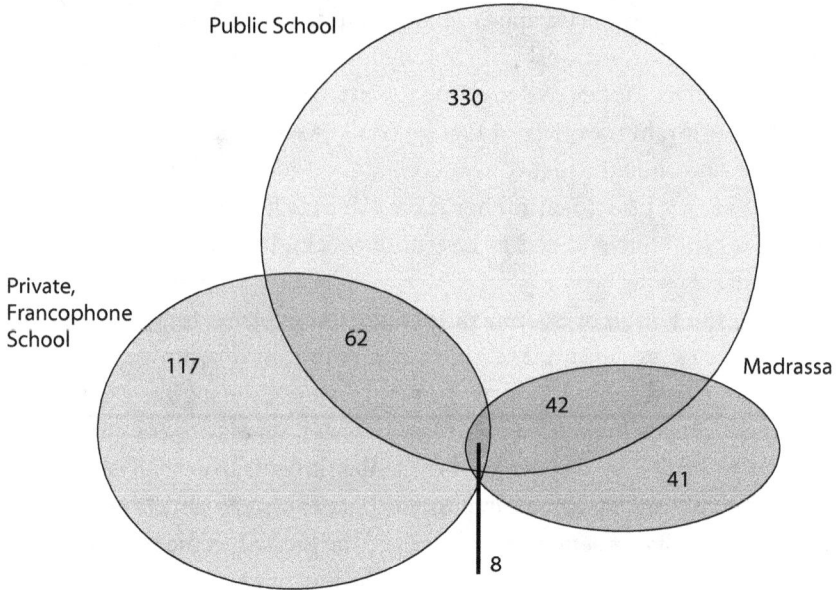

Figure 4.3. Overlapping enrollment between school types (*N* = 600)

(1997b:58) similarly finds that only 20% of guardians send their children exclusively to public school and only 13% send their children exclusively to Islamic school; the remaining 67% use some kind of mixed strategy. This strategy of diversification is consistent with findings in Pakistan, where a study finds that only 25% of families who send their children to madrassas do so exclusively (Andrabi et al. 2006). The majority of parents enrolling children in madrassas also enroll their other children in public or private schools.

Parents give multiple reasons for diversification, including a preference for religious education for girls and supplemental religious education for children who are not yet old enough to attend public school. For some parents, especially those who are reluctant to send their girls to school at all, madrassas represent a more culturally appropriate and conservative educational venue (interview with World Education employee, July 2007). Most madrassas in Mali are not gender-segregated, but they do require female pupils to cover their heads, which few Malian girls do outside of that context.[25] The willingness to enroll children in diverse schooling types suggests that parents' social spheres and political orientations are less segregated than we would assume if parents were only choosing one type of schooling.

Conclusion

These examples open up the possibility that some school choices might be independent of political beliefs or attitudes. At a minimum, the schooling experience might have the ability to influence parents with malleable educational preferences. While some of the most committed parents might see their first preference through, those parents who are a bit more ambivalent might find their children in their second- or third-choice school.

The dramatic increases in enrollment and the accreditation of non-state schools generate interesting questions about the impact of educational policy on democratization. Historically, we imagine the state monopoly over education as shaping citizens' political knowledge, experience, and expectations. What are the effects of a massive educational expansion on democratic citizenship? The growing role of Islamic education raises additional questions about the role of madrassa alumni in the future of Malian democracy. How might different types of school shape citizens' knowledge or patterns of political participation? In the next chapter I explore the relationship between citizens' educational experiences and their political knowledge and participation to forecast the effects of these policy changes.

CHAPTER FIVE

Can Education Empower Citizens?

In this chapter I examine two questions: Does education increase political knowledge and participation? Do all schools foster knowledge and participation in the same way? I introduce data from the 1,000-person household survey and from interviews with 200 university students to examine the relationship between education, political knowledge, and democratic participation in a context of low external efficacy (see chapter 3). The data demonstrate that citizens with any type of education are more knowledgeable about politics than their peers with no education. Contrary to my initial expectations, I find no significant differences in political knowledge and most forms of participation between the alumni of state schools and citizens who attended non-state schools, including madrassas and Quranic schools.[1] However, I find that education and participation do not have a simple linear relationship: the most educated citizens do not participate in all types of channel at higher rates than citizens with no education.

I demonstrate that higher levels of education are correlated with "difficult" forms of political participation. I argue that education empowers citizens to engage with political opportunities. Higher education, particularly French literacy, significantly increases both citizens' internal efficacy and their ability and willingness to navigate a flawed political system. This means that while greater educational opportunities might not directly translate into greater voter turnout, they do create a more knowledgeable population that is capable of discerning political opportunities. These empowered political consumers are ultimately necessary for accountable democratic institutions (Dahl 1971).

Education as a Prerequisite for Knowledge and Participation?

Many Malians believe that those who did not attend formal school are not fully empowered to engage with the relatively new, democratic political system. An encounter during the first day of our survey research illustrates this belief. Djenebou, the other female member of our research team, and I walked down a red dirt road in Niamakoro,[2] counting houses on a Sunday afternoon. At the fifth house, we saw Boubacar, a wealthy Soninke businessman, sitting outside drinking tea with his *grin*.[3] We approached the group, explained our mission, and asked those who lived in the household if they would be willing to participate in our survey. The group laughed at the sight of two women, an American and a Malian university student, speaking Bambara and inquiring about their opinions. Everyone who was over 18 agreed to participate, so we passed out playing cards in order to randomly select who was going to participate in the survey. Boubacar pulled the highest playing card and was thereby selected. Djenebou read the first series of questions about education and socioeconomic status. Like many Soninke, Boubacar had attended an informal Quranic school for a few years as a youth but had never gone to Francophone school.

Later in the process, as Djenebou broached the topic of politics, Boubacar grew impatient with us. I coded one "I don't know" response after another before he stood up from his metal chair, sipped some tea, and then explained that he was busy and needed to stop the interview. As we reluctantly packed up, he defended his early departure: "I never went to school, so I am not involved in politics. I don't know anything about politics—I focus on the market" (F70). As a consolation, he offered: "My children are in school, so maybe they can get involved in politics." Boubacar saw himself as unequipped to engage with the political system. He linked his lack of formal, French education with his ignorance about politics. A successful trader, Boubacar is actively engaged in business in Bamako, but his human and social capital does not flow over into the political realm. However, he sees different possibilities for his two boys and two girls, who attend an elite, private Francophone school in Bamako.

Boubacar's understanding of the relationship between education and politics mirrors that of many political scientists and policy makers: more educated citizens are better able to understand and participate in politics. His informal, Quranic education does not provide him with those skills. Will this assumption about the links between education, knowledge, and participation hold in a nascent, Muslim, African democracy with a diverse portfolio of accredited education providers? Can Islamic schooling also increase one's capacity as a citizen?

What Do Citizens Know and Why Do They Participate?

While schools are not the only locus for political socialization and development,[4] the political science literature identifies them as serving a key function as the purveyors of nationhood and democratic citizenship. Education can increase political knowledge through a number of mechanisms: democratic curriculum, literacy, cognitive empowerment, socialization, and exposure to centrally connected figures (see Dahl 1967; Lipset 1959). First, citizens may learn political facts in school through the curriculum. In the US context, schools have traditionally been seen as the venues where students learn about the duties and rights of citizenship.[5] Second, increased literacy skills enable citizens to access written information. In places like Mali, where the predominant language in the bureaucracy is spoken by a minority of the population, understanding the language of the state enables Malians to access a greater range of political information. Third, education might also work indirectly to increase citizens' awareness of the world around them, as well as their interest and ability to cull political information from their environment (Neuman, Just, and Crigler 1992).[6]

The literature on US political participation demonstrates that the most educated citizens are also the most active in all forms of politics due to a democratic curriculum, heightened socialization, increased literacy, political mobilization by teachers, increased internal efficacy, and increased cognitive development (see, for example, Almond and Verba 1963; Lipset 1959; Nie, Junn, and Stehlik-Barry 1996; Rosenstone and Hansen 1993; Verba, Schlozman, and Brady 1995). With greater education, students might feel more capable as democratic citizens, increasing their internal efficacy (Converse 1972). This internal efficacy is particularly important in systems characterized by low external efficacy such as the Malian context where people doubt the responsiveness of the political system.

Education, especially at state schools, might instill a sense of obligation to participate in democratic institutions (Dahl 1967). Similarly, if schooled in French, the language of the state, citizens might be less fearful of exploitation by the system. Citizens who speak French are more capable of engaging with government and bureaucratic institutions (Laitin 1992). In addition, students' experiences on school campuses might connect them to key political mobilizers and political movements through socialization. Scholars have described the powerful role of teachers and students in shaping the democratization movements across Africa (Smith 1997; Wing 2008). Frequent teacher and student strikes are a testimony to the legacy of political activism in schools. Finally, education—especially at the tertiary level—could expose students to networks of political power, which, like socialization in schools, facilitate participation in politics (Nie, Junn, and Stehlik-Barry 1996).

While empirical evidence from Africa shows that educated respondents are more able to formulate political opinions and criticize authority figures and institutions (Mattes and Mughogho 2009; Mattes and Shenga 2007; Mc-Cauley and Gyimah-Boadi 2009; Moehler 2008), there does not appear to be a consistent linear relationship between education and all forms of participation. In their analysis of Afrobarometer data, Kuenzi and Lambright (2005) do not detect a consistent relationship between education and participation. Survey data from Ghana and Côte d'Ivoire demonstrate that higher levels of education are correlated with a greater likelihood of contacting an elected official and with collective participation, but not with voting (MacLean 2011). Bratton and his collaborators (1999) find civic education in Zambia to have a positive effect on citizens' knowledge and values, but they find no consistent increases in political behavior; the authors find that prior levels of education and information mediate the effect of the civic education programs. Relatedly, participants in civic education were less trusting of public officials than were the general public (ibid.). Similarly, Isaksson's (2013:9) analysis of cross-national Afrobarometer data reveals that respondents with secondary and university education are significantly less likely to vote, but that respondents with any level of formal education are significantly more likely to attend a political meeting than their peers with no education.

When probing the relationship between education and participation in the developing world, it is important to acknowledge that incentives could obfuscate or inflate the relationship between education and participation. Voters are often mobilized by political entrepreneurs through the use of short-term incentives, such as bribes and threats (e.g., Collier 2009; see also Bratton 2008). These types of voting environments are far removed from a citizen's autonomous expression of policy preferences or belief in a candidate.

During election week, the streets of Bamako are filled with layers of party posters, roving teams of party supporters on motorcycles, and professional "animators" who are paid to dance on the back of rented trucks. *Kalata wati* (the time period associated with election campaigns) is often viewed as a narrow window when one may extract resources from a typically aloof and unaccountable political system. In recent years, citizens have complained that parties are not giving out as many gifts in urban zones; there have been fewer T-shirts and household supplies distributed. In rural areas, citizens are increasingly dissatisfied with the distribution of salt or sugar, which is a pre-requisite for even launching a campaign; they view these commodities as insufficient and unsustainable. These rural constituencies are starting to demand more durable public goods (interviews with leadership in two villages in the Koulikoro region, October 2011). Young people, typically unemployed students, earn a couple of dollars rounding up voters to go to the polls. Political parties continue to hold high-profile soccer matches in most urban neighborhoods. The Alliance for Democracy in Mali (ADEMA)—the political party that led the transition to democracy in 1992, dominated the first two presidential elections, and also dominated the 2009 municipal elections—reportedly paid a ₵1,000 prize to the winner of one of these soccer tournaments (informal interview with participating soccer player, March 2009).

In this context, voting and declaring partisan support are not always the best indicators of empowered democratic agency. As Ahmed, a 70-year-old Kayes resident, explains, "I don't know who I voted for; they just brought me the paper" (K54). While conducting exit polls during the 2009 municipal elections, the research team observed voters being rewarded with breakfast sandwiches or money upon exiting the polls. During the same campaign period, I often observed people in my neighborhood—sometimes adorned with a party T-shirt—who were uncertain whom they were voting for. When I asked about their vote choice for the municipal elections, they often turned to another member of the compound to ask: "Which party is it that I support?"

It is possible that those who are educated or have the most resources might be less likely to participate in an environment of short-term incentives. If, as some research suggests, educated voters are less reliant on political party mobilization or less likely to be targeted by political entrepreneurs, they might be less likely to turn out to the polls than their less educated peers (Blaydes 2006; Dalton 2007; Isaksson 2013; Kramon 2010). These imperfect electoral conditions make it difficult to assess how education might increase empowered participation.

One strategy to deal with the presence of the noise introduced by these short-term incentives is to distinguish between easy and difficult participation. The scholarship on participation in environments of low external efficacy provides additional theoretical reasons to disaggregate difficult from easy participation. If education manages to increase citizens' assessments of their own political competence, some political scientists argue, then internal efficacy can motivate political action in low-trust or cynical environments, such as present-day Mali (Craig 1980; Fraser 1970; Gamson 1968). However this participation tends to be high initiative (in other words, *difficult*) or unconventional. Pollock (1983:401) explains, "Individuals who harbor feelings of personal political competence (high internal political efficacy) and relatively cynical assessments of the responsiveness of the political system (low external political efficacy) are more prone toward unconventional, nonconformist participation. However, they also engage in high initiative conventional participation closely connected with the ongoing political process." Although unconventional, or contentious, politics would be theoretically interesting to explore, especially given the Islamic community's use of protest tactics in the democratic context, I did not feel that a survey instrument could capture candid responses about contentious participation—such as boycotts or protests—accurately. I thought that questions about those topics might invoke suspicion and fear in the respondents and contaminate the other data. Ethnographic data collection or a different, more anonymous method of soliciting this sensitive information could better elicit sincere responses on this type of issue. Therefore, I omit a discussion of contentious politics despite its theoretical importance.

Building on Nie, Junn, and Stehlik-Barry's (1996) definition of "difficult" participation[7] as activities that require greater time and resources, I stress the greater skill level required for difficult participation regardless of the incentives offered. I categorize the following behaviors as difficult: campaigning, running for office, and contacting a government official. These activities contrast with voting or expressing partisanship in that they require skills beyond stating one's party preference or stepping into one of the rented *sotramas* that transport voters to the polls. There is still the possibility that more difficult activities are also incentivized by short-term benefits, but the skill threshold serves as an impediment to those who are less educated. Therefore, we should observe that higher levels of education increase difficult participation but have no effect on easier forms of participation. Since most Malians have never attended any school, I compare Malians who were able to obtain any level of schooling, including informal education, to a reference category of Malians who never attended school. I hypothesized that educated Malians will know more about politics and that they will be more likely to participate in difficult political activities than Malians who never attended any school. As discussed above, I anticipated the effects of education to be less pronounced in the domains of "easy" political behavior—voting and partisanship.

Do All Schools Shape Citizenship Equally?

The declining quality of state schools and the liberalization of the education sector could temper expectations of education's impact on knowledge and participation. Malian students attend accredited non-state schools, such as secular private schools, Christian schools, and madrassas, as well as Quranic schools, and they all use different languages of instruction. Do these different schooling providers affect knowledge and participation differently?

One could speculate that private schools are less invested in democratic or civic ideologies and discourage students from learning about secular politics; they also may teach in languages other than French (the language of the bureaucracy). Private schools, which are primarily profit-seeking enterprises, could be less committed than state schools to the project of state-building.[8] Students who attend private school therefore might be less dependent on or familiar with the state and thus be less inclined to participate in democratic politics (Hirschman 1970). However, when private schools endow students with fluency in the bureaucratic language of the state, they may be equally capable of honing students' skills for political engagement.

Islamic schools offer neither the bureaucratic ties nor the language skills offered by public schools. Due to the history of contention between religious authorities and the secular state in West Africa, Islamic schools may be less invested in state-building and might even discourage students from learning about politics (Brenner 2001; Idrissa 2008; Manchuelle 1997). Dahl's (1967) argument that education creates better democratic citizens was predicated on the assumption that schools are committed to liberal democratic ideals. However, schools that embody hierarchical norms or reinforce allegiance to traditional or religious figures might be less committed to liberal democratic values. For many years, Islamic schools embodied resistance to the foreign-imposed, colonial state. This further suggests that alumni of Islamic schools might be less willing to follow or engage in a political system that traces its heritage and legitimacy directly to that colonial state.

Unlike many Muslim countries where Islamic clerics mobilize voters, there has not traditionally been effective political mobilization in formal electoral channels by religious leaders in Mali (Sears 2007). Therefore, students who attend religious schools might be more committed to solidarity with religious and traditional leaders and hesitant to express their preferences directly to the secular authorities (Brenner 2001; Gandolfi 2003; Soares 2006). In addition, learners in Islamic schools are at a linguistic disadvantage. Despite government requirements that madrassas teach French, few madrassas provide comprehensive French instruction.[9] Therefore, alumni of Islamic schools are less likely to have the linguistic skills needed to engage in difficult forms of political participation compared to those citizens who attended Francophone schools.

For these reasons, I expected students who attend state schools to be more informed about politics and more willing to participate in politics than students who attend non-state schools, particularly Islamic ones.

Measuring the Relationship between Education, Knowledge, and Participation

The survey included questions about political knowledge and political participation as well as questions about respondents' education profiles and socioeconomic status. I assessed respondents' education in two ways: the highest level of education attained and the schools they had attended, which I labeled the *length of schooling* and the *type of provider*.

We asked four Afrobarometer questions to evaluate the first dependent variable, citizens' political knowledge: (1) What is the name of the president of the National Assembly? (2) What party has the majority of seats in the assembly? (3) What are the term limits for the president? (4) Who is your local mayor? These indicators are general so that they can be used in many different contexts, but because of that they do not capture awareness of current events. During my stay in Mali, citizens and news outlets were engaging in heated debates over issues such as the revised Family Code and the secondary school promotion system. While the Afrobarometer questions only scrape the surface of political debates or national issues of interest, they do offer insight into citizens' abilities to name important and relevant political players and one basic rule in their constitution.

I used multiple Afrobarometer indicators in order to capture a broad range of formal political participation. In my analysis, I separate participation into two categories based on the skills required: easy and difficult. *Easy* behaviors refer to voting and the expression of partisan identification, while

TABLE 5.1.
Dependent variables

Political knowledge	Political participation
Who is the mayor of (name of locality)?	Did you vote in the 2007 presidential elections? (easy)
Who is the president of the National Assembly?	Do you feel close to a political party? (easy)
What party has the most seats in the National Assembly?	Did you participate in a campaign for the 2007 presidential elections? (hard)
How long can someone serve as president?	Would you run for political office? (hard)
	Have you ever visited a government official to express an idea or to resolve a problem? (hard)

Note: If citizens reported engaging in these activities, they were coded as 1; if they did not know or responded that they had not engaged in these behaviors, they were coded as 0. For voting behavior, I excluded respondents who were ineligible to vote in 2007. I coded nonresponses as 0 except for instances where the respondent noted that they were prevented from voting, which I excluded from the sample. All nonresponses were dropped from the sample.

difficult behaviors refer to campaigning, being willing to run for office, and contacting a government official. Many scholars see partisan identity as a determinant of other forms of political behavior.[10] However, in a context of extreme skepticism about parties, the willingness to claim attachment to a political party—which is a symbol of democratic or state authority—rather than exclusively aligning with religious or traditional authorities can be considered a political act.

The dependent variables measuring knowledge and participation are listed in table 5.1.[11] These measures of participation are far from inclusive, but provide insight into some fundamental political behaviors. As mentioned earlier, I did not feel that a survey instrument could capture candid responses about contentious participation, such as protests or boycotts, so the dependent variables focus on participation in formal channels.

I have included control variables for factors that might obscure or inflate the relationship between education, knowledge, and participation: gender, age, rural or urban, school district, and a poverty measure based on an index of possessions. Historically, many fewer women than men have attended school, and simultaneously women have been less active in the public sphere, thus it is important to separate gender effects from education (Logan 2010:17; MacLean 2011:17). Afrobarometer data also reveal that older citizens are more likely to vote (Kuenzi and Lambright 2005; MacLean 2011) and less likely to identify with a party (Ishiyama and Fox 2006). Age might obscure the relationship between participation and education in Mali, where primary school enrollment has increased dramatically since the 1990s.[12] Older respondents were less likely to have attended school, but they generally vote more often and might identify less strongly with a party.

MacLean (2011) has found higher levels of poverty to be correlated with higher rates of reporting contact with a politician. Because higher levels of education and household wealth are generally correlated, I have included a proxy for poverty in an attempt to separate these effects.[13] I code all respondents as urban or rural since I anticipated distinct patterns of mobilization and participation in those zones that could be differentially affected by education (Ishiyama and Fox 2006; Logan 2010:17; MacLean 2011:21). Finally, I added a control for school districts to parse out regional effects.[14]

I have included two additional controls from models for political participation: membership in a secular organization and membership in a religious organization. Scholars of West Africa have found that "agencies of mobilization"— which include parties and civil society organizations—play an important role in encouraging turnout (Beck 2008; Ishiyama and Fox 2006; Koter 2013; Kuenzi and Lambright 2005). I observed this phenomenon while sitting in on campaign meetings for a municipal candidate in Bamako in 2009. The primary strategy for getting voters to the polls was to target patrons or associational presidents who could mobilize their vertical networks of members to vote. Prospective campaign members would tout their ability to access specific demographics, such as neighborhood youth organizations, as a way to court support from political parties. This vertical system of organizing and voting is even more exaggerated at the village level (interview with executive members of the National Independent Electoral Commission, May 2009; interview with Malian academic, March 2009). If better educated citizens are found to be more or less likely than average citizens to join organizations, correlations might capture the effect of participation in these organizations rather than of education itself. Therefore I have included membership in both secular and religious organization as a control to exclude these potential confounders.

Table 5.2 provides summary statistics from my sample and from Round 3 of the Afrobarometer survey, which was administered in 2005. I caution that these surveys are not wholly comparable since the Afrobarometer data reference the presidential election in 2002, while respondents in my sample reference the 2007 elections. But the summary enables a comparison between my sample and a nationally representative one.

TABLE 5.2.
Summary statistics

	Bleck sample, 2009 (%)	Afrobarometer, 2005 (%)
Education Level		
None	17	43
Informal	29	22
Primary	34	24
Secondary	16	9
University	3	2
Knowledge		
Can name the mayor	50	65
Can name president of the National Assembly	36	41
Can name majority party	41	12
Can name term limits	70	60
Participation		
Voted in 2007 (2002)	66	78
Identifies with a party	52	61
Campaigned in 2007 (2002)	29	NA
Would run for office	34	NA
Contacted a government official	23	30
Other Variables		
Woman	54	42
Rural	20	73
N	1006	1244

Note: NA = non-applicable

Analysis: Does Schooling Increase Knowledge and Participation?

I generated dummy variables for each level of education and regressed the knowledge variables on the level of education and controls for sex, poverty, rural, age, and school district. Bamako was used as the regional reference category for all regressions except for the question on the majority party, which compares all school districts to Timbuktu, where ADEMA has a strong presence.

The evidence uniformly shows that educated citizens are more likely than those with no education to know about politics. Any level of formal education (primary, secondary, university) has a positive and significant ($p < .01$) effect on the predicted probability that the respondent will answer any of the political knowledge questions correctly as compared to the reference category. In addition, informal education has a significant, positive predicted effect on political knowledge for all questions except knowing the name of the president of the National Assembly ($p < .05$). In other words, Malians who received informal education—which includes Quranic education and indigenous-language literacy instruction—are more likely than Malians who attended no school to answer the knowledge questions correctly, except for the question about naming the president of the assembly.

I calculated the impact of obtaining each level of education on the probability of providing a correct response to the political knowledge questions by using Gary King's CLARIFY software. Figure 5.1 graphs the predicted increase in probability of a correct response for each level of education that I found to have a significant effect. The predicted probability that a respondent will answer a political knowledge question correctly increases with each level of education. For example, depending on the question, a respondent with a primary education has a 13%–27% higher predicted probability of knowing the correct answer than a peer who did not attend school. Respondents who attended high school or vocational training had an even higher predicted probability of providing a correct response to the political pop quiz, between 35% and 56% higher, than their peers who did not attend school. Having attained secondary or tertiary education levels has the greatest effect on levels of political knowledge—particularly a respondent's ability to name the president of the assembly and the majority party. One can observe that the effects of higher education are stronger in relation to political phenomena in the capital city compared to knowledge of the rules of the democratic game or localized political knowledge about the mayor. Note that I could not graph the university students' responses for president of the National Assembly because I had a case of complete separation: every university-educated respondent correctly named Dioncounda Traoré.

Despite the positive effects of education on knowledge, being a woman had a consistent negative and significant ($p < .001$) effect on the probability of the respondent providing the correct answer to any political knowledge questions. Controlling for all other characteristics, the probability of giving a correct response was 15%–26% lower for a woman than for a man. Living in a rural zone increased the likelihood that citizens could correctly name their mayor, which suggests the greater visibility of the mayor or the salience of that municipal office in the village context. Living at a higher level of poverty was associated with a lower likelihood of naming the president of the National Assembly or correctly stating the executive term limits. Older residents were also more likely to be able to name the president of the National Assembly. While Traoré was largely assessed as less charismatic than his predecessors, older citizens may remember his prominent role as an ADEMA activist during the transition to democracy in the early 1990s.

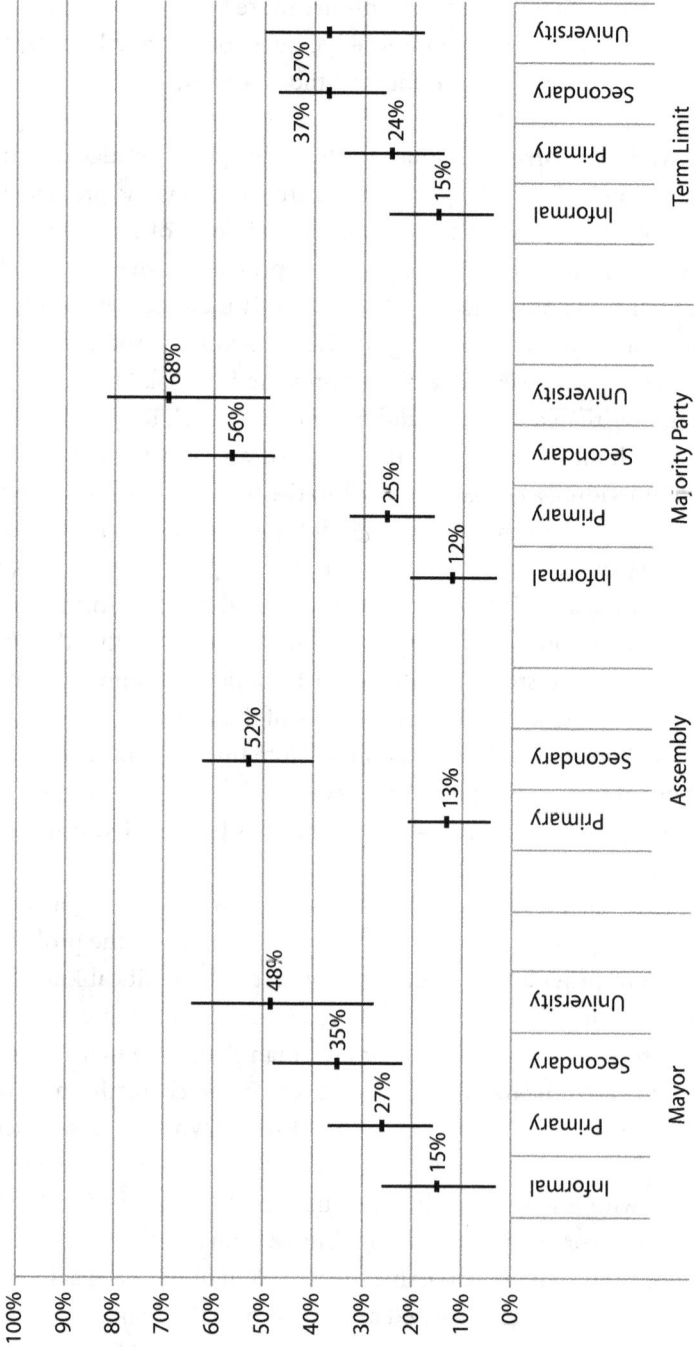

Figure 5.1. Increase in predicted probability of correct answer by level of schooling. Full regression tables are available under the data tab at www.jaimiebleck.com.

To test the impact of education on political participation, I conducted a maximum likelihood estimation that regressed "voted," "party ID," "campaigned in 2007," "would run for office," and "contacted government official" on the different levels of education and the controls, including membership in an association (religious and secular). All levels of formal education have positive, significant predicted effects on campaigning and willingness to run for office as compared to no education. Only the highest levels of education—secondary and tertiary—were significantly correlated with a greater likelihood that a respondent had contacted a government official. This finding suggests that primary school education is not enough to affect this aspect of political behavior and may indicate the importance of French-language acquisition, which typically happens after primary school, to a citizen's willingness to contact a government official. Figure 5.2 graphs the model's predicted increases in the probability of participation in difficult activities for each level of formal education with significant effects as compared to a reference category.

University education appears to have a particularly strong effect compared to other forms of education. For instance, the model predicts a 16% higher probability that secondary students will contact a government official compared to citizens with no education and a 22% higher probability that university-educated respondents have contacted a government official compared to their peers with no education. Similarly, university respondents have higher predicted probabilities of campaigning and willingness to run compared to peers with no education.

As theorized, the highest levels of education do not affect voting or party identification. However, citizens with limited levels of education were more likely than those with no education to state that they voted in 2007 or identified with a party. Reporting voting in 2007 is positively correlated with primary and informal education, while party identification is correlated exclusively with primary education. The inverted U-shaped findings related to easy participation could suggest that political entrepreneurs target those with enough education to have some political consciousness but who require partisan assistance for expression.[15]

These findings loosely support Russell Dalton's work on the evolution of citizenship. Dalton (2007) demonstrates that those who have higher levels of education are sophisticated enough to use "cognitive mobilization" based on independent information rather than relying on "partisan mobilization." He argues that better educated citizens participate directly through "engaged"

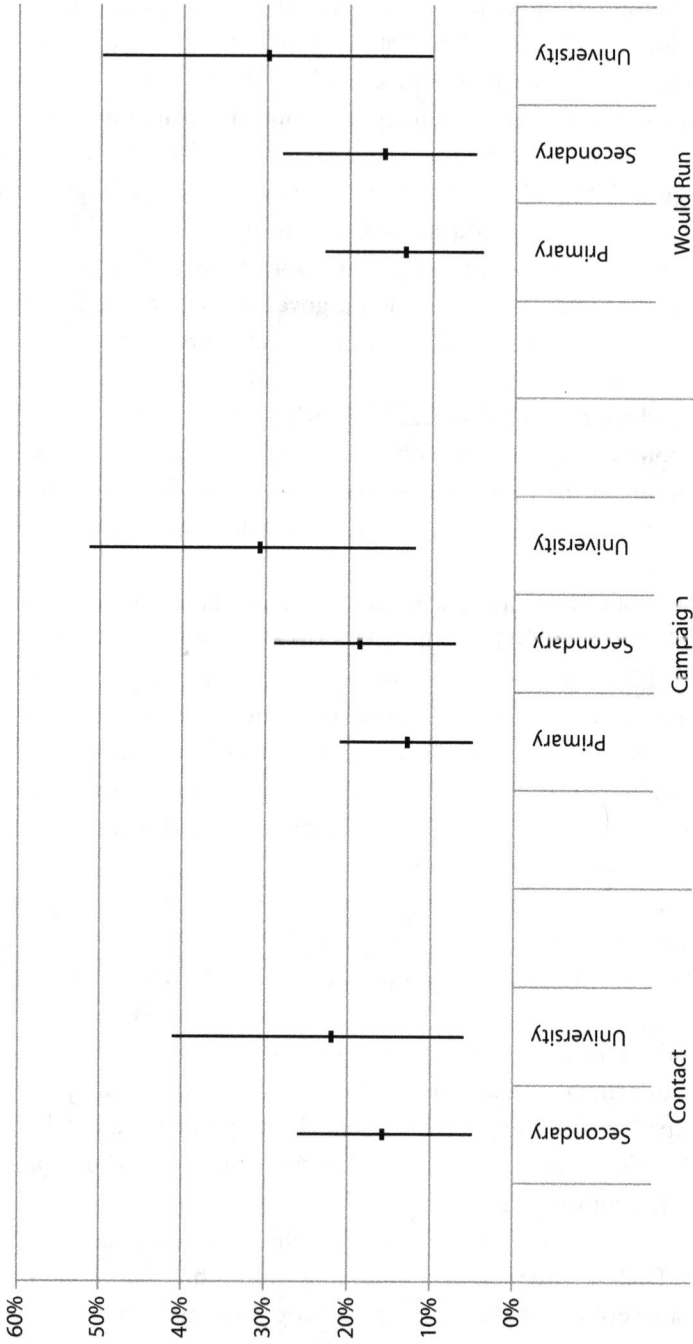

Figure 5.2. Increase in predicted probability of participation by level of education

citizenship instead of voting out of duty-based citizenship, which ties them to political parties (Dalton 2008). This might also reflect educated voters' disdain for electoral mobilization in general. While these findings speak roughly to Huntington's (1968) thesis about the political alienation of the educated class, I caution against reading too much into a negative connection between higher education and easier forms of participation, since this relationship was not significant in my study.

In addition, better educated Malians' refusal to turn out at the polls might also be linked more to their own voting calculus than to political dissent. During the municipal elections, I asked some "middle-class" Malians if they planned on voting. Most expressed apathy, stating that the $2 that was being handed out certainly could not buy their vote or that they were "too busy" to turn out. For unemployed students and lower-class Malians, the promise of $2 or an egg sandwich might be enough of an incentive to jump in a van and go to vote. Perhaps the economic control variables in my analysis are not properly capturing these differences. Informed but skeptical political consumers are in contrast with more marginalized citizens, who take what they can of the cash and goods that circulate during election time but are generally uninformed about politics.

Two control variables had strong, consistent effects on participation: gender and associational membership. Being a woman is negatively associated with the likelihood that a citizen identifies with a party, is willing to run for office, contacted a government official, or will campaign. At times, our survey team was refused interviews by women who feared violent reprisals from their husbands if they spoke to us when the men were not home. Women's survey responses confirmed the gender barriers to participation. Djeneba, who lives in a village outside of Kayes, explicitly describes the issue: "I have never seen a woman run for any office here. It's because they are scared, and the men won't allow them to run" (K6). Consistent with theories of mobilization associations, membership in a secular association has a positive and significant effect on all forms of political participation, except the willingness to run for office. (Membership in a religious association does not have a significant effect.) This is consistent with qualitative evidence that many Malians imagine group membership to be the key vehicle for political engagement. As described in chapter 1, many Malians gain strength and empowerment from group participation. They feel more comfortable engaging with traditional or bureaucratic authorities when they do so together.

Additionally, age has significant, but divergent, effects on participation.

Being a member of the oldest age category increases the predicted probability of voting by 29% compared to the youngest cohort (18–28). Age is positively correlated with contacting a government official, but negatively associated with campaigning or willingness to run for office. Interviews revealed that older citizens' hesitancy to campaign or run for office stems in part from the high level of effort and energy that is required for these activities. Many older respondents said they are too tired or too old to run for office or that they wanted to focus on religious activities at this stage in life.

Does School Type Matter?

In order to evaluate the effects of different types of education on political knowledge, I ran two regressions. The first compared learners who attended public schools to learners in four other school types: madrassas, private schools, community schools, and Christian schools. I restricted my analysis to citizens who only attended primary school since only nine respondents in my sample attended madrassas at the secondary level. I also restricted the analysis to the primary level because government sponsorship of students at private secondary schools confuses any attempt to differentiate between the school types at the secondary level.

The results do not show that public schools educate more knowledgeable citizens than other types of school at the primary level. The only statistically significant difference between Malians who attended government schools and those who attended private schools is that the latter were less likely than the former to be able to name the executive term limits. Respondents who attended community schools performed slightly better than those who attended public schools. Contrary to my theoretical expectations, I found no statistically significant differences between respondents who attended Islamic schools and those who attended public schools at the informal or primary levels.

I repeated the regression, restricting the sample to respondents with informal education in order to compare those who attended Quranic schools with alumni of literacy programs. I found no significant differences in the political knowledge of respondents in these two groups. Both Quranic education and literacy programs appear to be contributing to political knowledge.

I used the same models—still restricting the sample to primary and informal learners only—in order to compare the political participation of learners from state and non-state schools. I found no evidence that public school alumni participate more than respondents who attended private schools, community schools, or madrassas. The only significant difference that I found among primary-educated respondents is that community school alumni are more likely than respondents who went to public school to say they campaigned, would run for office, and identified with a party. Since community schools are typically in rural areas, I included an interaction term in the model to assess whether education has greater returns for people living in places where comparative literacy rates are lower. Not only was I unable to reject the null hypothesis, but I found the inverse to be true: there is a significant, positive correlation between education and living in a city. This suggests, at a minimum, different patterns of mobilization in urban and rural environments. Perhaps students are mobilized at a greater rate in urban centers, while villages mobilize all inhabitants regardless of education levels.

There are no significant differences between alumni of informal schools except the lower predicted likelihood that Quranic alumni will run for office when compared with graduates of literacy programs. The similarity of responses between alumni of Islamic and secular schools is surprising because of the historical separation between secular and religious authorities. Graduates of Islamic schools know as much about politics as public school alumni with comparable amounts of education.

Contrary to my theoretical expectations, many religious school alumni claim they "get their hands dirty" in secular politics. Again, I stress that I only made this comparison for students with comparable levels of education and do not have data on alumni from various school types at the secondary level. Yet, given the large percentage of Malians with only informal or primary education, roughly 46% of all Afrobarometer respondents compared to only 11% who had attended secondary school or higher, these findings are important (Afrobarometer data 2005, www.afrobarometer.org). The data show that the effect is strongest at the secondary and university levels, but there is not enough variation in enrollment at that level to explore the difference between Francophone schooling and Islamic schooling at that level. The increasing number of students attending religious, Arabic-language schools at the secondary level raises interesting questions about these students' political futures. Will madrassa education qualify students to participate in the elite world of secular politics now that the state endorses and accredits these schools? To investigate this important question, we must have a better idea about which aspects of education facilitate political participation.

Refining and Isolating Mechanisms

The survey results demonstrate a relationship linking education to knowledge and participation. Existing theories suggest multiple mechanisms through which schooling creates greater political knowledge and increased participation in difficult activities: democratic curriculum, heightened socialization, increased literacy, political mobilization by teachers, increased internal efficacy, and increased cognitive development. I searched for observable effects of various pathways to knowledge—including curriculum, language skills, and cognitive empowerment—and participation, such as internal efficacy, higher skill levels, socialization or mobilization, and closer connections to central nodes of political power. Below, I argue that in the Malian case, schooling empowers citizens to gain new political knowledge rather than transmitting information through an explicit curriculum. Second, I argue that education increases citizens' internal efficacy, and in the case of Francophone schooling, it expands their ability to interact with the government, which further heightens internal efficacy.

Before I proceed, it is important to briefly discuss endogeneity concerns. Most children are in an educational track before their political coming of age, which largely rules out reverse causation (i.e., higher political engagement affecting the levels and types of educational enrollment). One concern is the possibility that parental preferences could play a confounding role, determining both school choice and their children's subsequent political orientation (Franklin 1984). Two findings from my data suggest that this is not the case. First, given the historical separation between the secular and religious spheres, I theorized that parents who choose to send their children to state schools should be more likely (and capable) to teach their children about politics and to urge them to participate in institutional channels due to their underlying political beliefs or access to certain socioeconomic resources. However, as discussed earlier, there is no significant difference between the knowledge and participation of people who attended state or religious schools. I make this claim based on data from the primary level; it is possible that parents with students at the secondary or university level may play a role in transmitting civic values, but there is no reason that we should not also see these differences reflected at the primary level.

Second, due to the increase in educational enrollment over time, a child who went to school in the twenty-first century is more likely than a child in prior generations to have an educated parent. If parents transmit knowledge about politics, the youngest cohort of educated respondents should know more about politics than older cohorts of educated respondents, whose parents are less likely to be educated. I tested this observable implication by creating an interaction term for education and age, which allowed me to compare levels of education for each 10-year age cohort. I did not find the interaction term to have a significant effect on correct responses to any knowledge question. The evidence that I was able to generate suggests that parents are not, at least entirely, responsible for spreading political knowledge or spurring participation.

Curriculum

The Traoré dictatorship struck civic education from the curriculum in 1972, and despite discourse about education as a tool for democratic citizenship, the Malian Ministry of Education did not reintroduce civic education until 2009 (Bleck and Guindo 2013). Only the first decade of post-independence students received lessons about how the government functions and the duties and rights of citizens. If civic education matters for knowledge and participation, students who were exposed to this curriculum should be better able to answer political knowledge questions and should have a greater likelihood of participating in politics than students who did not experience the curriculum. I generated a variable called "civic education" for those learners who attended school between 1960 and 1972. I regressed the political knowledge questions on education level, the controls, and a new interaction term that tested the effects of civic education and education level together. This interaction term is not significant for any aspect of political knowledge and therefore does not provide evidence for support of the democratic curriculum mechanism.

I repeated the regression to assess the effect of the interaction term on participation. The test does not provide evidence for support of the democratic curriculum mechanism as fostering duty-based participation. The interaction term also is insignificant for campaigning and for willingness to run for office.[16] This is not to say that a democratic curriculum would not have further improved educated citizens' knowledge and participation, but the current evidence cannot speak to the role of civics curriculum in explaining why educated citizens have greater knowledge and participation in the Malian case.

Socialization

Greater political knowledge and participation could be caused by socialization in the schooling environment rather than by the educational experience itself.[17] Children could learn about politics by talking to peers or by being exposed to new experiences and information. In this scenario, knowledge is not linked to curriculum, but to the experiences and interactions that happen in the schooling environment. I tested the mechanism of socialization by exploiting differences in Malian gender norms. Generally, Malian girls have more limited social interactions than boys due to their greater responsibility for household chores and stricter societal regulations. The gender segregation—women at home and men in the public sphere—continues as girls grow older.[18] Since boys have more opportunities to socialize outside of the home, the socialization effect of school should be greater for girls, who have more limited exposure to new experiences and ideas except in the schooling space. I ran a logistic regression with an interaction term for woman and education level. The effect of education on women's political participation and political knowledge is not consistently different from the effect on men.[19] However, this could also mean that the average family that allows their daughter to attend school also allows her greater freedom of movement than is permitted by the average Malian family, which suggests that there is less of a difference in the socialization opportunities between boys and girls who attend school.

It is possible that the experience of exchanging ideas with peers, as much as the experiences in the classroom, generates political knowledge and curiosity for further knowledge. It might also generate norms for political participation. However, the current evidence does not allow me to separate socialization from the general schooling experience apart from the lack of significance of the interaction between gender and schooling.

Political Mobilization

Scholars have described the powerful role of teachers and students in shaping the democratization movements in the early 1990s across Africa (Wing 2008). Frequent teacher and student strikes and battles over school conditions are a testimony to the legacy of political activism in schools (Diakite 2000; Smith 1997). The only female presidential contender in 2007, Sidibé Aminata Diallo, is a university professor who ran her campaign largely by using her base of students as a support network. She was later named the minister of education in ATT's government. Given the politicized school environment, I explored the possibility that students in schools are targeted and mobilized by teachers and political leaders. I drew on data from interviews that we conducted with 203 university students at the various campuses of the University of Bamako in February 2009.[20]

Our team asked students a series of questions about their expected political participation prior to the municipal elections. The questions were slightly different from those posed in the household survey: we asked the students about participation in municipal elections, while we asked the survey respondents about participation in presidential elections.[21] Only 33% of the university students claimed they would participate in the 2009 municipal elections, while 29% of survey respondents said they had participated in presidential campaigns.[22] If students are mobilized by teachers and political parties on campuses, there should be a much greater difference in reported participation rates between active university students and average respondents.

It is possible that participation patterns are different for national and local elections and that students play a larger role in national-level elections. It might also be that secondary school students, rather than university students, play a more significant role in the physical mobilization of voters. I caution that my data can only speak to the 2009 cohort of university students and may reflect their apathy toward elections as compared to earlier, more engaged, and more hopeful peers from the 1990s. While I do not rule out the role of other mechanisms, I do not find substantial evidence for alternative mechanisms.

Education and Empowerment

I argue that education stimulates empowerment, which can create greater political knowledge and enhanced internal efficacy. There are four components of political empowerment: meaning, competence, self-determination, and impact (Hur 2006:533). In other words, the process of becoming empowered starts with access to information, which increases awareness of one's own ability and of the possibilities for and constraints on one's actions. Doug McAdam (1982:34) refers to the similar concept of "cognitive liberation" as being able to identify the conditions of oppression and the belief that this condition can change. I define individual empowerment as a citizen's greater awareness of the environment around her and of her own capabilities.

Empowerment does not contribute to a linear form of political socialization, but rather equips citizens with the tools to understand and question their political environment and adapt their behaviors to it. This empowerment promotes citizens to the status of democratic agents, which Guillermo O'Donnell (2004:27) argues are critical components of democratic regimes. Empowerment is elusive and difficult to measure since many of the processes are internal to individuals. However, the finding that any level of education, regardless of school type, increases political knowledge suggests the empowerment mechanism. This blanket correlation suggests that through the process of education, regardless of curriculum, citizens develop greater awareness about the political environment around them. Certain types of pedagogy or schooling might be better at generating empowered democratic agency, but according to the Malian data educated citizens, regardless of school type, will be more empowered than citizens who were not able to attend school. Like Boubacar, who was introduced at the beginning of this chapter, many respondents have reservations about their agency and capabilities. Respondents lament that they have never been to school and that they do not know much about politics. These statements are consistent with O'Donnell's (ibid.:11) argument that agency requires the attainment of some basic capabilities.

One proxy for political empowerment, or increased internal efficacy, is a citizen's ability and willingness to discuss political issues. In order to further test the empowerment mechanism and to assess whether education actually stimulates political debate and conversation, I created a dichotomous dependent variable—"discuss politics"—based on citizens' responses to an Afrobarometer question of whether they ever talk about politics. Individuals with any level of formal education—primary, secondary, or university—are significantly more likely than those with no education to discuss politics. Educated citizens appear to have greater interest, ability, and comfort in discussing political material.

The Resilience of Colonial Language

The lack of French literacy restricts citizens' access to pluralistic news sources such as newspapers, the internet, French-language debates, and information on the radio or television.[23] Mobido, a farmer in the Sikasso region who scored one out of four on our political knowledge quiz, feels excluded from politics and from the media: "I don't have confidence in politics. Politicians do not take the time to look at farmers' problems. ATT hasn't done anything to help us [farmers]. I never watch television because I don't speak French" (SR11).

In order to assess the power of the French language on political knowledge, I generated a variable based on the language the interviewee used during the survey: "any French" or exclusively an "indigenous language." Typically, respondents were greeted by the survey team in a local language and were offered a choice about which language they preferred for the survey. While the majority of Malians who speak French fluently went to university or secondary school, there are other factors that contribute to a citizen's ability and comfort in using French. For example, someone who has traveled *en exode*, perhaps looking for work in a neighboring country like Côte d'Ivoire or Senegal, is more likely to speak French. Those in the tourism or service industries are also more likely to feel comfortable speaking French.

Reinforcing the primacy of indigenous languages in Malian life, less than 14% of all respondents chose to use any French during the survey. I created a dichotomous variable, "French interview," for all respondents who used any French in their interview and ran it in a regression with all variables, except education, on the knowledge questions. Speaking French in an interview is associated with significantly higher predicted probabilities of providing a correct response to our political pop quiz, ranging from a 14% increase in the predicted probability of being able to name the local mayor to a 37% increase in correctly naming ADEMA as the dominant party in the National Assembly. Speaking French appears to have a large and significant effect on political knowledge and may reflect French-speakers' greater access to political information. Note that these increases are slightly larger than those associated with primary education, yet not as large as those associated with secondary education.

Literacy and Participation

In many African countries, including Mali, the political sphere uses a language that citizens do not speak in their homes. The qualitative data from our survey suggest that illiteracy in colonial languages dampens internal efficacy. While Mali has no formal education requirements for candidates to run for office, most citizens reveal the imagined barrier of French fluency as a necessary condition for running for office. Respondents repeatedly describe themselves as incapable of running for municipal office because they are not able to speak French or did not go to school. For instance, when we asked

Kadiatou, an informed woman from Kayes, if she had ever run for office or would consider running for mayor in the future, she retorted: "I can't speak French. Do you think that someone with no [French] education can run for office?" (K39). Kindie, another Kayesian, also said that she would not run for office because she had not gone to school. She then suggested that perhaps her children, two of whom are receiving government scholarships to attend high school, might be able to run (K40). Dadel, another female respondent from Kayes, gave an eloquent lecture about the poor performance of the current municipal government, but she will not run for office: "No, you need to have studied" (KV78). When the enumerator questioned why someone so informed and articulate would not run, Dadel responded: "Yes, I do [know how to speak well], but I didn't go to school" (KV78). The following quotes, all responses to the question of whether the respondent would ever run for office, demonstrate that this mentality stretches beyond the borders of Kayes:

> I didn't go to school, so I cannot run.
> —Modibo, 50-something Senoufou man,
> village in the Sikasso region (SR11)

> I didn't study, so I can't run for office.
> —Kadi, 40-something woman, Quranic education (M71)

> If you can't write your own name, can you be mayor?
> —Samba, 60-something Senoufou man,
> village in the Sikasso region (SR60)

> [I can't]. . . . I'm not educated.
> —Seydou, village in the Mopti region (SV81)

In the colonial and post-independence era, citizens prized French-language skills because they helped to navigate the bureaucracy and to avoid exploitation and deception by government officials (Bergmann 1996; Gérard 1997b). Remnants of these ideas remain, and most respondents avoid the police and the formal legal system because of the perception that these groups only cater to the most powerful. French literacy also enables participation by building internal efficacy so that Malians can navigate the bureaucracy without fear of exploitation or nonresponsiveness.

Our survey reveals that people who report frequent contact with the mayor's office have a high school or university education. As the best educated members of their families and communities, these citizens often serve as spokespeople for a friend or relative. Mariam is from Bamako and is university-educated; she contacted a government official on behalf of her cousin, who had a problem with her market stall (BC81). Amadou, a 60-year-old Songhai man in Timbuktu with some university education, frequently visits the mayor to discuss the poor quality of the roads during the rainy season because "in Timbuktu, people are passive and scared" to approach the authorities on their own (T20). University education qualifies citizens as French-speakers, but also provides access to networks of advocacy in case of potential injustice.

Speaking French during the survey is also positively correlated with the variables that best measure internal efficacy. All respondents who spoke French in the interview were significantly more likely to say that they would run for office and more likely to claim that they discussed politics. There is a 17% increase in the predicted probability that French-speakers would run for office as compared to those who did not use French in their interviews. Those respondents who spoke in French have a 29% increase in predicted probability that they discuss politics as compared to their peers who used local languages in the interviews. There is no significant relationship between speaking French and the other participation variables (campaigning, partisanship, voting, or contacting a government official). I might have expected language fluency to be positively correlated with contacting a government official, but if the broader category of French-speakers includes highly mobile individuals who travel abroad frequently, those individuals may be less likely to interact with politicians back in their village or country of origin.

Education, Internal Efficacy, and Empowerment in Environments of Low External Efficacy

Education appears to build internal efficacy through empowerment and, at higher levels, language skills. To further understand the effect of higher education on internal efficacy, I compared the qualitative justifications for political behavior from the typical survey respondents—85% of whom had either no, informal, or primary education—with the survey of university students. While most respondents, regardless of level of education, express dissatisfaction with "politics," less educated respondents express a greater feeling of helplessness and frustration, which indicates low internal efficacy. Most participants, regardless of their level of education, express skepticism about political accountability or responsiveness. While most respondents deftly identify the core power relations between the elites and the masses, many Malians struggle to give productive examples of how politics or democratic practices might improve. In most citizens' depictions, the inner workings of politics are far removed from their lives or their realm of understanding. However, there is a tangible difference between how university-educated Malians and other respondents react to political skepticism.

Among less educated respondents, there is a pervasive feeling of helplessness that often leads to their exit from political activities. Salah, an Arab respondent from the Mopti region, explains his reason for not coming out to the polls: "I do not vote because nothing is transparent" (M60). Fatoumata, a 50-something respondent in Sikasso, never attended school. She has a disdain for politics: "I no longer need the president or any other candidate any more; that's enough. There has been no change, I am struggling.... I have had enough difficulty already. I don't even trust you who are asking these questions right now" (S4). Moussa, who attended Quranic school in Sikasso, says, "They [elected officials] know our problems, but nothing is ever developed to help us. They know what is going on [in our lives]; they just close their eyes" (S1). A primary school–educated respondent, Diakaridian, in Bamako says, "Officials are not accessible. Outside of elections, they never come visit; we don't see any trace of them" (DC10). Dintou is in her mid-30s and attended public primary school; her deceased husband was in the Malian army. She describes the difficulty of getting government officials to be responsive to her requests for his pension payments: "Up until [the] present, I haven't been able to benefit from inheritances from when my husband passed away. It's the law of the strongest" (S17).

University respondents are also critical of the political system, harboring low levels of external efficacy, but they display much higher levels of internal efficacy. University students who dislike politics offer specific, concrete justifications for their non-participation, and some of the non-participators justify their inaction in terms of empowered protest. Fatogoma, a medical student, explains: "If we vote, then they do what they want" (U98). Oumar was born and raised in Bamako. He complains: "The elected don't do anything, so I won't vote.... But I am going to campaign. I am going to sensitize young people to tell them that they shouldn't vote!" (U179). Other students claimed that they would cast empty ballots in order to protest complacent politicians. These quotes are consistent with the earlier finding of no significant relationship between university education and a higher probability of voting, but reveal that the decision not to vote is an empowered choice. They are also consistent with the US politics literature on the ability of internal efficacy to empower certain types of participation, particularly in difficult and contentious channels, that is, in environments characterized by low trust. Citizens might abstain from other political activities as an empowered choice.

A second key distinction between the university respondents and respondents from the household survey is that there is a sizable population of university students who can imagine their future selves in the highest echelons of Malian politics. They display characteristics associated with greater internal efficacy. Some respondents claim to be involved in electoral politics in order to learn about the political system so that they can run for office one day (U132, U84, U85). In some instances, increased internal efficacy translates into support for the regime. Tiecouran has achieved French fluency and is eager to take advantage of political opportunities. He wants to work for the government in order to "fix his country." He says he plans on voting and campaigning in the municipal elections: "I want a good mayor in my commune; I want to participate in the development of my commune" (U171). Issouf, a 20-year-old medical student, grew up in Mopti, where he attended public school. He rates the Malian state's performance in the education sector as "10 out of 10" and even says "the educational system is perfect" in Mali. His optimism may reflect his own success; the medical school is the most competitive university in Mali. In the future, Issouf hopes to be employed by the Malian state because he wants to contribute to "the construction of his state." He says that he will participate in a campaign because one day he hopes to become a politician (U154). These examples offer direct evidence of education empowering democratic agency through heightened internal efficacy.

Empowerment, as discussed above, is generally conceptualized as having two steps: first, gaining awareness and competence, and second, mobilizing or becoming willing to act. This empowerment may then translate into internal efficacy, which may be applied to the political realm. But if we use a broader definition of internal efficacy as increased self-confidence as a capable agent, it may also apply to other venues: family relations, community exchanges, and economic activities. The second step—participation—is complicated in an atmosphere of low external efficacy, which may explain why the predicted effect of education is higher on knowledge than on participation. My findings reveal that better educated citizens are most likely to exhibit higher levels of what Pollock terms "high-initiative" and Nie and colleagues (1996) call "difficult" forms of participation: campaigning, willingness to run for office and contacting a government official. The evidence I have presented regarding how education increases participation in difficult activities supports Pollock's general claim: in environments of low external efficacy, increased internal efficacy is most likely to bolster high-initiative forms of political participation.

What Does Mass Education Mean for the Future of Democracy?

My findings suggest that by expanding education to the masses, the Malian government is creating more savvy and empowered citizens. Even with only informal or primary education, respondents know more than their peers with no education about their political system. At a primary or informal level of education, this political knowledge and internal efficacy might not be enough to encourage citizens to engage in difficult political activities, but they could help citizens to better understand political opportunities and to communicate their needs in the electoral context. Education does not guarantee engagement with poorly performing democratic institutions nor support for specific regimes,[24] but it helps citizens to amass more information about their political system and also provides the necessary tools for citizens to initiate crucial engagement.

At lower levels of education, attending an Islamic school instead of a state school does not appear to stymie political participation. Malian madrassas appear to be capable of shaping informed citizens who are as willing to vote and participate as their Francophone counterparts. These findings are encouraging given similar government partnerships with madrassas in Niger, Senegal, and Gambia (Villalón 2012). The research can speak to how Islamic education might encourage citizens' engagement in politics, but it cannot specify what the content of citizens' political demands will be. If students of madrassas get more involved in the political realm, they may be more likely to seek political representation of a broader set of value systems, including some of the more religiously conservative ideas, rather than the current political dominance by the secular elite (Bleck and van de Walle 2011; Villalón 2010). However, the continued importance of French literacy raises significant questions about the future of Islamic education in the democratization process. The lack of French-language skills could continue to be an obstacle for madrassa-educated citizens who want to get involved in the highest levels of politics.

My findings also suggest that the French language penetrates Malian politics at a deep level in the imagination of everyday Malians. Elite, secular political power is clearly associated with French and Western education. Mastery of the French language dictates who can fully participate in politics. Experts have lauded African elections for their early embrace of universal suffrage, but when we dig more deeply we uncover a massive rift that divides the politically empowered from the dispossessed. Even if indigenous- or Arabic-language education builds citizens' internal efficacy, people are constrained by their inability to directly communicate with formal bureaucratic institutions. Knowledge of the French language helps to overcome this constraint by helping people to feel capable of exercising their voice beyond the ballot box in more difficult venues. In the minds of many Malians, French fluency is a necessary condition to run for elected office. If primary education is not enough to achieve command of the French language, then government efforts to expand basic education might not be enough to bridge the gap between elite secular power and the masses.

CHAPTER SIX

Schooling and Parents' Engagement with the State

In this chapter I examine parents' school selection and consumption as it is linked to their own patterns of political participation. First, I seek to understand whether state provision of schooling as a welfare service impacts the ways that parents engage with the state. Social service provision, especially in weak states, represents a venue for political authorities to connect with constituencies. The literature on policy feedback mechanisms suggests that state schooling might be able to foster participation even in environments of low external efficacy. I find that public schooling—a state-sponsored welfare service—increases citizens' electoral participation. The data suggest that public school parents are more likely to participate due to two different mechanisms: a policy feedback mechanism and a linguistic brokerage mechanism.

Given the liberalization of the Malian education sector described in chapter 4, I assess whether state and non-state school provision have different impacts on participation. Specifically, do parents who send their children to Islamic schools (madrassas) participate differently than those who have children enrolled in Francophone public schools? The question of Islamic schooling communities is salient due to their historic marginalization by West African states. In addition, most madrassas use a different language of pedagogy (Arabic), which is not recognized as an official government language. On a practical level, the parents of students who attend madrassas are not equipped with the same skills as the parents of learners at public schools to engage with Malian democracy. In this chapter I demonstrate that madrassa consumers are reluctant to participate in electoral channels. Parents who enroll their children in madrassas are less likely than Malian citizens who do not have children enrolled in school to report that they participate in electoral politics. Evidence from exit polling in the 2009 municipal elections confirms these general trends.

These findings suggest a need to broaden the conceptualization of political constituencies beyond the narrow realm of regional and ethnic politics that is typically applied to Africa. They also raise important questions about the inclusion and representation of Islamic schooling communities in Mali. Finally, the findings offer evidence to further support MacLean's (2011) claim that public services link parents to political—in particular, electoral—participation.

Islamic Politics in Mali

On August 22, 2009—the first day of Ramadan—more than 50,000 citizens packed the national soccer stadium and overflowed into the surrounding streets of Yirimadio in protest of the recently legislated Family Code. Weeks earlier, the National Assembly had passed the code with a nearly unanimous vote: 117–5 with 4 abstentions. The code contained more than 1,000 amendments to existing family law, including raising the minimum age limit for legal marriage, restrictions on religious marriage, and changes in inheritance laws. Many Malian citizens were outraged by the government's entrance into personal matters that had been historically regulated by religious and traditional authorities (interview with Malian think tank director, August 2009). The contentious bill divided Malian society. Women's associations and NGOs had spent years lobbying for the passage of the bill in order to increase legal equality between Malian men and women. Protestors decried their representatives' disregard for their constituencies' preferences, Western donors' stranglehold on the political agenda, and the lack of transparency surrounding the political decision-making process.

Mosques, religious associations, and madrassas played a primary role in organizing the stadium protests and the marches in Bamako and Kayes the previous weekend. They facilitated meetings and organized buses to take congregations to the protest sites. Religious leaders lashed out against members of the assembly in televised commercials and bought full-page editorials in local newspapers. The members of the High Council of Islam issued a direct appeal to the Malian president, Amadou Toumani Touré, to reverse the code. In a televised speech on August 29, ATT announced that he would send the code back to the National Assembly so that the members could revisit the most contentious elements. In the interim, Islamic actors were allowed to provide input on revisions to the code. The Malian government eventually passed a tempered version of the code, which reflected many of the changes championed by the religious mobilization, in December 2011. Women's rights groups and the international community lamented the new code as doing far less to promote women's rights (http://www.rfi.fr/afrique/20111205-mali -moins-droits-femmes-le-nouveau-code-famille).

The Family Code protests demonstrate an effective use of contentious political action to achieve political reform. Religious leaders played a key role as brokers for mass opinion against the code. While their efforts to inform and mobilize constituencies around a salient issue helped citizens to achieve more representative political outcomes, the significant role of religious groups in disseminating political information also highlights the chasm between political parties and their constituencies. This was not the first time that religious groups have exerted their political muscle. In the twenty-first century, public protests led by major religious groups, such as the HCI, have overturned an amendment to annul the death penalty and gender quotas for political parties.

Mali, like many nascent African democracies, still harbors multiple forms of political authority, including traditional and religious authorities. As described in chapter 2, religious authorities have strong legitimacy in the eyes of the Malian population, but they rarely engage in formal, electoral politics. In chapter 4, I discussed the tumultuous relationship between Islamic schooling and the secular state. Until democratization, the government authorities tried to co-opt, control, or subjugate these schools. In the democratic era, Islamic organizations have exercised their activism through protests rather than at the ballot box. The contentious relationship between Islamic schooling and secular government authority in Mali raises questions about their current collaboration. Do parents who send their children to Islamic schools have different patterns of political participation and interaction with the state than parents who send their children to different types of school?

Hypothesis Building: Public Provision Engenders Active Citizenship

For numerous reasons, I anticipated that parents who send their children to public school would be more likely than other types of Malian citizens to engage with the government. In the past, governments have used state education to gain legitimacy and allegiance, build credibility, and extend their reach into the popular imagination.[1] This legitimacy is even more important in a weak state setting that harbors multiple forms of authority. Primary school provision represents one of few, if not the only, venue for citizens to interact with governing authorities in weak democratic states. A trip to most rural villages in Mali reveals, at a minimum, a school with a Malian flag as a symbol of the state even if no other government infrastructure is visible. Could the state, through social service provision, induce citizens to give formal political participation a try?

The policy feedback literature suggests multiple mechanisms, including providing resources and incentives for participation as well as affecting interpretive aspects of citizenship, that might lead parents who use public services to be more likely to interact with the government (Pierson 1993). Additionally, parents with a child in public school should be more likely to exercise their political voice because it is in their political interest to do so (MacLean 2011). Expanded public provision provides incentives to parents to express their political opinions about the administration of state schooling or other public services. As direct social service consumers of the state, these citizens are more invested in the performance of the state and will therefore be more active in politics compared to other citizens with less at stake during elections.

During our survey work, I often noted that respondents cited evaluations of the state's capacity (or lack thereof) in their calculation of whether or not to vote. In Kayes, where voting rates are habitually low, I asked respondents, taxi drivers, and other people I met why so few people were showing up to vote. To paraphrase their responses: "Look at the quality of our roads. Look at how dirty our city is. Our politicians do not do anything. We have no reason to campaign for them." Rather than using the ballot box to punish incumbents, many Kayesians chose to exit or forgo politics altogether. State inaction or incompetence might heighten citizens' low external efficacy and alienate them from politics.

The Malian state took significant steps to increase access to education through former president Alpha Konaré's "one school or adult education center in every village" campaign during the late 1990s and early 2000s. Because the Malian state has gone to great lengths to sensitize populations about the importance of education, most Malian citizens—especially those receiving public school services—are likely to view education in a positive light. Studies in the US context show that social service programs have the ability to shape political behavior by generating an empowered and active beneficiary base—particularly if those social service programs have a positive association (see Campbell 2003; Mettler 2005). By enrolling their children in Malian schools, parents are activating their positive citizenship status through an interpretive mechanism; increased political participation could be built upon this base of positive citizenship actions. Citizens might be encouraged to pursue other activities, such as voting, that validate their status as "good citizens."

From the beginning, before a parent enrolls a child in public school, she is forced to interact with the state in order to obtain a birth certificate for her child. Since many children are born at home and lack documentation, this often requires a trek down to the municipal government office and a request for a legal document. This simple act engages the parent with her local government, which might otherwise be viewed merely as an abstract symbol of state power. Parents, at a minimum, learn where state buildings are located and gain a sense of what the process is. This knowledge might result in greater contact with the state bureaucracy or a greater willingness to participate in state politics. The connection between enrolling a child in public school and political participation is more than symbolic: public schools also serve as polling stations during elections.

In an atmosphere of pervasive skepticism about politics, government services could provide citizens with tangible evidence of a functioning state, which could in turn make citizens perceive their vote as more relevant. While a demonstration of state capacity is not commensurate with citizens' belief that a state will be responsive and accountable to their demands, it is a first step toward realizing the possibility of external efficacy. The Malian government concentrated its efforts on developing school infrastructure in order to increase enrollment. Although public school is not free in practice,[2] parents with children in public schools can observe the state at work. Concrete proof of a state's work sensitizes citizens to the functioning of the government bureaucracy, increasing their perception of the state's external efficacy. Evidence of state welfare provision might incite engagement with the state as citizens see the state to be capable of responding to their exercise of voice. Consistent with this thesis, MacLean's (2011) analysis in Côte d'Ivoire and Ghana shows that citizens' consumption of public social services is correlated with greater political participation.

In line with the resource mechanisms in the policy feedback literature, parents whose children receive Francophone instruction—in public schools or private secular schools—might benefit from greater access to the government through the education of their children as linguistic or social brokers. In a low-literacy environment like Mali, language education for their children endows families with a resource for engaging with the state bureaucracy. An emerging literature on recent immigrants to the United States suggests that political socialization can be transmitted from children to parents, a companion idea to the traditional conception of political ideas traveling from parents to children (Bloemraad and Trost 2008; De Ment, Buriel, and Villanueva 2005; Parke and Buriel 2006). Malian parents—like newly immigrated parents who do not speak the language of the state—could benefit from their children's linguistic skills when interacting with the government bureaucracy. As I demonstrated in the previous chapter, Malians who do not speak French feel stigmatized as second-class citizens. By endowing a child with the skills to participate, education could impact the political capability of the entire family. Therefore, we can imagine educated children bringing their parents into the political process. This suggests that *parents who enroll(ed) their children in public school will be more likely than other citizens and other parents to engage with the Malian government.*

Islamic Schooling as Political Cleavage

Are consumers of religious education just as likely to participate in bureaucratic and electoral channels as their peers who were not exposed to religious education? An emerging comparative literature suggests that exposure to non-state social services provided by different actors could influence political behavior (Cammett and MacLean 2011). For instance, Thachil (2011) has demonstrated the Hindu nationalist Bharatiya Janata Party's use of schooling in India as a successful strategy to court voters from outside of its traditional base. Similarly, Cammett and Issar (2010) have revealed the use of schooling as a recruitment strategy by parties and by more radical groups in Lebanon. Relatedly, rebel groups have consistently used social service provision to win the support of host communities and recruits (Keister 2011; Weinstein 2007).

There are reasons to believe that parents who enroll their children in madrassas would be more likely to turn to contentious or informal participation—mediated by their mosques and religious leaders or a focus on self-directed improvement—than engage in traditional, institutional political channels. Since formal political participation is associated with secular, Western power, it is possible that parents who align themselves with religious authorities, including Islamic education, will forgo formal channels of political expression. The history of hostility, co-optation, and oppression of religious education and religious leadership by the colonial and postcolonial regimes suggests that Islamic schooling consumers would be particularly reluctant to engage with the state. Islamic schooling, in either modern madrassas or Quranic schools, represents a realm of knowledge and power distinct from the secular, Francophone state. I anticipated that parents whose children receive education from these venues might be less likely to contact the formal, secular political realm and more likely to engage with traditional or religious leaders. This could be due to two factors. First, parents' religious piety could lead them to simultaneously pursue religious education and avoid electoral politics; and second, the act of joining an Islamic schooling community could dissuade citizens from independent participation in party politics.

As I discussed in chapter 3, Islamic actors have profited from the opening of the public sphere facilitated by democracy, but have failed to capitalize in the formal political sphere. As a result, politics are viewed as the inverse of religion, and many devout Malians claim to abstain from politics due to their faith. Islamic organizations have been more effective in applying pressure on the executive and other top policy makers outside of formal political channels. Religious leaders have been extremely successful at organizing people to protest, but Islamic political movements and candidates have not mobilized these constituencies for elections. Therefore, Islamic schooling communities might be expected to encourage their members to avoid "dirty politics."

Madrassa schooling is unique because of its religious focus and because the primary language of instruction, Arabic, is not recognized as an official government language. If public schools and private Francophone schools endow students and their families with a linguistic broker capable of dealing with the government, parents who send their children exclusively to madrassas or Quranic schools will forfeit access to these resources. This, in and of itself, might make a parent at an Islamic school less likely than parents at Francophone schools to engage with the state bureaucracy.

I chose to disaggregate madrassa schooling consumers from those parents with children in Quranic schools because the two types of school are theoretically distinct.[3] Many of the parents who send their children to Quranic schools are from rural areas and do not have access to other types of educational infrastructure, or they do not have the means to pursue other types of education. In contrast, parents who enroll their children in madrassas come from a wider socioeconomic spectrum. They cite quality or religious reasons, rather than pragmatic reasons such as cost or proximity, for enrolling their children. Therefore, I generated the following hypothesis: *Parents who enroll their children in madrassas will be less likely than other Malian citizens to engage with the Malian government through formal electoral channels.*

The Political Perceptions and Behavior of
Islamic Schooling Communities

As already mentioned, I draw on an original survey of 1,000 individuals from 10 school districts. All respondents were asked if they had children who were at least 7 years of age.[4] If they had children, they were asked if their children had ever been enrolled in school and, if so, what school type(s). Each respondent was asked their reason(s) for enrolling their child(ren) in each relevant school, their evaluations of the schools, and their general attitudes toward the Malian education system. In our sample, 694 respondents reported having at least one child 7 years of age or older.[5] Of the parents with children who attend(ed) school,[6] 362 respondents had children who attend(ed) public school, 169 had children who attend(ed) private secular school, 38 had children who attend(ed) exclusively a madrassa, 51 had children in community school, 31 had children in Quranic school, 7 had children at both Quranic and public schools, and 46 had children at both madrassas and public schools. Our sample includes parents who were benefiting from a state service at the time of the survey, but also parents who previously benefited from state services. These data enable us to compare the behavior of parents who send their children to madrassas and those who send their children to public schools to other Malian citizens.

I included control variables, as described in the previous chapter, for factors that might obscure or inflate the relationship between social service consumption and participation: gender, age, rural or urban, school district, and poverty. I coded all respondents as urban or rural since I anticipated distinct patterns of mobilization and participation in those zones and since there is a greater availability of schooling options in urban zones (Ishiyama and Fox 2006; Logan 2010:17). I also controlled for parents' level of education, since this variable is likely to influence parents' decision to enroll their child in school and parents' level of political participation (MacLean 2011). I included controls for membership in a secular organization and membership in a religious organization, as explained in the previous chapter. Membership in organizations could also affect school choice (see Koter 2013 for Benin, Mali, and Senegal; see Beck 2008 for Senegal).

I assessed formal participation through a series of measures: whether the respondent identified with a party, reported campaigning or voting during the 2007 presidential elections, and reported contacting a government official. Each variable was coded dichotomously and evaluated independently.

Additionally, I included whether or not a citizen had a voting card as another measure of electoral participation.

I compared parents who send their children to different school types to citizens who do (or did) not have a child enrolled in school.[7] This strategy allowed me to compare different types of schooling consumers with a neutral category of non-consumers in order to simultaneously evaluate the effects of different types of schooling on parents. I regressed the dichotomous outcome variables for political participation (party identification, campaigning, voting, having a voting card, willingness to run for office, and contacting a government official) on each schooling dummy and the controls: age, education level, gender, urban or rural, school district, associational membership(s), and poverty.[8]

Enrolling a child in public school has the expected positive and significant relationship with parents' political participation. As demonstrated in table 6.1, having a child in public school increases the likelihood of respondents stating that they campaigned ($p < .01$) or voted ($p < .01$) in the 2007 presidential elections as compared to respondents without children enrolled in school.[9] Having at least one child enrolled in public school increases the likelihood that a parent campaigned by 10% and increases the likelihood of voting by 12%. Having a child enrolled in public school significantly increases the predicted probability of a parent having a voting card by 17% ($p < .001$).

As I suspected, parents who send their children exclusively to madrassas are less likely to vote than Malians without children enrolled in school. If a respondent's child attends (or previously attended) a madrassa, there is a lower predicted likelihood ($p < .01$) that the respondent reported voting as compared to the reference category. If a parent's children are enrolled exclusively in a madrassa, this is associated with a 25% decrease in the parent's predicted probability of voting. However, madrassa enrollment is associated with decreases only in that category of participation. There are no significant differences between madrassa consumers and the reference category for any other type of participation: campaigning, contacting a government official, or willingness to run for office.[10] I ran additional tests to see if those with children enrolled in madrassas were more broadly isolated from the political system and less likely to have documentation that is legible to the state. However, the data suggest that parents with children in madrassas are not less likely to have bureaucratic documentation. I found that having a child enrolled in a madrassa had no significant effect on having a birth certificate or national identification card.

TABLE 6.1.
Schooling consumers' participation

Where child enrolled	Voted in 2007	Campaigned in 2007	Voter ID card
Public school	.55**	.52**	.86***
	(.18)	(.19)	(.18)
Madrassa	−1.03**	−.29	−.57
	(.39)	(.38)	(.37)
Private secular school	.29	.17	.10
	(.21)	(.20)	(.20)
Community school	.60	.88**	.49
	(.41)	(.34)	(.37)
Quranic school	.16	.36	.35
	(.44)	(.45)	(.38)
Private Christian school	−.04	.68	.13
	(.08)	(.50)	(.56)
Public and madrassa	.22	−.24	.94^d
	(.36)	(.46)	(.38)
Public and Quranic	−.02	−.56	perfect
	(.90)	(1.13)	failure
Controls			
Education	.06	.15**	.07
	(.05)	(.05)	(.05)
Woman	−.32	−.70**	−.51**
	(.17)	(.17)	(.16)
Urban	−.32	−.20	−.53*
	(.21)	(.21)	(.21)
Poverty	.04	−.01	−.15*
	(.07)	(.07)	(.17)
Age	.25***	−.19**	.18**
	(.06)	(.06)	(.06)
Association member	.24**	.32***	.24**
	(.08)	(.07)	(.08)
Religious association member	.04	.11	−.07
	(.10)	(.09)	(.10)
Constant	.1–.15	−1.17	.59
	(.34)	(.34)	(.34)
McFadden's pseudo R-squared	.08	.08	.09
Log likelihood	−523.43	−519.22	−545.93
Observations	889	936	931

*$p < .05$, **$p < .01$, ***$p < .001$.

Parents with children enrolled in both madrassas and state secular schools appear to behave more like parents with children only in state school. Parents who enroll their children in both madrassas and public schools are more likely than people in the reference category to report having a voting card. Having children enrolled in both public schools and madrassas increases the probability of having a voting ID card by 15% ($p < .05$).

A second category of non-state schools, community schools, has a significant, positive relationship to campaigning. Parents with children enrolled in community schools were significantly more likely to have campaigned in 2007. Having a child in a community school increases the predicted probability of campaigning by 20% ($p < .01$). Enrollment in these non-state schools, typically run by NGOs, appears to foster participation in campaigns.

No other category, including mixed schooling and enrollment in secular private school, had a significant effect on voting or participation compared to the population of parents with children who did not attend school. Education ($p < .01$) and non-religious associational membership ($p < .001$) are positively associated with campaigning, while being a younger respondent and a woman are negatively associated with voting ($p < .01$). Being a woman, living in an urban zone, and poverty decrease the likelihood of someone having a voter identification card, while age and associational membership increase the likelihood of having a voter ID.

In sum, there is a strong correlation between sending a child to public school and electoral participation in terms of voting, campaigning, and having a voter identification card. These results largely confirm the hypothesized relationship between public schooling consumption and political participation in the electoral realm.

The evidence also reveals that parents who have children in madrassas are less likely to report voting. The negative, significant correlation between parents who send their children to madrassas and voting does not hold, however, for other types of political participation (party identification, willingness to run for office, or contacting a government official). In addition, the control variable, religious membership, has no significant relationship to participation. These findings suggest that the negative relationship between enrolling a child in a madrassa and participation is restricted to the narrow electoral realm, rather than being representative of a broader, more diffuse disengagement from the state. There are no comparable findings for Quranic education, which raises interesting questions about the specific relationship between the constituencies that use madrassas and the broader populations that enroll their children in Islamic schools.

Leveraging Additional Data: Focus Group Interviews and Exit Polling

Since all participation data from the survey were self-reported, I have no way of knowing if correlations with participation represent actual behavior or just how respondents wanted to characterize themselves. If public school parents know that "good citizens vote," then they might want to overrepresent that behavior. Similarly, if there is a stigma associated with voting for members of certain religious communities, then they might want to downplay their own "dirty" electoral participation. In order to generate more data to evaluate the proposition that parents who send their children to different types of school have different types of political behavior—and to examine the mechanisms behind these behaviors—I introduced into my analysis two other types of data: exit polling during the community elections in 2009 and a focus group I conducted with current university students in the spring of 2011.

Municipal Election Polling 2009

I collected exit poll data on the school enrollment choices of voters during the 2009 municipal elections in three school districts in Bamako. All school districts were located in zones near where we conducted our surveys to capture potential variation in schooling experiences. I organized three teams to stand outside a large polling station (usually a public school) in each of the districts. Each team was composed of three members, primarily university students and recent graduates, who were tasked with interviewing every third person who exited from the polls to see if they had children and what school, if any, those children were enrolled in. The teams conducted their interviews from the time the polls opened at 8 a.m. until they had collected 150 total responses.[11] Of the 457 voters responding, 261, or 57%, claimed to have school-age children, and 92% of those parents enrolled their child in school.

It is important to note that these data were taken during the municipal elections, while our survey references the presidential elections of 2007. There is a possibility that municipal elections, described as "elections of proximity," attract a wider swath of participation since candidates often recruit family members and neighbors. In the context of familiarity, there could be greater incentives for madrassa consumers to be involved in these elections rather than the national elections, which cater to elite politicians. In presidential elections, where contenders are unfamiliar and generally secular, Western-educated elites, madrassa consumers would have a lower likelihood of a personal allegiance or connection that would overcome the societal stigma about voting. In this sense, municipal elections are a more challenging test of non-turnout among madrassa parents since local elections may be less stigmatized.

I restricted the data in order to compare the voter turnout of those par-

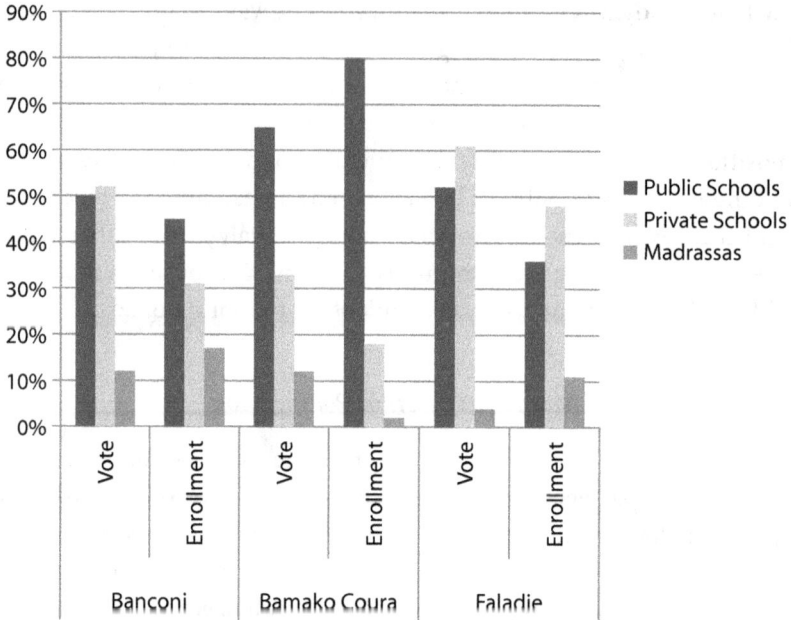

Figure 6.1. Percentage of voters with children in each school type compared to percentage enrollment in district

ents who enroll their children in different primary school types with the percentage of children who are enrolled in that particular school type.[12] To do so, I drew on the Ministry of Education's annual report (Annuaire National 2009–2010). If the survey data presented earlier in this chapter are correct, there should be a large number of public school parents at the polls as compared to a much smaller percentage of parents who enroll their children in madrassas. There should be public school parents overparticipating relative to district enrollment, and similarly there should be madrassa parents underparticipating. Figure 6.1 shows the percentage of voters who claimed to have enrolled their child in each of three primary school types: public, private, and madrassa.

As I predicted, the largest turnout was among parents with children in public and private Francophone schools. Many fewer voters reported sending their children to madrassas. At the three polling stations, the percentage of voters claiming to have children enrolled in public school ranged from 49% to 65%, compared to only 4%–12% of voters who had children enrolled in madrassas. When I looked at turnout by school type and compared that to general enrollment in each district, parents of private school students made up a higher percentage of voters than they did for total district enrollment; public school parents "overperformed" in two of the three districts, Banconi and Faladie; and parents who sent their children to madrassas "underperformed" except in Bamako Coura.[13] These findings generally mirror the results from my regression analysis of our survey except that private school parents voted at higher rates than expected. The exit poll data suggest at a minimum that in Bamako private school parents are coming out to vote.

It is also important to remember that Bamako, the national capital, might not be representative of larger national trends. For instance, while age is generally positively correlated with people stating that they have voted, the large number of respondents in our exit polls who claimed that they did not have children suggests that many young people came out to vote. It may be that mobilization in Bamako targets youth at a higher rate than in other regions. Earlier, I noted that 33% of all parents in our sample had children enrolled in Francophone secondary school. Given that net attendance in secondary schools in Bamako is only 31%, this number seems extremely high, especially considering that the denominator—parents—includes anyone who has a school-age child, not necessarily a child who is old enough to attend secondary school. The data suggest that parents with children enrolled in secondary education are overrepresented at the polls, which lends support to the idea that two mechanisms link public education to higher turnout: linguistic brokers and, possibly, policy feedback effects.

Focus Group with University Students

As mentioned earlier, Francophone education in a public or private school could endow a family with a child who is a qualified linguistic broker. Children who have received secondary or university education could help their families, especially those families who are illiterate and living in rural zones away from the capital, to interpret and understand parties' electoral promises. In order to probe the linguistic mechanism directly, I ran a small focus group in Bamako in the spring of 2011 with university students from regions outside the capital to determine how their grandparents, uncles and aunts, parents, and neighbors back home in the village access political information and get involved in politics.[14]

The students' responses were nearly unanimous: they (the educated children) tell their parents and other relatives how to vote. More concretely, students and former students in Bamako participate in campaigns as brokers for political parties. They act as guides, introducing candidates and party representatives to traditional leadership in the villages. The students stressed their French-language skills as legitimizing their role as party brokers. They had connections to the community, and therefore could be trusted to apply their education to decipher the intricacies of party politics and to lobby for the local community. Even when students were not actively involved in traveling to villages to campaign for parties, their relatives often called their cell phones to get the students' opinions on whom they should vote for.

These findings suggest that, at least in rural areas, educated children play a role in bringing their parents into the political arena through linguistic brokerage. This mechanism benefits not only public school parents, but any parent whose child receives a French-language education. My experience of trying to recruit research assistants for exit polling during community elections also confirms the active student participation on election day. In order to get six extra pollsters to complement my team of three research assistants, I had to pay more than what the political parties were offering to students who were mobilizing voters. This wage was higher than what I would typically pay a temporary research assistant in Mali for a half day's work—emphasizing the demand for young students to mobilize communities to vote.

Causation: Policy Feedback through Schooling Experience, Linguistic Brokerage, or Existing Political Predisposition?

There are different causal paths that might lead to the correlation between consumers of different schooling options and increased or decreased political behavior. First, parents' political attitudes could determine both enrollment and political behavior. Second, the schooling experience itself might drive participation or non-participation. This could happen through a policy feedback mechanism, as MacLean (2011) has suggested, or through the acquisition of linguistic skills that benefit the entire family, as in the case of Francophone schools. I first review these two mechanisms and then turn to the negative relationship between sending a child to a madrassa and voting.

There is little evidence that parents who are more civic-minded purposefully enroll their children in public schools and simultaneously are more active in politics. Few parents interviewed claimed to have enrolled their children in public school because it was their first preference. The majority of parents enrolled their children in public schools for practical reasons: 63% claimed to have enrolled their child in a public school due to proximity and

14% due to affordability.[15] My qualitative data on citizens' justifications for schooling decisions demonstrate that many parents enroll their children in public schools for non-ideological or non-strategic reasons, such as cost, a friend's recommendation, or proximity. These justifications are coupled with the fact that many Malians express a desire to enroll their child in private school if they had the means. The majority of schooling choices appear to be based on external constraints rather than on a desire for state education, suggesting that parents' preferences do not drive both school choice and political participation.[16] It is possible that parents who are interested in government affairs or democratic institutions would be more invested in ensuring that their children learn French and, consequently, in enrolling their children in a public or private Francophone school. If this were the case, private enrollment would have been correlated with higher reported rates of voting, but the regression demonstrated that private Francophone schooling was not significantly related to higher rates of reported voter turnout.

Turning to the schooling experience itself, I found evidence that causation could work through a policy feedback mechanism or through educated children as political brokers. In either case, having a child enrolled in school longer is more likely to have an effect on citizen participation than if the child only attends school for a few years. Greater exposure to a social service would mean a greater experience of policy feedback. In addition, the higher the grade level children attain, the greater the likelihood that those children acquire French skills, which in turn increases their probability of working as an electoral broker.[17] A high percentage (20%) of respondents in the exit poll had children enrolled in secondary school. When I truncated the sample to parents, 33% of all respondents had children enrolled in Francophone secondary school—higher than the secondary enrollment rate in that school district. In addition, the qualitative data from the focus group provide evidence of the brokerage mechanism since the students are dictating their relatives' political action, not vice versa.

As recommended in the policy feedback literature, I ran an additional test to see whether parents' positive evaluation of their children's experience is correlated with higher reported turnout to the polls.[18] I restricted the analysis to parents with children who attend(ed) public school. During the survey, parents were asked to evaluate each child's experience in each school type on a scale of 0 (no quality) to 5 (very good). Surprisingly, despite the criticism that public school quality is declining (for Mali, see Bleck and Guindo 2013, and Diakite 2000; for Congo, Kenya, and Cameroon, see Boyle 1999; for

Ghana and Côte d'Ivoire, see MacLean 2007), the modal respondent rated their public school experience as good: 4. I included a public school rating variable in the logistics regression with the expectation that people who gave public schools the highest rating would be even more likely to vote. However, a high rating of a child's educational experience is not significantly correlated with a higher predicted likelihood of voting.

Mali has rapidly expanded access to basic education, in part through the construction of new schools. There is the possibility that parents view the act of school construction or their child's educational success—rather than the quality of the educational content—as fulfilling the state's role or that some parents are not capable of assessing the quality of their child's education. In most instances, parents justify their evaluation based on their children's relative rank in the classroom or on whether the children were able to pass to the next level. Parents may be less aware of the actual content of what is being taught at school and therefore be likely to rely more on visible infrastructure criteria than on the actual content of the curriculum or the quality of teacher performance when evaluating their child's education. This is consistent with the literature's emphasis on visibility, the degree to which citizens are able to observe the implementation of policy, as mediating the policy feedback effect (Harding and Stasavage 2014; Soss and Schram 2007). If parents are more responsive to highly visible indicators, like school construction and new opportunities for enrollment, then declining school quality, at least in the short term, might be less destructive to the policy feedback experience.

The Puzzle of Islamic Schooling

It is harder to disentangle Islamic schooling consumers' reasons for weaker participation. Fifty-four percent of parents in our sample report enrolling their children in madrassas for religious reasons, which suggests that madrassa parents are more likely to have ideological beliefs that dictate both schooling and political participation. I do not know if patterns of participation are a result of the receipt of schooling or an underlying characteristic that determines parents' school preference and their non-participation. The statistical evidence presented earlier suggests that madrassa schooling communities might be more likely to be drawn into the electoral process after they enroll their child in public school, since that act makes it more likely that they will obtain a voter ID. However, those parents might be less ideologically committed to religious education and thus their willingness to diversify their education portfolio may be simply an expression of their underlying ideology.

In order to assess the impact of ideology, I created dummies for the two types of justification that parents gave for enrolling their child in a madrassa: practical and religious. I ran a regression with a population of madrassa consumers—parents with children exclusively in madrassas—and with parents with children who are in public school. If religious reasons drive enrollment choices and behavior simultaneously, those respondents with religious reasons for enrollment should be less likely than their peers with more pragmatic justifications to participate.

I regressed the variables on voting in the truncated population of madrassa consumers, but I did not find those parents who provided religious justifications to be significantly less likely to vote than their peers who gave pragmatic justifications.

The sex of the respondent might also be used as a tool to leverage clues about causality. Conversations with survey respondents revealed that men typically make schooling choices for the household, so if ideological predispositions determine both schooling choices and political behavior, I would expect the correlation between male respondents' stated behavior and Islamic schooling preference to be more exaggerated than in the regular population. Therefore, within the subpopulation, women should be more likely to vote.

I did find women to be significantly more likely to say they voted; being a woman resulted in a 43% higher predicted probability of voting. However, these results should be interpreted with caution since women's responses may be subject to higher levels of social desirability bias. In sum, I found mixed evidence for ideology as a determinant of both enrollment and behavior. Further research will have to be done to uncover the exact reasons that Islamic schooling consumers are less likely to vote.

Discussion

I found evidence that public service provision induces citizens to participate in electoral channels through two different mechanisms: policy feedback (as suggested by MacLean 2011) and linguistic brokerage provided by educated students. Public education and other social services provide the state with a tool to connect with its citizenry and to encourage participation in electoral institutions. Furthermore, by increasing the number of children who make it into secondary or university schooling, policy changes endow families with linguistic brokers: family members who can speak the bureaucratic language.

Future research should explore the linkages between public provision and democratic participation with particular attention to the policy feedback mechanism. Stasavage (2005) and Harding and Stasavage (2014) have already demonstrated ways in which the state responds to electoral constituencies' demands. My study suggests that public social service expansion might create a feedback loop, which strengthens participation and accountability between the state and its constituencies. At the same time, the linguistic broker mechanism highlights French fluency as better linking citizens to the state; students' fluency becomes a club good for the entire family or village rather than just a private skill for the educated student.

I have also demonstrated that Islamic schooling consumers are less likely to vote, but they are not much different from other Malian citizens in terms of their broader relationship with the state. These results suggest that there is not a divisive counterculture emerging that might be sympathetic to the radical goals of the rebels, but rather that the receipt of social services has a particular correlation with electoral participation. The evidence presented here cannot determine if the schooling experience itself, or ideological self-selection by parents for madrassas, is what reduces the likelihood of voting. However, the descriptive finding that sending a child to a madrassa is negatively correlated with voting is an important contribution on its own. Whether the choice to abstain from voting reflects prior values or values cultivated within the schooling community, it is revealing that these constituencies are choosing to forgo electoral participation. Until now, Western-educated elites have held a monopoly over national-level politics in Mali. Parents who send their children to Islamic schools might be willing to participate in elections if the electoral landscape included some of "their" candidates, who reflect their values and background.

The Malian state's accreditation of madrassas creates the possibility of the emergence of "Islamic" candidates with state diplomas. In the previous chapter, I demonstrated that students who attend madrassas or Quranic schools know just as much about secular politics as their peers in state-sponsored schools with comparable levels of education and are just as likely to participate in politics. Students who were educated in state-accredited madrassas could potentially run as candidates, which raises the possibility that constituencies who send their children to madrassas might be more involved in politics if candidates more aligned with their values were running.

Other states—such as Gambia, Senegal, and Niger—have adopted similar policies to integrate madrassas into the national education system. By expanding the range of citizens who are exercising their political voice, this policy change has the potential to increase the representativeness of African democracies, but could also change the elite and secular values currently associated with West African politics.

These findings remind us about a central question of political representation and the importance of disaggregating the political behavior of particular constituencies, especially those who have been historically marginalized by the state. African politics are often viewed through the lens of ethnic (Mozaffar, Scarritt, and Galaich 2003; Posner 2005) and urban or rural constituencies (Bates 1981; Harding 2012), but few efforts have been made to understand the distinct patterns of political participation among religious communities.[19] The Afrobarometer data reveal that religious and traditional authorities continue to be the most respected authorities in African states. Political science should have a better understanding of how they nurture, discourage, or influence participation. In many countries where the government has not consolidated control as the exclusive authority, the existence of traditional or religious communities that do not engage with the state—or do so in a distinct or limited capacity—raises important questions about the level and scope of representative and inclusive democratic participation.

CHAPTER SEVEN

Educational Expansion and Democratization in Africa

Since the founding elections of the early 1990s, African governments have vastly expanded access to education. In the political science literature, education has long been thought of as a cornerstone of state-building and democratic citizenship. In the contemporary African context, education is a highly solicited welfare service. However, we know little about how this dramatic policy change has impacted the relationship between the state bureaucracy, the elected government, and constituencies. Will unprecedented educational opportunities change the future of democratic citizenship in Africa?

In this book I have investigated how the act of schooling could affect citizens' political knowledge and political participation in a country that has experienced one of the sharpest increases in enrollment—Mali. Following its first transition to democracy in 1992, Mali has almost tripled primary school enrollment due in part to a liberalization of the education sector, which includes government partnerships with Arabic-language Islamic schools. As the multiple crises of 2012 demonstrate, Mali is still far from a consolidated democracy. Even after 20 years of experience with elections and two peaceful turnovers of executive power, Mali suffered a coup d'état and a near-collapse of the state. Throughout the crisis, many citizens remained critical of democratic institutions.

In the context of Mali's general skepticism toward bureaucratic and elected authority, I have asked three questions about the way that education might shape political knowledge and participation. First, can education increase students' knowledge of electoral politics and engagement with the electoral system? Second, can public schooling connect parents, as social welfare consumers, with the state and encourage their political engagement? Finally, do all types of schooling—public and private, secular and religious—affect citizenship in the same way?

Students' Political Knowledge and Engagement

In chapter 5 I presented evidence that citizens with any type of schooling, including Quranic education and literacy training, were on average better informed about politics than their peers with no education. These findings are consistent with a comparative literature that suggests that better educated citizens also tend to be best informed about politics, but my research has broadened the scope to include informal and Islamic education. My results, which are consistent across different school types, suggest that increases in knowledge are less related to a specific curriculum and more linked to a set of skills with which schooling endows students to collect and process new information.

Citizens' levels of political knowledge increase with each subsequent level of education: primary, secondary, and university. The vast majority of respondents in my sample who attended secondary or university education did so at a Francophone school. I have argued that at higher levels of education, enhanced fluency in French enables citizens to access a wider diversity of news sources directly. These citizens can read newspapers, search online for Malian and international news sources, and tune into both local language and French news broadcasts on Malian radio and television.

Unlike the vast literature in US politics, the Malian data suggest that there is no clear linear relationship between education and all types of formal participation. The differences may stem largely from the quality of the democratic institutions in each context. Consistent with literature from other environments where citizens are skeptical of state responsiveness to their demands (i.e., low external efficacy), secondary and university education are only associated with significant increases in difficult forms of participation: campaigning, contacting a government official, and willingness to run for office (see Craig 1980; Craig and Maggiotto 1982; Fraser 1970). Those with secondary or university education are no more likely than peers with no education to vote or identify with a party. In contrast, citizens with primary education, from any school type, are more likely than those with no schooling at all to vote and identify with a party.

My qualitative data reveal that a lack of French fluency poses an important obstacle to participation in the most difficult political activities for those with levels of educational attainment that fall short of French proficiency. Many respondents with informal and even primary education balked at the idea of running for mayor because they did not feel qualified due to their discomfort with French. In contrast, some university-educated respondents presented themselves as brokers for their illiterate family members. Those university and secondary school students who obtain French skills not only know more about the workings of bureaucracy, but also feel more confident and skilled when interacting with that system of governance. They approach the state bureaucracy not only to pursue their own needs and goals, but also on behalf of others who are fearful or intimidated by the state. While education levels do not impact the way that a citizen feels about contacting a religious leader or a traditional chief, the strong association between the state bureaucracy and French education gives the highly educated a comparative advantage in the state's political realm.

This is a departure from the way that scholars typically imagine schools contributing to state-building—as communal institutions teaching and re-inforcing the importance of democracy or nationalism. Instead of instilling uniform messages through different curricula, the Malian schooling ex-pansion since the 1990s has created more capable citizens by heightening individuals' ability to process and evaluate political information. At higher levels of education, schooling in the former colonial language offers students a comparative advantage in interacting with and understanding the state bu-reaucracy, but it does not necessarily indoctrinate students into values or be-haviors that support the state regime.

Parents' Political Knowledge and Engagement

In this book I have also revealed that schooling, as a welfare service, can foster connections between parents and the state. In chapter 6 I introduced data to demonstrate that, holding all other factors constant, parents who enroll their children in public school are significantly more likely to vote, to campaign, and to have a voter ID card than parents who do not or citizens who do not have school-age children. Exit poll data from the 2009 elections confirm an overrepresentation of public school parents, particularly those with children enrolled (or previously enrolled) in secondary school. I have suggested two potential mechanisms. First, public school enrollment of their children fos-ters a policy feedback mechanism that makes parents want to engage at the ballot box. Second, families reap the benefit of their children's French-lan-guage skills. They are better able to interact confidently with political parties and the bureaucracy by relying on students' linguistic brokerage.

This study joins an emerging literature that demonstrates that welfare provision might induce citizens' engagement with the state (Cammett and MacLean 2011, 2014) and political allegiance (Harding 2012; Zucco 2011), but approaches the question of service provision from the perspective of consumers. I build on Lauren MacLean's work on the impact of service provision on political behavior, but disaggregate citizens by the categories of service they engage with, state and non-state, and whether they do so as direct beneficiaries (students) or as indirect beneficiaries (parents). By doing so I have brought greater precision to the measurement of how citizens are exposed to services and the subsequent effects of exposure as a direct or indirect beneficiary. Some evidence in this book highlights how different types of state and Islamic education have distinct and inverse effects on parents.

My findings also draw parallels to the role that educated, first-generation American children play in connecting their non-English-speaking parents with the political system. Previous studies of the Malian education sector have emphasized the role of educated students as political brokers,[1] but mine is one of the first to demonstrate the general effect on parents' political participation. In doing so, I raise the larger question of the importance of bureaucratic language literacy as a tool for engaged citizenship.

Variation by School Type

Despite the historical antagonism between Islamic leaders and secular, bureaucratic authorities, political scientists have not yet explored the implications of this rift on subsequent political behavior. In this book I have explored different schooling trajectories, including secular and Islamic, to see how they might impact citizens' knowledge and political participation. At the primary level, I did not find any differences in the political knowledge or political engagement of students who attended Islamic schools, public schools, or Francophone private schools. My findings suggest the potential role that Islamic education, even Quranic schools, can play in generating active and informed citizenship. However, since the vast majority of respondents attended Francophone schools at the secondary and university levels, the data cannot speak to how different educational trajectories at the secondary level might generate different types of political knowledge and engagement. As I have mentioned, it is likely that French fluency affects the ease with which citizens can approach the state without fearing exploitation. Therefore, difficult participation might require not only a secondary or university degree, but also French literacy.

In chapter 6 I revealed the different patterns of participation among parents who send their children to different school types. Parents who send their children to madrassas claim that they vote less than a reference category of parents who do not enroll their children in school and citizens without school-age children. I noted that there are not comparable differences in participation among parents who send their children to Quranic schools. Those parents are not any less likely to participate in politics than other types of parents.

It is important to contextualize these findings. The religious protests that have characterized Malian politics in the twenty-first century suggest that madrassa parents are not necessarily withdrawing from politics, but could be choosing contentious politics mediated by religious brokers over direct engagement with the state at the ballot box. This alternative pattern of participation is significant because it reflects the lack of inclusivity of formal political institutions and representation in Mali. It reminds us that contentious politics are often more effective means to make demands on the state than appeals to political parties or national representatives. It also might reflect the paucity of ideological diversity among the field of candidates as much as citizens' indifference toward the state as a primary political authority.

Post-Coup Mali: Relevance of This Research for Mali's Future Democratic Trajectory

Three years after the fieldwork for this book, the Malian state experienced a dramatic democratic reversal that nearly brought about the state's collapse. The research for this book was conducted prior to these tumultuous political events, but many of the themes and trends I outline inform Mali's current political challenges.

In January and February 2012, the National Movement for the Liberation of Azawad (MNLA)—a Tuareg rebel group with secessionist aims—as well as two hardline Islamist groups—Ansar al Dine and AQIM—clashed with Malian forces. In one battle, the government soldiers were rumored to have run out of ammunition. International media reported executions of government soldiers by the rebels even after they had surrendered. This prompted a series of protests by soldiers' wives at the presidential palace in Koulouba, foreshadowing the events to come. The Malian government had developed a regional reputation as a weak link in the "war on terror" due in part to its public role in negotiating the release of foreign hostages. Many Malians in the south were concerned that Touré would continue to rely on negotiations and compromises with northern actors rather than resort to the use of force.

On March 21, 2012, one month before Mali was slated to experience its third change of presidential power, military officers seized control of the national radio and television stations. Soldiers stormed the presidential palace at Koulouba, prompting the presidential guard to evacuate the president and his wife. The national airwaves went silent, and 14 million Malians speculated about what had happened. The following morning, the officers, calling themselves the Committee for the Restoration of Democracy and the State, announced that they had launched a coup d'état with the aim of restoring territory in the north of the country. The seizure of the radio station and the presidential palace formally ended almost 20 years of democracy in Mali.

Initially, many Malians welcomed the regime change as a way to retake portions of the north and regain territorial integrity. A survey conducted in Bamako in the wake of the coup found 65% of Malians supported the junta's actions (Guindo 2012). The coup leaders pledged to stabilize a burgeoning rebellion in the north of the country, but also announced a broad range of populist objectives, including education sector reform. The junta embraced the language of democracy to challenge the legitimacy of the previous governing system. The leaders underscored that democracy under the previous regime had failed ordinary citizens and profited a small political elite. They attempted to link the rebellion to ATT's poorly performing democracy; they claimed that systematized corruption had brought Mali to the brink of disaster.

In the context of the chaos in Bamako, three rebel groups moved quickly to occupy the northern half of the country. Within days of the coup, rebels captured three regional capitals: Gao, Kidal, and Timbuktu. Eventually, the MNLA was sidelined by groups that claimed a fervent Islamist agenda, including a new AQIM spin-off. Infighting between the presidential guard and pro-junta military officers obliterated hopes of a swift counterattack. Malians watched as the government and the country they knew unraveled. In January 2013, after rumors that Islamist rebels were traveling south toward Bamako, the government of France intervened in Mali. More than 4,000 French troops pushed rebels out of Gao and Timbuktu.

In the summer of 2013, the Malian government prepared for a late July election deadline to usher Mali back into an era of "democracy." At that time, there were still more than 400,000 people displaced from their homes, and the government still did not have full control of Kidal. However, Mali held democratic elections with unprecedented participation rates. The former prime minister and perennial political challenger, Ibrahim Boubacar Keita, won a second-round runoff against Soumaïla Cissé. Keita, considered an authoritative and decisive candidate, campaigned on "Mali first" and "restoring Mali's honor," which evoked patriotism and the need to restore Mali's dignity. In the November 2013 elections, Keita's party, Rally for Mali, won 61 of 147 seats, while Cissé's party took 18 seats. The elections opened up foreign aid flows, which had been frozen for nearly two years.

During Mali's first era of multiparty democracy, the state did not invest tremendous resources in democratic pedagogy or civic education. As Mali embarks on its second democratic transition, the new government has a unique opportunity to actively support students' civic education and theoretical appreciation of democracy in the classroom. The 2012 coup d'état offers an excellent teaching opportunity for Malians to talk about what democracy should provide to citizens, how to engage with the state, and democratic values in the Malian context. Studies of civic education initiatives have shown that such programs can increase participants' political knowledge, democratic values, expectations of politicians, and willingness to participate, but also that participants often share these lessons with others in their social networks (Finkel and Smith 2011; Gottlieb 2014). Mali is well placed to benefit from this addition to its curriculum, but a larger national conversation is also needed about what citizens should expect from democracy.

Education as a Tool to Foster Empowered Citizenship and Electoral Engagement

Despite Mali's return to democracy, the country still faces the governance challenges that were present when the junta instigated the coup. I have offered evidence of the pervasive skepticism, or low external efficacy, that characterized the pre-coup era. Education is not an elixir that can force students to engage with a system that they view as unresponsive or incompetent. If the newly elected government continues to expand access to education, but does little to foster transparency and accountability with the Malian public, we should not anticipate that students will be socialized into blind allegiance to and political engagement with an underperforming regime.

The evidence in this book demonstrates that education can foster political empowerment, both as a way to gain more knowledge about politics and as a boost to internal efficacy. Hopefully, an increasingly educated youth population will have the skills and self-confidence to engage with the state and make their voices heard. This may take time since Mali continues to experience a crisis of sovereignty; while I am writing this, the future governance of the Kidal region remains uncertain, and the government is still in negotiation with armed actors.

Based on my research, I suggest that the newly elected government use expanded service provision as a tool to generate legitimacy and spur citizen engagement. My findings highlight a policy feedback effect: citizens exposed to state welfare services will be more willing to engage with the state at the ballot box. Exposure to concrete proof of the state's capacity can help citizens to overcome skepticism about democracy and to make their voices heard. If the new regime manages to leverage donor aid and improve the efficiency of government spending to expand citizens' access to basic services, such as health facilities, education, roads, and electricity, this could foster greater citizen engagement in elections. Expanded Francophone education would offer citizens an additional push toward electoral engagement since it increases the number of families with a child who is fluent in the language of the state.

Citizens' engagement is important for electoral institutions. Some scholars posit that the act of participating increases citizens' support for a democratic system. As part of our survey of 450 Malians during the March 2009 municipal elections in Bamako, we asked an open-ended question: Why did you come out to vote today? The responses were sorted and grouped into qualitative categories (see figure 7.1).

Originally, I was interested in seeing if respondents' level of education influenced the justification that they gave for coming out to vote. For instance, were those voters with higher educational levels more likely to espouse democratic justifications for voting instead of more materialistic motives? To test this expectation, citizens' justifications for voting are grouped by their highest level of educational attainment (from no schooling to university degree). The data demonstrate that regardless of education, respondents claimed to have voted because of a sense of patriotism and civic duty.

Figure 7.1 shows that politically active Malians in Bamako share a basic understanding of the importance of elections as an element of a multiparty democracy. The data only capture citizens who decided to come to the polls; there is a likelihood that this population is more optimistic than other groups about their democratic participation. However, since citizens are often mobilized to go to the polls by material incentives or familial allegiance, exit polls should capture a broader swath of people than just idealist citizens or staunch partisans. These sentiments do not preclude the possibility that the

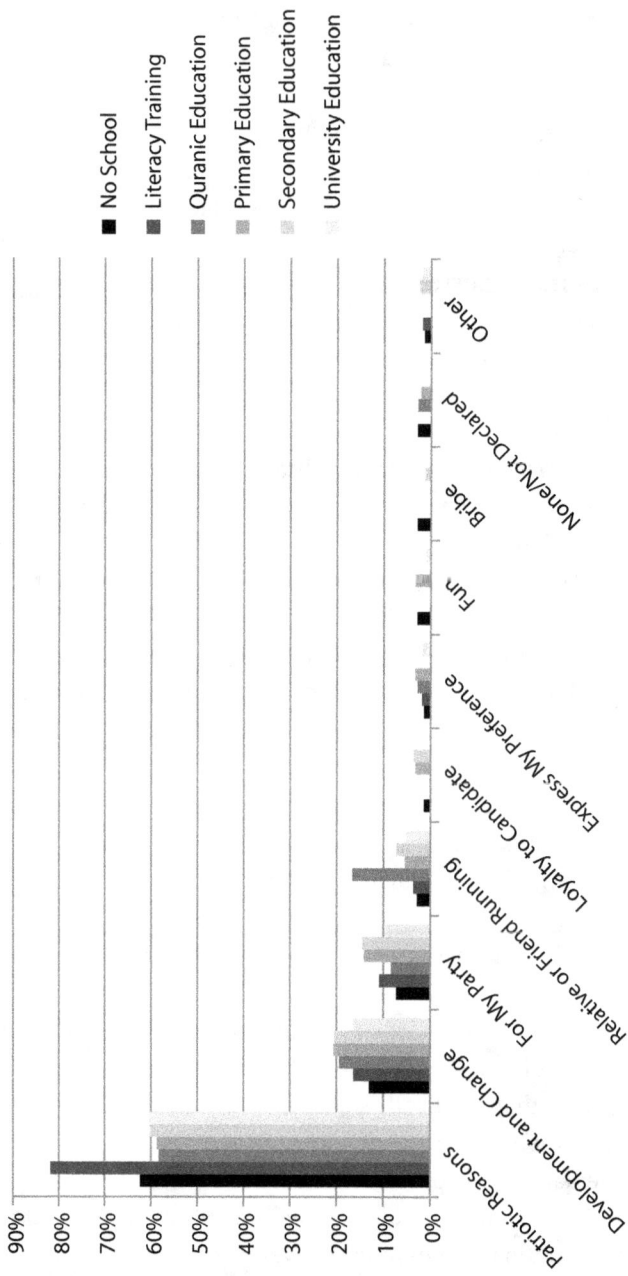

Figure 7.1. Citizens' reasons for voting in 2009 municipal elections by education level

voter received a bribe or voted for a boss; receiving short-term incentives for voting and the act of voting as an expression of citizenship are not mutually exclusive. But despite the widespread mistrust discussed in this book, those who are engaging in democratic politics express a civic appreciation for their act and for the process.

Given the irregularities and the group mobilization for voting in Mali, it is tempting to deride voting as artificial or inauthentic in the atmosphere of weak parties and widespread clientelism. However, my findings suggest that those citizens who engaged in the act of voting, regardless of how they ended up at the ballot box or what they knew about politics, felt as if they were fulfilling their civic duty to the country.[2] This is consistent with evidence that participation in the democratic process, as well as the experience of electoral alternation, can breed a greater trust in democracy (Cho and Logan 2013) and that democratic participation fuels greater external efficacy (Finkel 1985). Getting people out to the polls is an important step in improving democratic governance in Mali.

Citizen voice is critical for legitimizing democratic institutions and for making them more accountable (Norris 1999, 2012). This case study of Mali has revealed citizens who feel largely isolated from the democratic institutions that claim to represent them. I suspect that this cynicism plagues many other African democracies, especially among the less educated and the less powerful. While it might take decades before we see change at the national level, there is some evidence of progress at the municipal level. As data from this book and from Afrobarometer demonstrate, the majority of Malians can name their mayor. This familiarity and the visibility of the mayor's policy outputs on a localized, tangible scale make it easier for constituencies to judge them. Conversations with hundreds of Malians during the research for this book revealed that citizens are willing to issue judgments of their mayor's performance, even though they tend to be hesitant to criticize deputies or the president. The high turnover rate of municipal officials and the high turnout rate among voters in municipal elections relative to other election cycles suggest that healthy competition exists at the decentralized level and that citizens are already holding officials accountable for their performance.

If educational expansion generates a pool of more and more citizens who feel eligible and willing to run for municipal posts, as well as a larger electorate that feels competent and capable of assessing the growing pool of candidates, then education's effect might be evident sooner at the local level. In contrast to the dramatic, national-level events in capital cities that led to democratic transitions in the 1990s, the future of democratic consolidation may be in these quiet, decentralized processes in rural zones.

Islam and Politics in Mali

The Islamist incursion into the north has raised questions about the future of political Islam in Mali.[3] In this book I have suggested that citizens who attend Islamic schools or send their children to these schools have a similar relationship to the state as other members of the Malian population; in other words, there is no immediate threat of a hard-line counterculture emerging through Islamic schooling within Malian society. Students who attend Islamic schools are no less knowledgeable about secular politics than their peers with primary or informal education in state schools nor are they less likely to participate in politics. For the most part, the political behavior of parents who send their children to Islamic schools resembles that of parents who send their children to state schools. The primary sphere of difference is electoral politics: madrassa parents vote less often than other Malian citizens. While these communities might effectively mobilize through contentious politics, their lack of electoral representation suggests potential marginalization by the formal democratic system.

Partnership with Islamic education providers was a groundbreaking departure from the suspicions and hostility that have plagued collaboration between the government and Islamic schools since colonial times. The current system—which acknowledges madrassas as accredited institutions of state education, mandates that they teach French, and offers Arabic-language testing options—attempts to incorporate those who prefer Islamic education into the citizenship project. For the first time, constituencies that support Islamic education have gained access to higher education and government employment.

The current collaboration between the state and Islamic schooling in the democratic context sends signals to Islamic actors that their preferences are recognized and legitimated by the state. If the current system continues, it may move Muslims from the contentious sphere into more formal participation. State support for Islamic education and the newly instituted Arabic-language university entrance exam could change the future political terrain of Mali. Until now, Western-educated elites have held a monopoly over national-level politics because higher education was synonymous with

Francophone education. It remains to be seen if highly qualified candidates with Islamic schooling backgrounds emerge.

The data do not allow me to determine whether parents self-select into madrassas and specific forms of political action due to their religious attitudes or if the experience of enrolling a child in a madrassa decreases the likelihood of electoral participation. In either case, it is important to explore this issue because there are differences in the ways Islamic schooling consumers and secular consumers participate in electoral politics. The descriptive evidence confirms a popular view in Mali that the most pious Malians choose Islamic schooling and simultaneously abstain from politics. More broadly, my findings are a reminder about the central question of political representation, particularly among communities that have been historically marginalized by the state. In many countries where the government has not consolidated control as the exclusive authority, the existence of communities that do not engage with the state—or do so in a distinct or limited capacity—raises concerns about representative and inclusive democratic participation. In Mali, these questions have become particularly salient since some groups have turned to violence to express their policy preferences.

Women and Politics

My findings suggest that the expansion of education on the continent through privatization and liberalization has increased citizens' capabilities as it has increased the number of children who are attending school and the number of learners who are continuing to secondary and university education. Many of these changes are positive externalities of efforts to reach development goals rather than a calculated government strategy to improve the quality of democracy by building citizens' capacity. The increase in girls' and rural-dwellers' enrollment and partnership with Islamic schools, though driven in part by citizen demand, was also largely engineered to reach development targets. The democratic gains have happened accidentally. Unlike the immediate post-independence era, democratic expansion has not been accompanied by national efforts to inculcate citizens and shape their democratic behavior. Given the young age and the scarce resources of African democracies, inattention to building more representative or participatory democracy is unsurprising. After all, many politicians and theorists of fledgling democracies might prefer less citizen participation so as not to overwhelm nascent institutions (Almond and Verba 1963).

In countries like Mali, where primary school enrollment still excludes 20% of eligible children and where the vast majority of adults cannot read the bureaucratic language, the question of education and empowerment is particularly salient. Education is not the only way for citizens to achieve empowerment nor do formal politics offer the most important and relevant venue for the expression of political preferences. It is clear that many citizens receive "education" through travel or apprenticeship or informal learning and that many rural Malians who have never been to school can articulate the intricacies of the Malian political scene. However, education—through both formal and informal schooling—is a tool that the state can offer to systematically improve the agency of its citizens.

The educational expansion since the 1990s is particularly interesting in that it enabled many more girls to attend school. My study, as well as much of the secondary literature on Africa, has shown that women are less knowledgeable and less likely to participate in formal politics (Isaksson 2010; Isaksson, Kotsadam, and Nerman 2014; Kuenzi and Lambright 2005; Logan 2010). All African states adopted universal suffrage at independence, but the ability to vote did not translate into equal political opportunities. It is important to acknowledge that women exercise political power in other—often informal—domains (Hirschmann 1991; Tripp 2001), but their participation in the formal democratic system is of utmost important to a democracy's level of inclusion.

Since the increases in access and enrollment have targeted women, I might interpret the story of greater educational access as being about laying the foundations for girls' political empowerment. My study has shown how education instructs and empowers citizens, including women, to be able to engage in politics. If a larger subset of girls is educated, this bodes well for their ability to participate and to be represented in democracy. Currently, women hold fewer than 10% of all mayoral posts in Mali. However, women who manage to attain the highest levels of education are able to compete with other educated elites. Mali's first female prime minister, Cissé Mariam Kaidama Sidibé, took office in the spring of 2011, setting an example for future generations of educated Malian girls. In the future, hopefully we will see a greater number of highly educated women—endowed with an educational comparative advantage—competing in national politics. Africa now boasts three women presidents, Ellen Johnson Sirleaf of Liberia, Joyce Banda of Malawi, and Catherine Samba-Panza of the Central African Republic (serving as acting president), offering hope for girls that educational credentials can translate into elite political opportunities for African women.

Despite the pushes for greater girls' enrollment, there are many barriers to education that remain. Girls make up 60% of the children who are not in school; they constitute less than 40% of students enrolled in secondary school (Pearce, Fourmy, and Kovach 2009). As of 2005, only 46% of girls who were enrolled in school in sub-Saharan Africa were able to complete primary school (*Citing Girls' Education in Africa* 2005). Given the importance of secondary and tertiary education for empowerment as a complete citizen, it is imperative that programs continue to focus on girls' retention and completion in order for them to gain the skills and self-confidence necessary for full democratic participation. Focus should also be placed on what happens inside Malian classrooms. VonDoepp's (2002) work in Malawi has demonstrated that local power relations and outdated gender norms can often creep in and obstruct women's opportunities for participation. If schools are plagued by these limitations on women's expression and development, they cannot be expected to contribute to women's political efficacy.

Education, Knowledge, and Participation in Environments of Political Skepticism

In African contexts where much of the political action happens outside of formal venues and where traditional, religious, or other types of unelected authorities play a large role in governance (Englebert 2000; Logan 2013), citizens have fewer incentives to invest in learning about the bureaucratic political system. There is a tremendous need to make the state relevant and accessible. If schooling makes the state more visible and more familiar to students and their parents, educational expansion plays an important role in making the state more useful for citizens. State-building literatures have long stressed the role of education in familiarizing citizens with the state and orienting them toward the state as an important source of authority. This is still relevant in many countries in Africa, where citizens are least likely to turn to an elected official or civil servant to express a need or idea, and much prefer to lobby traditional authorities, economic players, or religious officials.

The Primacy of Political Knowledge

Education also offers an important venue to improve citizens' abilities to gain knowledge about politics and to improve their sense of internal political efficacy—or self-confidence in their ability as democratic citizens. The presence of short-term incentives and political brokers in most African elections makes it difficult to distinguish between those citizens who are voting for better political representation and those who are mobilized to the polls for less constructive reasons. Political acts that look equivalent could be expressions of political voice or could have no direct link to any kind of policy or institutional feedback loop.

Behavioral research in nascent democracies can, at a minimum, disaggregate the political competencies of respondents who report participating in easy activities in order to better understand what this participation might indicate. Even if we cannot determine a person's exact motivations for involvement, it is important to distinguish informed from uninformed participation. In other words, participation should not be isolated from knowledge. Given rampant group mobilization, especially in rural zones and among hierarchically stratified groups, this kind of disaggregation is essential because informed political actors are a necessary, albeit insufficient, condition for productive political engagement. For example, a household survey could assess an actor's degree of political competence in addition to standard questions about expected participation. Do they know for whom they voted? Do they know the party of that candidate? Do they know anything about the party or candidate? What policy or expressive feature of the candidate mattered most to them? Then researchers could analyze determinants of projected behavior among subgroups of the most and least informed citizens.

The conceptual distinction between informed and uninformed citizen participation stretches far beyond Africa and nascent democracies. A study of voters in the United States used a political competence test to sort the knowledgeable from the uninformed citizens. Fowler and Margolis (2014) found that ignorant citizens voted in ways that were inconsistent with their preferences and that when they were provided with information, these voters shifted their partisan affiliation. If uninformed participation means that people mobilize along lines other than their political preferences, this poses a major threat to representative democracy. In contexts where there are high percentages of uninformed voters, high participation rates become a poor proxy for the quality of democracy.

In the majority of the political science literature, education is said to simultaneously build skills, inculcate values, and socialize citizens toward participation. As my study has demonstrated, all of these relationships are contingent upon political context and opportunity.[4] Instead of rapidly building from the micro mechanisms of participation and knowledge to an assessment of democracy, analysts need to problematize their assumptions along the way. I have made explicit the differing motivations for political participation and emphasized some of the factors, like vote buying and mass mobilization, that we would expect to be negatively linked to education. While the motivations for participation are diverse, when political action is coded as citizens participating or not, these contextual factors are collapsed, and all behavior looks the same.

There is evidence that suggests that some of the most historically marginalized citizens vote at higher rates (Isaksson 2013; Kuenzi and Lambright 2005), which underscores the need to contextualize the motivation, mobilization, and political information behind political behavior. An analysis of Afrobarometer data reveals that people with secondary or post-secondary education are actually six or seven percentage points less likely to vote (Isaksson 2013). Other studies have found higher rates of partisan attachment (Ishiyama and Fox 2006; Kuenzi and Lambright 2005) and voting (Kuenzi and Lambright 2005; MacLean 2011) among those in rural areas. At the same time, empirical work tells us that educated voters have distinct patterns of political participation and respond to information differently. They are most likely to change their vote choice when presented with new information, place more weight on policy criteria, and are less vulnerable to short-term clientelist pressures (Kramon 2010; Weghorst and Lindberg 2013:727).

Before we make assumptions about the relationship between education and regime type, political scientists might first analyze how education helps citizens to obtain representation and accountability at the local level regardless of the overarching governance scheme. Education should be thought of as stimulating citizens' capabilities. These capabilities are relevant far beyond the narrow political sphere and can move into broader venues of localized engagement. Cornwall and Coelho (2007:8) describe how citizens acquire the means to participate in "processes of popular education and mobilization that can enhance the skills and confidence of marginalized and excluded groups, enabling them to enter and engage in participatory arenas." Citizens can apply these skills for substantive and meaningful participation in venues as diverse as hospital facility boards, national deliberative processes, policy councils, and forums offered through community groups, NGOs, and social movements (ibid.). While these marginal increases in skill might prove insufficient initially for citizens to make demands on the national government or to influence institutional quality, they are necessary for that type of change to happen in the future.

Orienting citizens toward underperforming electoral institutions may prove to be more challenging, but it is ultimately very important for institutional strengthening. Participation in the political system can foster skills and encourage support for democracy (Lindberg 2006). If educated citizens and their families are more active participants in politics, and if African democracies spend more than non-democracies on primary education due to mass demands (Stasavage 2005), we can imagine a generative cycle in which a greater number of citizens are educated and thus are more supportive of democracy as the governing system.

Language Fluency and Democratic Governance

My findings emphasize the importance of fluency in the former colonial language and suggest that basic education might not be enough to help citizens realize their full citizenship in Mali. Although Mali's literacy rates are among the lowest in Africa, the dichotomy between indigenous languages, used in popular culture and everyday interactions, and the colonial language that is required for citizens' interaction with the government persists. Many institutions operate exclusively in French, so in order to file a complaint, get a land title, register your child at school, or get a prescription filled, you need the assistance of someone who speaks French or someone who knows how to navigate the system informally. Malians are quite adept in locating someone who knows the system or finding a language broker to assist with these formalities. However, these intermediaries create distance between citizens and the governing system.

Post-colonial theorists have long warned of the danger of the colonial language as a lingering force of personal subjugation and as a threat to indigenous languages and culture (Achebe 1965; Fanon 1965; Gandolfi 2003; Thiong'o 1985). The analyses I have presented in this book suggest that the continued use of the colonial language has practical implications for democratization in countries where literacy rates remain low. Most states do not have formal education requirements for political participation, although some countries, such as Nigeria and Gambia, require a certain level of educational attainment or language competency in order to run for office (Bleck and Patel 2015). In the Malian context, the political constraints of language are largely imposed through a societal understanding of linguistic power. The power of French as a necessary condition for full political participation is both a product of the Malian population's collective imagination and understanding of politics and a direct effect of French-language colonial institutions. Further, language fluency is not equally distributed across populations. Women, rural residents, and those with fewer resources are comparatively disadvantaged by the dominance of the former colonial language in the political realm.

In this context, information becomes hierarchical. Knowledge from reading a source directly or hearing an international news broadcast in French could be judged as more valuable or more authoritative than information gleaned from local language media. This hierarchy of information reflects the harsh reality facing most illiterate Malians: they are excluded from written or spoken information in French unless they can contract the help of an interpreter or information broker who can translate the primary source material. Language fluency limits news sources and makes any information subject to the whims and reliability of information brokers: local radio DJs, chiefs, or relatively educated people in the villages. A citizen who speaks a meta-trading language, like Bamana or Songhai, might have access to greater information than someone who speaks Bozo or Tamasheq, but in order to achieve complete, autonomous citizenship, people must deal in the currency of the former colonial language (Laitin 1992).

Brock-Utne argues that European languages used by the state and political elites are only spoken by a minority of the African population. This has an impact on citizens' potential as participants in democracy (2003). How can we expect citizens to fully engage with a political system that is largely out of their linguistic reach? While Mali has one of the highest illiteracy rates on the continent, as figure 7.2 demonstrates, less than 70% of adults are literate in the state language in many African countries. Only in a few places does literacy hover near 90%. This linguistic dilemma of governance is also applicable to other countries where the government policies and programs are enacted in a language other than that of mass, popular discourse.[5] Emerging research suggests that the language of governance is likely to affect citizens' trust in institutions. Drawing on World Values data, Liu and Baird (2012) find a significant and robust relationship between the languages used in courts and popular confidence in the justice system.

The power of the colonial language to delimit complete citizenship suggests that governments should put a premium on official language instruction for students in all schools, including madrassas, and consider the ways that French literacy classes for adults might help them to gain political autonomy. However, since education is unlikely to reach the poorest of the poor, those in remote rural areas, and many adults, a complementary—and more

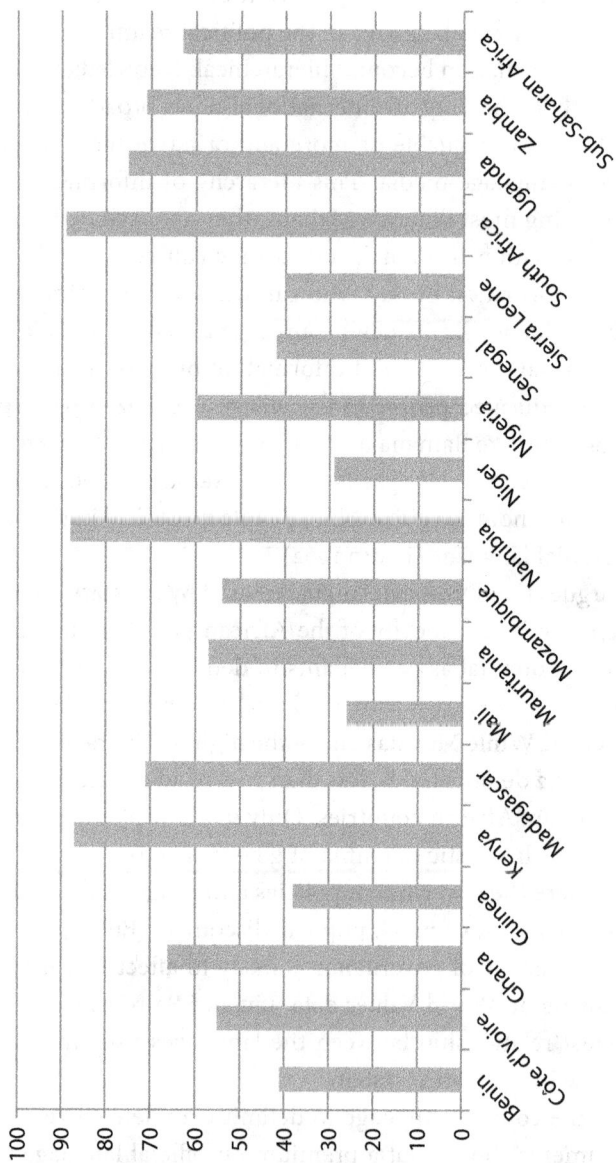

Figure 7.2. Percentage of adult literacy in the state language in selected African countries, 2005–2008.
Source: http://www.unicef.org/statistics/index_step2.php?

radical—strategy would be to reshape the nature of democratic politics in Africa to embody and reflect more widely the local indigenous languages. While this might be a more challenging option in places where linguistic fractionalization is high, it is possible in places like Mali, Kenya, and states in Nigeria where meta-trading languages, like Bambara, Swahili, and Hausa, are widely spoken.

As David Laitin (1992) demonstrates, language is extremely politicized and thus very difficult to change. Further, Albaugh's (2009) work shows that most moves toward local language schooling have come from international, rather than domestic, forces. I cannot anticipate that African citizens—eager to connect with scapes beyond their own borders—want to replace former colonial language with indigenous languages. But this type of reform does not necessarily require a linguistic renationalization of democratic spaces, and there could certainly be greater efforts in the translation and dissemination of resources in local languages and Arabic. For instance, only two courts in Mali—one in Ségou and one in Bamako—offer offices of operational assistance that translate and explain judicial information to everyday citizens. The state could undertake efforts to make these kinds of resources more accessible to citizens, especially rural populations. While these initiatives would take scarce resources away from the Malian state, it is critical that average Malian citizens be able to relate to and understand their democratic institutions.

Emerging Religious Constituencies as a Political Bloc

African politics are often viewed through the lens of ethnic, urban, or rural constituencies, but few efforts have been made to understand the distinct patterns of political participation among religious communities. In many instances, religious communities, particularly those with transnational ties and access to resources and social mobility distinct from the state, can overshadow or compete with traditional state or bureaucratic actors.[6] I urge political scientists to consider religious constituencies and their patterns of political behavior, particularly in contexts where religious authority is evolving in ways that depart from historic regional or ethnic configurations.

An analysis of the role of Islam and religious actors in Muslim-majority democracies is critical to understanding political trajectories. As political science moves past reductionist questions about the compatibility of Islam and democracy, researchers can begin to ask other interesting questions about the behavior, ideological aspirations, and representation of religious constituencies in nascent democracies. My study joins emerging work that focuses on the ways that Islam and the political opportunities offered by democratization affect each other (see Idrissa 2008; Kendhammer 2013; Villalón 2010).[7]

There has been much debate about the role of madrassas in state-building and in the proliferation of "terrorism," but little has been said about their democratic potential. My study suggests that incorporating Islamic schooling into the state's education system has two potential effects on democracy. First, Malian madrassas appear as capable as their Francophone counterparts in shaping informed citizens who are willing to vote and participate. Islamic schooling thus has the ability to encourage more informed and more active democratic citizens from communities that prefer religious education. Quranic schools are typically disregarded as archaic centers of rote memorization that preserve social hierarchy and distract students from productive classroom time by forcing them to beg for alms in the street. However, the results from my research suggest that Quranic schools have the potential to empower students to become more aware of their political environment. Policy makers might reexamine how they could engage with Quranic teachers to offer short courses on citizenship and democracy in order to make students more aware of their rights and obligations in the current political system.

My research can speak to how Islamic education might elicit and encourage citizens' engagement in politics, but I cannot specify what the content of their demands will be. No one can guarantee that madrassas or Quranic schools will produce democrats with liberal values, although one study of madrassas in Mali found that the majority were teaching content on "peace and tolerance" (Moussa et al. 2007). Religiously educated citizens could have a very different sense of what "democratic values" should look like. For instance, Kendhammer (2013) shows how activists in northern Nigeria used democratic discourse to justify the implementation of sharia as ultimately more accountable to citizens' demands. If Islamic schooling graduates get more involved in the political realm, there will likely be a greater demand for the political representation of a broader set of value systems, including some of the more conservative ideas in reformist schools of Islam.

The emergence of Islamist candidates in West African politics could prompt secular candidates to engage with populist issues that are typically housed in religious venues. This might lead to greater debate and contestation in electoral politics and in the National Assembly. My research suggests that this will depend both on candidates' French language acquisition and on the government's language policy toward Arabic. Other states, such as

Gambia, Senegal, and Niger, have adopted policies similar to Mali's: integrating madrassas into the state education system in national efforts to expand enrollment. In these cases, the government's willingness to partner with Islamic providers—favored by subsets of the population who may have been hesitant to participate in secular politics—is one step toward incorporating these communities into electoral processes and democratic representation. By expanding the range of citizens who are exercising their political voice, this policy change has the potential to increase the representativeness of African democracies and to change the elite, secular values currently associated with West African politics.

Chapter 1 · Introduction

1. The author notes the other prominent English-language spelling, *madrasa*, and the French spelling, *médersa*. *Madrassa* is used throughout this book to refer to schools that are synonymous with these two terms.

2. Uchendo (1979:29) argues that education offers opportunities for a few non-elites, but it also extricates them from the struggle of their less educated peers.

3. Other analyses of citizen-state relations in Africa include Moehler's (2008) exploration of citizens' engagement with the Ugandan state during the constitution-building process, Ashforth's (2005) study on the limitations that witchcraft imposes on citizens' engagement with the justice system in South Africa, MacLean's (2010) work on non-state welfare strategies among citizens in Côte d'Ivoire and Ghana, and Kendhammer's (2013) analysis of citizens' understanding of sharia in Nigeria.

4. Empowered democratic participation is synonymous with Bratton, Mattes, and Gyimah-Boadi's (2005) concept of "autonomous participation."

5. By "consolidated democracies," I refer to systems that are responsive and accountable to their citizens.

6. Hydén (2006) also adopts Hirschman's language about citizen-state relations in Africa.

7. The Human Development Index is calculated using a range of indicators of human well-being and economic prosperity; see http://hdr.undp.org/en/statistics/.

8. Tilly and Tarrow (2006:4) define contentious politics as "interactions in which actors make claims bearing on someone else's interests, leading to coordinated efforts on behalf of shared interests or programs, in which governments are involved as targets, initiators of claims, or third parties."

9. Many citizens, when asked if they went to school, replied, "No, but I traveled," asserting that their former expatriate status rivaled the sophistication and learning found in a formal classroom.

10. I employ David Easton's (1975) concept of "specific trust," which refers to trust in democratic actors.

11. Mattes and Mughogho (2009) do not find consistent general trends linking

citizens with political information or education to all forms of participation. Mac-Lean (2011:1250) finds that citizens with the highest levels of education and those with no education are less likely than their peers to vote.

12. Vicente (2013) found that a voter education program in São Tomé actually reduced turnout.

13. *Mission civilisatrice* refers to the French "civilizing" mission that sought to turn "educated" Africans into French subjects through an assimilation process.

14. Johnson's (1975:224) study of Guinea highlights the French attack on Quranic education. In 1910, Labé had 1,945 Quranic schools with a total of 5,538 pupils. By 1940, there were only 1,823 pupils in Quranic schools, while 6 French schools had 704 pupils.

Chapter 2 · *Research Design and Methodological Approach*

1. The United Nations estimates that approximately 33% of the adult population speaks the official language, French. See http://www.unicef.org/infobycountry/mali _statistics.html.

2. Thad Dunning and Lauren Harrison (2010) document the power of cousins' relations, which are as strong as ethnic affinities in citizens' positive assessments of candidates.

3. Examples of immersive surveys include Devra Moehler's (2008) work in Uganda, Claire Adida's (2014) study on violence in Nigeria, Adam Auerbach's (2013) work on slums in India, and John McCauley's (2013) work on evangelical clientelism in Ghana.

4. Surveys were also conducted in Arabic, Tamasheq, and Peul through simultaneous interpretation from French; there was no formally translated script in those languages. However, the research team spent time discussing the consistent phrasing of these questions.

5. Due to kidnappings and instability, as well as a US government travel ban to Timbuktu, I was unable to accompany the team to Timbuktu, Mopti, and Sévaré. I did conduct one monitoring visit to Timbuktu and was able to meet with the additional team members who were recruited and trained to help with the survey implementation.

6. Responses were only coded in instances when they were provided; coders were also encouraged to capture contextual details and behavioral observations during the interviews.

7. I suspect that complementary Quranic education, in which students attend both Quranic and French schools, was still vastly underreported in our survey.

8. As advocated by King, Keohane, and Verba (1994:140), I chose districts to maximize potential variation on the independent variable without knowledge of the variation on the dependent variable—political knowledge—or the reported participation of respondents.

9. At the time of the survey, Google maps' street view was unavailable for Mali.

10. Unlike Afrobarometer's method, I did not alternate the selection of respondents by gender nor conduct callbacks if the respondents were not home. However, we still managed to achieve near-parity in gender (54% of respondents were women

and 46% were men). Since we did not conduct callbacks, it is possible that heads of household and others engaged in the labor market are underrepresented in the survey. We did include domestic workers among the respondents.

11. This strategy is less desirable since respondents might feel restricted when speaking in the *dugutigi*'s compound, and there is usually an oversample of men. It took significant time and resources to reach those villages, and thus I did not have the budget to select replacement villages. Further, if I only selected villages with compliant chiefs I would have biased the results away from a more authoritarian local setting, which is a cultural reality in rural Mali. I have run all regressions without these districts included to ensure that they do not impact the results.

12. Statistics on Quranic and Christian enrollment were not available. Quranic schools are not monitored by the Malian Ministry of Education, and Christian schools are aggregated into the larger category of private schools.

13. *Sotramas* are green public transport vans that operate on preestablished routes.

14. Similarly, Gérard (1999:158) in his study of education in Burkina Faso also finds that trading communities prefer madrassas.

15. Many of our survey respondents in Timbuktu noted that Gaddafi visited regularly to distribute aid. In a survey question about the importance of foreign aid from different countries, Timbuktuciens gave the most favorable ranking of Libya compared to Malian peers in other regions, who favored China and the United States.

16. See also http://whc.unesco.org/en/list/119.

Chapter 3 · *Politiki ni Fanga Mali la* / Power and Politics in Mali

1. The phrase *politiki man ɲi* is ubiquitous in Malian culture. It is the title of a popular song by the Malian singers Amadou and Mariam, and Tiken Jah Fakoly, a reggae musician, has a song with a similar title.

2. Mali was ranked fifth worst on the Human Development Index in 2009, but boasted a Freedom House score of 2 for political rights and 3 for civil liberties before the coup in March 2012.

3. I have changed all respondents' names and the names of their villages to maintain their anonymity. The letter-number combinations are unique identifiers for each respondent with the letters signifying the school district where the interview took place; see the list of abbreviations in the front of this book.

4. It is important to acknowledge the substantial regional variation within Mali. Voter turnout in the northern region is consistently higher than in the rest of the country. For presidential races, the regional disparities in turnout are even greater than at the municipal level.

5. I thank Kelly McMann for allowing me to use this item from her questionnaire.

6. An August 25, 2009, interview with a member of a leading democratic think tank also stressed the power of the culture of consensus.

7. Mali's unique history has shaped values of tolerance and produced conflict mitigation mechanisms, including *sananku* or, in French, *cousinage*. *Cousinage* links together certain last names—*jamu*—from different ethnic groups in a joking attempt to create cross-cutting relationships. Because cousins come from different ethnic

groups, depending on their last name members of the same ethnic group can have different sets of joking cousins.

8. Castes are related to Malian last names and are integrated into the *cousinage* system. There are no political limits for any particular caste, but some occupations are exclusively held by certain castes (i.e., griots or mediators). Salif Keita, the most famous Malian singer, defied the wishes of his father and became a singer even though he is not from a griot class. In other instances, people of historically marginalized castes have made requests of Malians who have historically dominated them.

9. Another respondent in Timbuktu gave a zero vote of confidence to traditional authorities and religious leaders: "They are ruined now. Even them—they take part in politics" (T6).

10. The question was phrased this way: "Which of the following statements is closest to your view? Choose Statement 1 or Statement 2. Statement 1: Traditional leaders must represent all of their people equally. They should remain nonpartisan, and not affiliate themselves with any political party. Statement 2: Traditional leaders are citizens like everyone else and have the right to decide for themselves whether to support a particular party."

11. See Benhabib 2002 for a discussion of the problem of representatives speaking as the authoritative voice of a particular cultural group.

12. This is the French word meaning the separation of church and state, which has a stronger connotation than the English word "secular."

13. After the 2013 presidential elections, many believed that backing from influential religious leaders in Nioro du Sahel helped IBK to be elected, but it is unclear if this backing was decisive in his victory.

14. This is consistent with the Afrobarometer results (72%).

15. Interviews with DJs (July 2011) from private and community radio stations revealed that donors routinely transmitted messages about how to participate in politics.

16. Unfortunately, no data are available for Benin, which also boasts a large number of weak parties and would be the best direct point of comparison.

17. The questions are taken directly from Afrobarometer Rounds 3 and 4, available at www.afrobarometer.org.

18. This is common in any survey data on voting; see, for example, Holbrook and Krosnick 2009.

19. After initially including "ran for office" as a dependent variable for participation, I dropped it from my analysis since there was so little variation in how many people had run.

Chapter 4 · Mali's Evolving Educational Landscape

1. This 1991 figure does not include students enrolled in madrassas, which were not formally acknowledged by the state at that time.

2. The net enrollment rate was approximately 61% (Pearce, Fourmy, and Kovach 2009:7).

3. Some schools use a pedagogy that incorporates local languages—*pédagogie convergente*—as the language of instruction up until sixth grade. After being taught as a subject, French is used as the language of instruction after sixth grade.

4. During the 2011 UN–NATO attacks on Libya, local radio DJs in Bamako championed Gaddafi and criticized Malians for their lack of support for a "man who had paid for so many mosques and madrassas." There was a series of protests in Bamako during the beginning of the UN intervention in the spring of 2011.

5. On average, Francophone countries trailed their Anglophone counterparts in literacy rates at independence, and this trend continues today.

6. Two 70-something respondents to our survey said they had attained status as civil servants with only sixth-grade diplomas.

7. Teachers' salaries were estimated to be 13 times the GDP per capita at that time.

8. The French government associated madrassas with a Salafist school of Islam it found threatening, despite the fact that some madrassas had a Sufi orientation.

9. Most schools teach in indigenous languages using *pédagogie convergente*, but there are some NGOs, such as those sponsored by World Education, that use French-language immersion from the start.

10. However, one teacher also noted (interview, July 2009) the success of the World Food Program's school cafeterias and UNICEF competitions in increasing female student retention.

11. Louis Brenner (2007:209) explains that this process ended in the 1980s under structural adjustment reforms.

12. Gérard (1997b: 44) describes a similar hope for economic returns on French education in his study of a Malinke region in southern Mali.

13. Even with this reinstatement, few schools have actually implemented the reform (interview with educator, August 2013)

14. This is my translation from notes I took when I briefly had this textbook (by Keita et al.) in my possession. Unfortunately, I no longer have access to the original, and I did not record the publication information.

15. *Umma* is the global community of Muslims connected by their religious beliefs.

16. Gérard (1999) notes an increase in madrassas in Niger and Burkina as well.

17. The French labeled Salafists or reformists as Wahhabis, and eventually many of them came to accept this identity (Brenner 2007:211). Today, many Malians refer to reformists as Wahhabis.

18. The practice of sending children to live with friends and family is most common at the secondary and tertiary levels, because students must travel far distances to attend even the closest school.

19. This was the experience of all of my research assistants as they attended university in Bamako.

20. This description only represents a general trend; many women who are income earners, such as civil servants, also continue to support their own relatives.

21. Gérard (1997b) finds that public schooling is out of sync with the lives and rhythms of many Malians in the Sikasso region.

22. Parents could provide more than one justification for enrollment, so the total number of justifications exceeds the number of parents with children in each school type: public, N = 520; private secular = 299; madrassa = 75; Quranic = 39; community = 36; private Christian = 14.

23. Hopkins (1972) found the same pattern of Muslim enrollment in Christian schools in Kita in the 1960s due to the perception of the better quality of French instruction.

24. The Peul, or Fulani, are an ethnic group associated with herding and Quranic schooling. Of 42 parents who reported sending their children to Quranic school, 64% (27) said they spoke Fulani at home. Most of these respondents live in the Kayes region.

25. In Mali, it is uncommon to see young girls with covered heads. In most cases, head covering is not practiced until a woman marries.

Chapter 5 · Can Education Empower Citizens?

1. This analysis was conducted exclusively for citizens with a maximum of primary and informal schooling since only nine respondents in the survey attended secondary madrassas.

2. Niamakoro is a newer neighborhood in Bamako in the Faladie school district.

3. *Grin* is a Bambara word that refers to a group of friends who gather regularly to drink tea and hang out; the group can be same sex or mixed.

4. Other types of experience, such as travel, cultural exchange, and job opportunities, might also contribute to political knowledge and participation.

5. This idea was championed by Almond and Verba (1963), but has been touted by many scholars who study the relationship between schooling and participation in the US context.

6. Dalton (2007) describes educated citizens as less dependent on political parties for information.

7. I use this term as a synonym for "high-initiative" participation.

8. In their criticism of private schools, many public school educators made this assertion (interviews, Bamako, 2007).

9. Usually, a lack of French-language proficiency creates barriers for madrassa learners to switch over to Francophone schools. When students switch from Arabic to French schools, they usually have to repeat multiple grades in order to gain French-language skills.

10. Partisanship may very well increase some forms of easy political behavior, but I am more concerned with how citizens forge relationships with parties in the first place.

11. I keep all activities as isolated dependent variables since it is unclear which aspects of participation are associated.

12. Age is measured in 10-year cohorts because it was difficult to get precise ages from respondents.

13. This proxy is made from a possession index combined with questions about difficulties respondents have in obtaining food, water, and cooking fuel.

14. For instance, there are substantial regional differences in voter turnout in Mali.

15. Lauren MacLean (2011) similarly finds that only lower levels of education are correlated with a higher probability of respondents stating that they voted.

16. The interaction term is significantly negative ($p < .05$) for contacting a government official, the opposite of what I would expect if the democratic curriculum were the mechanism.

17. In this section, I am not referring to political socialization, but rather exposure to external stimuli through socialization or exposure to other people beyond the compound walls.

18. I do not want to suggest that gender segregation in Mali is as extreme as in northern Nigeria or Saudi Arabia nor that certain women do not navigate the public sphere with the ease and freedom of men.

19. It is significant for campaigning only at the university level, but not at the secondary level. I would expect consistent effects for the secondary and university levels if socialization were the determining factor.

20. The University of Bamako is the only national university and has students from all around the country; we surveyed at each of its four campuses.

21. The university students were surveyed approximately one month before the municipal elections, which I expected would inflate their predicted behavior compared to the survey respondents, who gave retrospective accounts of their participation. The majority of university respondents were men, which I also expected to inflate participation.

22. The university student interviews do not provide data about mobilization at the secondary level. The possibility that students are mobilized at the secondary level still exists.

23. There is indigenous language programming on Mali's state television channel (ORTM), but some programming and debates are exclusively in French.

24. On the distinction between specific and diffuse support, see Easton 1975:437: "The uniqueness of specific support lies in its relationship to the satisfactions that members of a system feel they obtain from the perceived outputs and performance of the political authorities." This performance is tied to individual leaders, parties, or regimes.

Chapter 6 · Schooling and Parents' Engagement with the State

1. Eugene Weber (1976) and Abram de Swaan (1988) discuss how public education spread the state's reach into the population. Many authors discuss the use of education to foster allegiance and support, including Anderson 1983; Gellner 1983; Hobsbawm 1990; Laitin 1977, 1998.

2. By law, Malian schools are free, but in practice all parents pay a nominal fee (around US$1) per month.

3. Additionally, madrassa enrollment is measured more accurately than enrollment in Quranic schools. I believe that enrollment in Quranic schools was under-

reported, especially in instances where parents enrolled their children in Quranic schools to supplement other forms of education.

4. Most Malian children are enrolled in school by this age; this is also the age required to enter Malian public schools.

5. The measurement of "children" reflects the shared childrearing in Malian homes. In some instances, respondents referenced extended family as their own: parents with grown children spoke regarding the experience of grandchildren, and aunts and uncles would answer the questions in reference to any school-age child living in the household even if he was a nephew rather than a son.

6. These numbers capture parents whose children already went through the educational system and those with children currently enrolled. Some of these parents are counted more than once because they have children enrolled in multiple schools.

7. This reference category includes non-parents, parents with no children enrolled in school, and parents whose children are too young to attend school.

8. I repeated the regression without controls and found that the schooling categories remain significant with the signs in the same direction.

9. Having a child enrolled in public school or community school drops to $p < .1$ significance if I exclude age from the regression. Since younger people are more associated with campaigning, and many of the people in the "no kids" category are young and do not yet have children, excluding the control inflates the likelihood that the reference category is campaigning compared to any other group.

10. This was initially negative and significant for madrassa consumers, but lost significance when I included the controls.

11. There is thus a potential for bias toward a subpopulation of early voters as compared to voters who come later in the day, but I have no reason to believe that this is correlated with the school type where voters enroll their children.

12. I restricted the analysis to parents with a child enrolled in primary school so that I could compare my percentages to those offered in the Ministry of Education reports.

13. A word of caution on the Ministry of Education data for Bamako Coura: only 271 students in the entire district are coded as attending madrassas. I suspect that a higher number of students are actually enrolled in madrassas, and if the data are corrected, my results in Bamako Coura might look more like the other two districts, where madrassa parents are underrepresented at the polls.

14. The focus group took place in March 2011 with six university students from San, Sikasso, and the Kayes region. All had gone through the public school system and were attending the public university in Bamako.

15. These findings are consistent with MacLean 2007 and Boyle 1999. They report that poorer citizens are "forced" into public services by financial constraints, while wealthier citizens use private services.

16. I did not find evidence of a significant relationship between income and voting, which rules out the possibility of poverty as a confounding variable for school enrollment and a higher voting rate.

17. I assume that parents who would benefit from children as linguistic brokers

would have to have children old enough to have completed at least sixth grade. In most instances, electoral brokers are at a minimum in their second cycle of primary school.

18. Conversely, it is possible that a poor rating, or dissatisfaction with existing service, might also drive citizens to vote.

19. Riedl's (2012) analysis of the interaction between religious groups and political parties, Grossman's (2015) research on the role of evangelical groups in lobbying for anti-homosexual legislation, and Dowd's (2014) exploration of religious diversity as driving variation in the ways religious groups foster political participation both offer exciting opportunities to understand the relationship between religion and political participation in sub-Saharan Africa.

Chapter 7 · *Educational Expansion and Democratization in Africa*

1. Gérard's (1997b) work highlights the importance of French fluency; work by Meillassoux (1970) discusses the class distinctions generated by differences in language fluency.

2. These findings are consistent with Staffan Lindberg's (2006) argument that elections fuel democratic consolidation.

3. Gilles Holder (2013) describes tensions within different Islamic communities in post-occupation Mali: http://www.sciencespo.fr/ceri/fr/content/dossiersduceri/mon-pays-sa-un-certain-retour-sur-la-democratie-exemplaire-du-mali-et-sa-derai son-islamique.

4. In a rare comparative assessment of the impact of education on democracy, Kamens (1988) underscores the need to take stock of the initial level of functioning of a democracy as well as the level of educational control by the regime.

5. Paulin Djité's (2011) work on Southeast Asia suggests similar dynamics in another complex multilingual environment where literacy in the state language is under 50%.

6. For instance, John McCauley's (2013) work in Ghana shows the growing pentecostal movement as detracting from other traditional clientelist networks.

7. Villalón, Idrissa, and Bodian (2012) examine the major education policy changes after the democratic transition, when many countries, including Mali, responded to the mass demand for state support of Islamic education.

Abernethy, David. 1968. *The Political Dilemma of Popular Education*. Stanford, CA: Stanford University Press.

Achebe, Chinua. 1965. "English and the African Writer." *Transition* (W. E. B. Du Bois Institute) 18:27–30.

Adcock, Robert, and David Collier. 2001. "Measurement Validity: A Shared Standard for Qualitative and Quantitative Research." *American Political Science Review* 95(3):529–546.

Adida, Claire. 2011. "Too Close for Comfort? Immigrant Exclusion in Africa." *Comparative Political Studies* 44(10):1370–1396.

———. 2014. *Immigrant Exclusion and Insecurity in Africa: Coethnic Strangers*. Cambridge: Cambridge University Press.

Ake, Claude. 1996. *Democracy and Development in Africa*. Washington, DC: Brookings Institution Press.

———. 2000. *The Feasibility of Democracy in Africa*. Senegal: Council for the Development of Social Science Research in Africa.

Akerloff, George, and Rachel Kranton. 2002. "Identity and Schooling: Some Lessons for the Economics of Education." *Journal of Economic Literature* 40(4):1167–1201.

Albaugh, Ericka A. 2007. "Language Choice in Education: A Politics of Persuasion." *Journal of Modern African Studies* 45:1.

———. 2009. "The Colonial Image Reversed: Language Preferences and Policy Outcomes in African Education." *International Studies Quarterly* 53(2):389–420.

Allison, P. D. 1999. *Logistic Regression Using the SAS System*. Cary, NC: SAS Institute.

Almond, Gabriel A., and Sidney Verba. 1963. *The Civic Culture: Political Attitudes and Democracy in Five Nations*. Princeton, NJ: Princeton University Press.

Amselle, Jean-Loup. 1985. "Le Wahabisme à Bamako (1945–1985)." *Canadian Journal of African Studies* 19(2):345–357.

Anderson, Benedict. 1983. *Imagined Communities*. London: Verso.

Andrabi, Tahir, et al. 2006. "Religious School Enrollment in Pakistan: A Look at the Data." *Comparative Education Review* 50(3):446–477.

Annuaire National. 2002–2003. Bamako: Ministère de l'Éducation.

———. 2004–2005. Bamako: Ministère de l'Éducation.

———. 2005–2006. Bamako: Ministère de l'Éducation.

———. 2006–2007. Bamako: Ministère de l'Éducation

———. 2009–2010. Bamako: Ministère de l'Éducation.

Arlin, Patricia Kennedy. 1975. "Cognitive Development in Adulthood: A Fifth Stage?" *Developmental Psychology* 11(5):602–606.

Ashforth, Adam. 2005. *Witchcraft, Violence, and Democracy in South Africa.* Chicago: University of Chicago Press.

Auerbach, Adam. 2013. "Demanding Development: Democracy, Community Governance, and Public Goods Provision in India's Urban Slums." PhD thesis, University of Wisconsin, Department of Political Science.

Ba, Oumar Issiaka. 2009. *Une histoire de l'enseignement au Mali: Entre réforme et réticences.* Paris: L'Harmattan.

Bagayoko, Shaka. 1987. "L'état au Malien: Représentation, autonomie, et mode de fonctionnement." In *L'état contemporain en Afrique*, ed. Terray Emmanuel, 91–122. Paris: L'Harmattan.

———. 1989. "Ba Lieux et théorie du pouvoir dans le monde mandé: Passé et présent." Bamako, Mali: Mission ORSTOM.

Baldwin, Kate. 2013. "Why Vote with the Chief? Political Connections and Public Goods Provision in Zambia." *American Journal of Political Science* 57(4):794–809.

Banégas, R. 1998. "Marchandisation du vote, citoyenneté et consolidation démocratique au Bénin." *Politique Africaine* 69:75–87.

Bast, Joseph, and Herbert Walberg. 2004. "Can Parents Choose the Best Schools for Their Children?" *Economics of Education Review* 23:431–440.

Bates, Robert H. 1981. *Markets and States in Tropical Africa: The Political Basis of Agricultural Policies.* Berkeley: University of California Press.

Baudais, Virginie, and Grégory Chauzal. 2006. "Les partis politiques et 'l'indépendance partisane' d'Amadou Toumani Touré." *Politique Africaine* 104:61–80.

Beck, Linda. 2008. *Brokering Democracy in Africa: The Rise of Clientelist Democracy in Senegal.* New York: Palgrave Macmillan.

Belli, Robert F., et al. 1999. "Reducing Vote Over-Reporting in Surveys: Social Desirability, Memory Failure, and Source Monitoring." *Public Opinion Quarterly* 63:90–108.

Bender, Penelope, et al. 2007. *Evaluation of the World Bank Assistance to Primary Education in Mali.* Washington, DC: World Bank.

Benhabib, Seyla. 2002. *The Claims of Culture: Equality and Diversity in the Global Era.* Princeton, NJ: Princeton University Press.

Bergmann, Herbert. 1996. "Quality of Education and the Demand for Education: Evidence from Developing Countries." *International Review of Education* 42(6):581–604.

Bernal, Jose Luis. 2005. "Parental Choice, Social Class, and Market Forces: The Consequences of Privatization of Public Services in Education." *Journal of Education Policy* 20(6):779–792.

Bernstein, Robert, Anita Chadha, and Robert Montjoy. 2001. "Overreporting Voting: Why It Happens and Why It Matters." *Public Opinion Quarterly* 65:22–44.

Bierschenk, Thomas. 2007. "L'éducation de base en Afrique de l'ouest francophone: Bien privé, bien public, bien global." In *Une anthropologie entre rigeur et engagement: Essais autour de l'œuvre de Jean-Pierre Olivier de Sardan*, ed. T. Bierschenk et al., 235–257. Paris: APAD-Karthala.

Bierschenk, Thomas, and Jean-Pierre Olivier de Sardan. 1997. "Local Powers and a Distant State in Rural Central African Republic." *Journal of Modern African Studies* 35(3):441–468.

Bingen, James, David Robinson, and John M. Staatz. 2001. *Democracy and Development in Mali*. East Lansing: Michigan State University Press.

Blaydes, Lisa. 2006. "Who Votes in Authoritarian Elections and Why? Determinants of Voter Turnout in Contemporary Egypt." Paper presented at the Annual Meeting of the American Political Science Association, August 31–September 3, Philadelphia, PA.

Bleck, Jaimie, and Mody Boubacar Guindo. 2013. "Education for All? Education for Whom? Education for What?" *Development in Practice* 23(8):1004–1017.

Bleck, Jaimie, and Kristin Michelitch. 2015a. "Capturing the Airwaves, Capturing the Nation: Citizen Response to Putschist-Controlled Radio." Unpublished paper in author's possession.

———. 2015b. "The 2012 Crisis in Mali: Ongoing Empirical State Failure." *African Affairs*, forthcoming.

Bleck, Jaimie, and David Patel. 2015. "Out of Africa: Why Islamists Do Not (Yet) Participate in African Elections." Unpublished paper in author's possession.

Bleck, Jaimie, and Nicolas van de Walle. 2011. "Parties and Issues in Francophone West Africa: Towards a Theory of Non-Mobilization." *Democratization* 18(5):1125–1145.

Bloemraad, I., and C. Trost. 2008. "It's a Family Affair: Inter-Generational Mobilization in the Spring 2006 Protests." *American Behavioral Scientist* 52(4):507–532.

Bogaards, Matthijs, Matthias Basedau, and Christof Hartmann. 2010. "Ethnic Party Bans in Africa: An Introduction." *Democratization* 17(4):599–617.

Boyle, Patrick. 1995. "School Wars: Church, State, and the Death of Congo." *Journal of Modern African Studies* 33(3):451–468.

———. 1999. *Class Formation and Civil Society: The Politics of Education in Africa*. London: Ashgate.

Bratton, Michael. 1989. "Beyond the State: Civil Society and Associational Life in Africa." *World Politics* 41(3):407–430.

———. 2008. "Vote Buying and Violence in Nigerian Elections." *Electoral Studies* 27:621–632.

Bratton, Michael, et al. 1999. "The Effects of Civic Education on Political Culture: Evidence from Zambia." *World Development* 27(5):807–824.

Bratton, Michael, Robert Mattes, and E. Gyimah-Boadi. 2005. *Public Opinion, Democracy, and Market Reform in Africa*. Cambridge: Cambridge University Press.

Bratton, Michael, and Nicolas van de Walle. 1997. *Democratic Experiments in Africa: Regime Transitions in Comparative Perspective*. Cambridge: Cambridge University Press.

Brautigam, Deborah. 1996. "State Capacity and Effective Governance." *Agenda for Africa's Economic Renewal* 1996:81–108.

Brenner, Louis. 1993. *Muslim Identity and Social Change in Sub-Saharan Africa.* Bloomington: Indiana University Press.

———. 2001. *Controlling Knowledge: Religion, Power, and Schooling in a West African Muslim Society.* Bloomington: Indiana University Press.

———. 2007. "The Transformation of Muslim Schooling in Mali: The Madrassa as an Institution of Social and Religious Mediation." In *Schooling Islam: The Culture and Politics of Modern Muslim Education,* ed. Robert Hefner and Muhammad Qasim Zaman, 199–223. Princeton, NJ: Princeton University Press.

Brock-Utne, Birgit. 2003. "The Language Question in Africa in the Light of Globalisation, Social Justice and Democracy." *International Journal of Peace Studies* 8(2):67–87.

Brown, Godfrey, and Mervyn Hiskett, eds. 1975. *Conflict and Harmony in Education in Tropical Africa.* London: George Allen and Unwin.

Buggenhagen, Beth Anne. 2004. "Domestic Object(ion)s: The Senegalese Murid Trade Diaspora and the Politics of Marriage Payments, Love, and State Privatization." *Studies on Religion in Africa* 26:21–53.

Bunce, Valerie. 2001. "The Postsocialist Experience and Comparative Politics." *Political Science and Politics* 34(4):793–795.

———. 2003. "Rethinking Recent Democratization: Lessons from the Post Communist Experience." *World Politics* 55(2):167–192.

Bunce, Valerie, and Sharon L. Wolchik. 2007. "Favorable Conditions and Electoral Revolutions." *Journal of Democracy* 17(4):5–18.

Cammett, Melani, and Sukriti Issar. 2010. "Bricks and Mortar Clientelism: Sectarianism and the Logics of Welfare Allocation in Lebanon." *World Politics* 62(3):381–421.

Cammett, Melani, and Lauren M. MacLean. 2011. "Introduction: The Political Consequences of Non-State Social Welfare in the Global South." *Studies in Comparative International Development* 46(1):1–21.

Cammett, Melani, and Lauren M. MacLean, eds. 2014. *The Politics of Non-State Social Welfare.* Ithaca, NY: Cornell University Press.

Campbell, Andrea. 2003. *How Policies Make Citizens: Senior Political Activism and the American Welfare State.* Princeton, NJ: Princeton University Press.

Campbell, David E. 2006. "What Is Education's Impact on Civic and Social Engagement?" In *Measuring the Effects of Education on Health and Civic/Social Engagement,* ed. Richard Desjardins and Tom Schuller, 25–126. Paris: Centre for Educational Research and Innovation / Organisation for Economic Co-operation and Development.

Carbone, Giovanni M. 2006. "Comprendre les partis et les systèmes de partis Africaines." *Politique Africaine* 104:18–37.

CATEK. 2010. *Rapport définitif: Enquête légère sur le niveau actuel de satisfaction des usagers des services publics.* Bamako, Mali: CATEK. http://www.cdi-mali.gov.ml/upload_etude/doc29.pdf.

Cho, Wonbin, and Carolyn Logan. 2013. "Looking Toward the Future: Alternations in Power and Popular Perspectives on Democratic Durability in Africa." *Comparative Political Studies,* doi: 0010414013488534.

Ciftci, Sabri. 2010. "Modernization, Islam, or Social Capital: What Explains Attitudes towards Democracy in the Muslim World." *Comparative Political Studies* 43(11):1442–1470.

Cissoko, Sékéné Mody. 1975. *Tombouctou et L'Empire Songhoy.* Abidjan-Dakar: NEA.

Citing Girls' Education in Africa. 2005. Education and Gender Equality Series, Programme Insights. Oxford: Oxfam.

Cleary, Matthew, and Susan Stokes. 2006. *Democracy and the Culture of Skepticism: Political Trust in Mexico and Argentina.* New York: Russell Sage Foundation.

Collier, Paul. 2009. *Wars, Guns, and Votes: Democracy in Dangerous Places.* New York: HarperCollins.

Collier, Paul, and Pedro C. Vicente. 2012. "Violence, Bribery, and Fraud: The Political Economy of Elections in Sub-Saharan Africa." *Public Choice* 153(1–2):117–147.

Converse, Philip E. 1972. "Change in the American Electorate." In *The Human Meaning of Social Change,* ed. Angus Campbell and Converse, 263–337. New York: Russell Sage Foundation.

Coppedge, Michael, et al. 2010. "Conceptualizing and Measuring Democracy: A New Approach." *Perspectives on Politics* 9(2):247–267.

Cornwall, Andrea, and Vera Schattan Coelho. 2007. *Spaces for Change? The Politics of Citizen Participation in New Democratic Arenas.* London: Zed.

Coulibaly, Massa, and Michael Bratton. 2013. "Crisis in Mali: Ambivalent Popular Attitudes on the Way Forward." *Stability: International Journal of Security and Development* 2(31):1–10.

Coulibaly, Massa, and Amadou Diarra. 2004. "Démocratie et légitimation du marche: Rapport d'enquête Afrobarometer au Mali, Décembre 2002." Afrobarometer Working Paper 35, www.afrobarometer.org.

County, Brandon, and Ryan Skinner. 2008. "*Faso* and *Jamana*: Provisional Notes on Mande Social Thought in Malian Political Discourse, 1946–1979." In *Mande Mansa: Essays in Honor of David Conrad,* ed. Stephen Belcher, Jan Jansen, and Mohamed N'Daou. Münster, Germany: LIT.

Craig, Stephen C. 1980. "The Mobilization of Political Discontent." *Political Behavior* 2(2):189–209.

Craig, Stephen C., and Michael A. Maggiotto. 1982. "Measuring Political Efficacy." *Political Methodology*, 85–109.

Dahl, Robert. 1967. *The Pluralist Democracy in the United States: Conflict and Consensus.* Chicago: Rand McNally.

———. 1971. *Polyarchy, Participation, and Opposition.* New Haven, CT: Yale University Press.

Dalton, Russell. 2007. "Partisan Mobilization, Cognitive Mobilization, and the Changing American Electorate." *Electoral Studies* 26(2):274–286.

———. 2008. "Citizenship Norms and the Expansion of Political Participation." *Political Studies* 56:76–98.

De La O, Ana. 2013. "Do Conditional Cash Transfers Affect Electoral Behavior? Evidence from a Randomized Experiment in Mexico." *American Journal of Political Science* 57(1):1–14.

Delarue, Jocelyne, et al. 2009. "The Sikasso Paradox: Does Cotton Reduce Poverty?" Unpublished paper in author's possession.

De Ment, Terii, Raymond Buriel, and Christina Villanueva. 2005. "Children as Language Brokers: A Narrative of the Recollections of College Students." In *Language in Multicultural Education*, ed. Farideh Salili and Rumjahn Hoosain, 255–272. Scottsdale, AZ: Information Age.

de Swaan, Abram. 1988. *In Care of the State*. New York: Oxford University Press.

Deutsch, Karl W. 1961. "Social Mobilization and Political Development." *American Political Science Review* 55(3):493–514.

Deutsch, Karl W., and William J. Foltz, eds. 1966. *Nation-Building*. New York: Atherton.

Diakite, Drissa. 2000. "La crise scolaire au Mali." *Nordic Journal of African Studies* 9(3): 6–28.

Djité, Paulin. 2011. *The Language Difference: Language and Development in the Greater Mekong Sub-Region*. Toronto: Multilingual Matters.

Dougnon, Isaie. 2013. "In a Time of Crisis, Why Are the Academics So Quiet?" *University World News* 262. http://www.universityworldnews.com/article.php?story =20130308124745395.

Dowd, Robert. 2014. "Religious Diversity and Religious Tolerance: Lessons from Nigeria." *Journal of Conflict Resolution*, doi: 0022002714550085.

Dunning, Thad, and Lauren Harrison. 2010. "Cross-Cutting Cleavages and Ethnic Voting: An Experimental Study of Cousinage in Mali." *American Political Science Review* 104(1):1–19.

Easton, David. 1975. "A Re-Assessment of the Concept of Political Support." *British Journal of Political Science* 5(4):435–457.

Education for All: Global Monitoring Report. 2007. Paris: UNESCO.

———. 2008. Paris: UNESCO.

———. 2010. Paris: UNESCO.

———. 2011. Paris: UNESCO.

Education Sector Medium Term Plan 2008–2011. 2008. Banjul: Republic of Gambia, Department of State for Basic and Secondary Education.

Eifert, Ben, Edward Miguel, and Daniel N. Posner. 2010. "Political Competition and Ethnic Identification in Africa." *American Journal of Political Science* 54(2):494–510.

Ekeh, Peter P. 1972. "Citizenship and Political Conflict: A Sociological Analysis of the Nigerian Crisis." In *Nigeria: Dilemma of Nationhood: An African Analysis of the Biafran Conflict*, ed. Joseph Okpaku, 76–117. New York: Third.

———. 1975. "Colonialism and the Two Publics in Africa: A Theoretical Statement." *Comparative Studies in Social History* 17(1):91–112.

Elman, Colin, Diana Kapiszewski, and Lorena Vinuela. 2010. "Qualitative Data Archiving: Rewards and Challenges." *PS: Political Science and Politics* 43(1):23–27.

Englebert, Pierre. 2000. "Pre-Colonial Institutions, Post-Colonial States, and Economic Development in Tropical Africa." *Political Research Quarterly* 53(1):7–36.

———. 2010. *Unity, Sovereignty, and Sorrow*. Boulder, CO: Lynne Rienner.

Esposito, John, and John Voll. 1996. *Islam and Democracy.* Oxford: Oxford University Press.

Evans, Geoffrey, and Pauline Rose. 2007. "Education and Support for Democracy in Sub-Saharan Africa." Unpublished paper, Michigan State University.

Fanon, Frantz. 1965. *The Wretched of the Earth.* New York: Grove. *Final Poverty Reduction Strategy Paper.* 2002. Bamako: Government of Mali.

Finkel, Steven E. 1985. "Reciprocal Effects of Participation and Political Efficacy: A Panel Analysis." *American Journal of Political Science* 29(2):891–913.

Finkel, Steven E., and Amy Erica Smith. 2011. "Civic Education, Political Discussion, and the Social Transmission of Democratic Knowledge and Values in a New Democracy: Kenya 2002." *American Journal of Political Science* 55(2):417–435.

Fish, Steven. 2002. "Islam and Authoritarianism." *World Politics* 55(1):4–37.

Fowler, Anthony, and Michele Margolis. 2014. "The Political Consequences of Uninformed Voters." *Electoral Studies* 34:100–110.

Fowler, Floyd. 2009. *Survey Research Methods.* Los Angeles, CA: Sage.

Fox, Jonathon. 1994. "The Difficult Transition from Clientelism to Citizenship: Lessons from Mexico." *World Politics* 46(2):151–184.

———. 1996. "How Does Civil Society Thicken? The Political Construction of Social Capital in Rural Mexico." *World Development* 24(6):1089–1103.

Franklin, Charles. 1984. "Issue Preference, Socialization, and the Evolution of Party Identification." *American Journal of Political Science* 28:459–478.

Fraser, John. 1970. "The Mistrustful-Efficacious Hypothesis and Political Participation." *Journal of Politics* 32(2):444–449.

Freese, Jeremy, and J. Scott Long. 2006. *Regression Models for Categorical Dependent Variables Using Stata.* College Station, TX: Stata Press.

Fridy, Kevin. 2007. "We Only Vote but Do Not Know: The Social Foundations of Partisanship in Ghana." PhD diss., University of Florida, Gainesville, Department of Political Science.

Friedman, Milton. 1955. *The Role of Government in Education.* New Brunswick, NJ: Rutgers University Press.

Friedman, Willa, et al. 2011. "Education as Liberation?" http://ipl.econ.duke.edu/bread/papers/working/299.pdf.

Gamson, William. 1968. *Power and Discontent.* Homewood, IL: Dorsey.

Gandolfi, Stefania. 2003. "L'enseignement islamique en Afrique noire." *Cahiers d'Études Africaines* 43(169–170):261–277.

Gandolfo, Andrew. 2009. "Education-Medium and African Linguistic Rights in the Context of Globalization." *Globalisation, Societies, and Education* 7(3):321–336.

Gazibo, Mamadou. 2006. "Les partis politiques d'Afrique: Retours sur un objet délaissé." *Politique Africaine* 104:1–17.

Gellar, Sheldon. 2005. *Democracy in Senegal: Tocquevillian Analytics in Africa.* Bloomington: Indiana University Press.

Gellner, Ernst. 1983. *Nations and Nationalism.* London: Blackwell.

Gérard, Étienne. 1992. "Entre l'état et populations: L'école, l'education, en devenir?" *Politique Africaine* 47:59–69.

————. 1997a. "Les médersas: Un élément de mutation des sociétés ouest-africaines." *Politique Étrangère* 62(4):613–627.

————. 1997b. *La tentation du savoir en Afrique: Politiques, mythes, et stratégies d'éducation au Mali.* Paris: Ostrom.

————. 1999. "Logiques sociales et enjeux de scolarisation en Afrique: Réflexions sur des cas d'écoles maliens et burkinabè." *Politique Africaine* 76:164–176.

Giné, Xavier, and Ghazala Mansuri. 2011. "Together We Will: Evidence from a Field Experiment on Female Voter Turnout in Pakistan." Washington, DC: World Bank Policy Research Working Paper 5692.

Glick, Peter, and David Sahn. 2000. "Schooling of Girls and Boys in a West African Country: The Effects of Parental Education, Income, and Household Structure." *Economics of Education Review* 19(1):63–87.

————. 2006. "The Demand for Primary Schooling in Madagascar: Price, Quality, and the Choice Between Public and Private Providers." *Journal of Development Economics* 79:118–145.

Glomm, J. 1997. "Parental Choice of Human Capital Investment." *Journal of Development Economics* 53(1):99–114.

Goldring, Ellen, and Rina Shapira. 1993. "Choice, Empowerment, and Involvement: What Satisfies Parents?" *Educational Evaluation and Policy Analysis* 15(4):396–409.

Gordon, Linda. 1994. *Pitied but Not Entitled: Single Mothers and the History of Welfare.* New York: Free Press.

Gottlieb, Jessica. 2014. "Greater Expectations: A Field Experiment to Improve Accountability in Mali." *American Journal of Political Science*, forthcoming.

————. 2015. "The Logic of Party Collusion in a Democracy: Evidence from Mali." *World Politics* 67(1):1–36.

Grandes orientations de la politique éducative: PRODEC. 2000. Bamako: Ministry of Education.

Grossman, Guy. 2015. "Renewalist Christianity and the Political Saliency of LGBTs: Theory and Evidence from Sub-Saharan Africa." *Journal of Politics*, forthcoming.

Guindo, Sidiki. 2012. "Résultats du sondage d'opinion sur la présidentielle de 2012." *L'Indépendant*, March 15.

Harding, Robin. 2012. "Democracy and the Provision of Rural Public Goods." PhD diss., New York University, Department of Politics.

Harding, Robin, and David Stasavage. 2014. "What Democracy Does (and Doesn't Do) for Basic Services: School Fees, School Inputs, and African Elections." *Journal of Politics* 76(1):229–245.

Harsch, Ernest. 2000. *Education in Africa: Schools Struggling in Crisis.* New York: Africa Recovery, Department of Public Information, United Nations.

Hefner, Robert, and Muhammad Qasim Zaman. 2007. *Schooling Islam: The Culture and Politics of Modern Muslim Education.* Princeton, NJ: Princeton University Press.

Hirschman, Albert. 1970. *Exit, Voice, and Loyalty.* Cambridge, MA: Harvard University Press.

Hirschmann, David. 1991. "Women and Political Participation in Africa: Broadening the Scope of Research." *World Development* 19(12):1679–1694.

Hobsbawm, Eric. 1990. *Nations and Nationalism Since 1780*. Cambridge: Cambridge University Press.

Holbrook, Allyson, and John Krosnick. 2009. "Social Desirability Bias in Voter Turnout Reports: Tests Using the Item Count Technique." http://comm.stanford.edu/faculty/krosnick/Turnout%20Overreporting%20-%20ICT%20Only%20-%20Final.pdf.

Hopkins, Nicholas. 1972. *Popular Government in an African Town*. Chicago: University of Chicago Press.

Huntington, Samuel. 1968. *Political Order in Changing Societies*. New Haven, CT: Yale University Press.

Hur, Mann Hyung. 2006. "Empowerment in Terms of Theoretical Perspectives: Exploring a Typology of the Process and Components Across Disciplines." *Journal of Community Psychology* 34(5):523–540.

Hydén, Göran. 2006. *African Politics in Comparative Perspective*. Cambridge: Cambridge University Press.

Idrissa, Abdourahmane. 2008. "The Invention of Order: Republican Codes and Islamic Law in Niger." PhD diss., University of Florida, Department of Political Science.

Ippolito-O'Donnell, Gabriela. 2006. "Political Clientelism and the Quality of Democracy." Paper presented at the International Political Science Association conference, July 9–13, Fukuoka, Japan.

Isaksson, Ann-Sofie. 2013. "Political Participation in Africa: The Role of Individual Resources." *Electoral Studies*, doi:10.1016/j.electstud.2013.09.008.

Isaksson, Ann-Sofie, Andreas Kotsadam, and Måns Nerman. 2014. "The Gender Gap in African Political Participation: Testing Theories of Individual and Contextual Determinants." *Journal of Development Studies* 50(2):302–318.

Ishiyama, John, and Krystal Fox. 2006. "What Affects the Strength of Partisan Identity in Sub-Saharan Africa?" *Politics and Policy* 34(4):748–773.

Jamal, Amaney. 2007. *Barriers to Democracy: The Other Side of Social Capital in Palestine and the Arab World*. Princeton, NJ: Princeton University Press.

Johnson, R. W. 1975. "Educational Progress and Retrogression in Guinea (1900–43)." In *Conflict and Harmony in Education in Tropical Africa*, ed. Godfrey Brown and Mervyn Hiskett. London: George Allen and Unwin.

Jourde, Cédric. 2005. "'The President Is Coming to Visit!': Dramas and the Hijack of Democratization in the Islamic Republic of Mauritania." *Comparative Politics* 37(4):421–440.

Kadzamira, Esme, and Pauline Rose. 2001. "Educational Policy Choice and Policy Practice in Malawi: Dilemmas and Disjunctures." Working Paper 124. Brighton, England: Institute of Development Studies.

Kamens, David. 1988. "Education and Democracy: A Comparative Institutional Analysis." *Sociology of Education* 61(2):114–127.

Kapiszewski, Diana, Lauren M. MacLean, and Benjamin L. Read. 2015. *Field Research in Political Science: Practices and Principles*. Cambridge: Cambridge University Press.

Keck, Margaret E., and Kathryn Sikkink. 1998. *Activists Beyond Borders: Advocacy Networks in International Politics*. Ithaca, NY: Cornell University Press.

Keefer, Philip, and Razvan Vlaicu. 2008. "Democracy, Credibility, and Clientelism." *Journal of Law, Economics, and Organization* 24(2):371–406.

Keister, J. 2011. "States Within States: How Rebels Rule." PhD thesis, University of California, San Diego, Department of Political Science.

Kendhammer, Brandon. 2013. "The Sharia Controversy in Northern Nigeria and the Politics of Islamic Law in New and Uncertain Democracies." *Comparative Politics* 45(3):291–311.

King, Gary, Robert Keohane, and Sidney Verba. 1994. *Designing Social Inquiry: Scientific Inference in Qualitative Research*. Princeton, NJ: Princeton University Press.

Koter, Dominka. 2013. "King-Makers: Local Leaders and Ethnic Politics in Africa." *World Politics* 65(2):187–232.

Kramon, Eric. 2010. "Vote-Buying and Political Behavior: Estimating and Explaining Vote-Buying's Effect on Turnout in Kenya." Paper presented at the Annual Meeting of the Midwest Political Science Association, September 2–5, Chicago.

Kramon, Eric, and Daniel N. Posner. 2013. "Who Benefits from Distributive Politics? How the Outcome One Studies Affects the Answer One Gets." *Perspectives on Politics* 11(2):461–474.

Krishna, Anirudh. 2002. *Active Social Capital: Tracing the Roots of Development and Democracy*. New York: Columbia University Press

Kuenzi, Michelle. 2006. "Nonformal Education, Political Participation, and Democracy: Findings from Senegal." *Political Behavior* 28(1):1–31.

Kuenzi, M., and G. Lambright. 2005. "Party Systems and Democratic Consolidation in Africa's Electoral Regimes." *Party Politics* 11:423–446.

———. 2011. "Who Votes in Africa? An Examination of Electoral Participation in 10 African Countries." *Party Politics* 17(6):767–799.

Künkler, Mirjam, and Julia Leininger. 2009. "The Multi-Faceted Role of Religious Actors in Democratization Processes: Empirical Evidence from Five Young Democracies." *Democratization* 16(6):1058–1092.

Kusch, Phillip. 2010. "Compulsory, but Meaningful Event." *Development and Cooperation* 2, http://www.dandc.eu/en/article/upsides-and-downsides-malis-local-government-elections-2009.

Laitin, David. 1977. *Politics, Language, and Thought*. Chicago: University of Chicago Press.

———. 1986. *Hegemony and Culture*. Chicago: University of Chicago Press.

———. 1992. *Language Repertoires and State Construction in Africa*. Cambridge: Cambridge University Press.

———. 1998. *Identity in Formation*. Ithaca, NY: Cornell University Press.

Landy, Marc. 1993. "Public Policy and Citizenship." In *Public Policy for Democracy*, ed. Helen Ingram and Steven Rathgeb Smith, 19–44. Washington, DC: Brookings Institution Press.

Lange, Marie-France, and Sékou Oumar Diarra. 1999. "Ecole et démocratie: L'explosion scolaire sous la IIe République du Mali." *Politique Africaine* 76:164–176.

Launay, Robert, and Benjamin Soares. 1999. "The Formation of an 'Islamic Sphere' in French Colonial West Africa." *Economy and Society* 28(4):497–519.

Leonard, David K., and Scott Straus. 2003. *Africa's Stalled Development: International Causes and Cures.* Boulder, CO: Lynne Rienner.

Lerner, Daniel. 1958. *The Passing of Traditional Society: Modernizing the Middle East.* New York: Free Press.

Lindberg, Staffan. 2006. *Democracy and Elections in Africa.* Baltimore, MD: Johns Hopkins University Press.

———. 2013. "Have the Cake and Eat It: The Rational Voter in Africa." *Party Politics* 19(6):945–961.

Lipset, Seymour Martin. 1959. "Democracy and Working-Class Authoritarianism." *American Sociological Review* 24(4):482–501.

Little, E., and C. Logan. 2008. "The Quality of Democracy and Governance in Africa: New Results from Afrobarometer Round 4." Afrobarometer Working Paper 108, www.afrobarometer.org.

Liu, Amy H., and Vanessa A. Baird. 2012. "Linguistic Recognition as a Source of Confidence in the Justice System." *Comparative Political Studies* 45(10):1203–1229.

Logan, Carolyn. 2008. "Rejecting the Disloyal Opposition? The Trust Gap in Mass Attitudes Toward Ruling and Opposition Parties in Africa." Afrobarometer Working Paper 94, www.afrobarometer.org.

———. 2010. "Citizens or Subjects? How Individuals Relate to the Local State in Democratizing Africa." Paper presented at the African Studies Association Annual Conference, San Francisco.

———. 2013. "The Roots of Resilience: Exploring Popular Support for African Traditional Authorities." *African Affairs* 112(448):353–376.

MacLean, Lauren. 2007. "The Micro Dynamics of Welfare State Retrenchment and the Implications for Citizenship in Africa." Paper presented at the Conference on the Micro-Foundations of Mass Politics in Africa, Michigan State University.

———. 2010. *Informal Institutions and Citizenship in Rural Africa: Risk and Reciprocity in Ghana and Côte d'Ivoire.* Cambridge: Cambridge University Press.

———. 2011. "State Retrenchment and the Exercise of Citizenship in Africa." *Comparative Political Studies* 44:1238–1246.

Magassa, Hamidou, and Stefan Meyer. 2008. "The Impact of Aid Policies on Domestic Democratisation Processes: The Case of Mali Donor Harmonisation: Between Effectiveness and Democratisation: Case Study IV." Brussels, Belgium: FRIDE Working Paper.

Mäkinen, Maarit, and Mary Wangu Kuira. 2008. "Social Media and Postelection Crisis in Kenya." *International Journal of Press/Politics* 13(3):328–335.

Mali Ministry of Education. 1993. "Portant organization du Diplome d'Etudes Fondamentales (DEF)," July 19, Arête 228, National Archives, III.1G.I323.

Mamdani, Mahmood. 1996. *Citizen and Subject: Contemporary Africa and the Legacy of Late Colonialism.* Princeton, NJ: Princeton University Press.

Manchuelle, François. 1997. *Willing Migrants: Soninke Labor Diasporas, 1948–1960.* Athens: Ohio University Press.

Marcus, R., and A. Ratsimbaharison. 2005. "Political Parties in Madagascar: Neopatrimonial Tools or Democratic Instruments?" *Party Politics* 11:495–512.

Mattes, Robert, and Dangalira Mughogho. 2009. "The Limited Impacts of Formal Education on Democratic Citizenship in Africa." Afrobarometer Working Paper 109, www.afrobarometer.org.

Mattes, Robert, and Carlos Shenga. 2007. " 'Uncritical Citizenship' in a 'Low-Information' Society: Mozambicans in Comparative Perspective." Afrobarometer Working Paper 138, http://www.afrobarometer.org.

McAdam, Doug. l982. *Political Process and the Development of Black Insurgency, 1930–1970.* Chicago: University of Chicago Press.

McCauley, John F. 2013. "Africa's New Big Man Rule? Pentecostalism and Patronage in Ghana." *African Affairs* 112(446):1–21.

McCauley, John, and E. Gyimah-Boadi. 2009. "Evidence from the Afrobarometer Surveys." Afrobarometer Working Paper 113, www.afrobarometer.org.

McKie, Kristin. 2012. "Reining in the Big Men: The Politics of Executive Constraints Across Sub-Saharan Africa." PhD diss., Cornell University, Department of Government.

Meillassoux, Claude. 1970. "A Class Analysis of the Bureaucratic Process in Mali." *Journal of Development Studies* 6(2):97–110.

Mettler, Suzanne. 2005. *Soldiers to Citizens: The G.I. Bill and the Making of the Greatest Generation.* Oxford: Oxford University Press.

Mettler, Suzanne, and Joseph Soss. 2004. "The Consequences of Public Policy for Democratic Citizenship: Bridging Policy Studies and Mass Politics." *Perspectives on Politics* 2(1):55–73.

Mettler, Suzanne, and Jeffrey Stonecash. 2008. "Government Program Usage and Political Voice." *Social Science Quarterly* 89(2):273–293.

Moehler, Devra. 2006. "Participation and Support for the Constitution in Uganda." *Journal of Modern African Studies* 44(2):275–308.

———. 2008. *Distrusting Democrats: Outcomes of Participatory Constitution-Making.* Ann Arbor: University of Michigan Press.

Moehler, Devra C., and Staffan Lindberg. 2009. "Narrowing the Legitimacy Gap: Turnovers as a Cause of Democratic Consolidation." *Journal of Politics* 71(4):1448–1466.

Moehler, Devra C., and Naunihal Singh. 2011. "Whose News Do You Trust? Explaining Trust in Private versus Public Media in Africa." *Political Research Quarterly* 64(2):276–292.

Moore, Mick. 2004. "Revenues, State Formation, and the Quality of Governance in Developing Countries." *International Political Science Review* 25(3):297–319.

Morgan, David L. 1996. "Focus Groups." *Annual Review of Sociology* 32:129–152.

Moulaye, Zeïni, and Amadou Keïta. 2007. *L'Assemblée nationale du Mali sous la troisième république: Un guide à l'usage des élus, des citoyens et des partenaires extérieurs.* Bamako: Friedrich-Ebert-Stiftung.

Moussa, Laouali Malam, et al. 2007. "A Synthesis of Studies of Madrassas and Other

Quranic Schooling Centres in Gambia, Mali, Niger and Sénégal." Unpublished paper, Réseau Ouest et Centre Africain de Recherche en Education.

Mozaffar, Shaheen. 1999. "Mali." In *Elections in Africa: A Data Handbook*, ed. Dieter Nohlern, Michael Krennerich, and Bernard Thibaut, 567–584. Oxford: Oxford University Press.

Mozaffar, Shaheen, James R. Scarritt, and Glen Galaich. 2003. "Electoral Institutions, Ethnopolitical Cleavages, and Party Systems in Africa's Emerging Democracies." *American Political Science Review* 97(3):379–390.

Nie, Norman, Jane Junn, and Kenneth Stehlik-Barry. 1996. *Education and Democratic Citizenship in America*. Chicago: University of Chicago Press.

Neuman, W. Russell, Marion R. Just, and Ann N. Crigler. 1992. *Common Knowledge: News and the Construction of Political Meaning*. Chicago: University of Chicago Press.

Norris, Pippa. 1999. *Critical Citizens: Global Support for Democratic Government*. Oxford: Oxford University Press.

———. 2012. *Making Democratic Governance Work: How Regimes Shape Prosperity, Welfare, and Peace*. Cambridge: Cambridge University Press.

Obichere, Boniface. 1979. "Politicians and Educational Reform in French-Speaking West Africa: A Comparative Study of Mali and the Ivory Coast." In *Education and Politics in Tropical Africa*, ed. Victor Uchendu, 196–210. London: Conch Magazine.

O'Donnell, Guillermo. 2004. "Human Development, Human Rights, and Democracy." In *The Quality of Democracy: Theory and Applications*, ed. Guillermo O'Donnell, Jorge Vargas Cullell, and Osvaldo M. Iazzetta, 9–92. Notre Dame, IN: University of Notre Dame Press.

———. 2010. *Democracy, Agency, and the State*. Oxford: Oxford University Press.

Ouedrago, B. 2008. "Le Système éducatif Malien." Cours Education Comparé (Exposition de Groupe 1). Bamako: University of Bamako

Pande, Rohini. 2011. "Can Informed Voters Enforce Better Governance? Experiments in Low-Income Democracies." *Annual Review of Economics* 3:215–237.

Parke, Ross, and Raymond Buriel. 2006. "Socialization in the Family: Ethnic and Ecological Perspectives." In *Handbook of Child Psychology: Social, Emotional, and Personality Development*, vol. 3, ed. William Damon, Richard M. Lerner, and Nancy Eisenberg, 429–504. Hoboken, NJ: Wiley.

Pearce, Caroline, Sebastién Fourmy, and Hetty Kovach. 2009. *Delivering Education for All in Mali*. N.p.: Oxfam.

Pepinsky, Thomas B., and Bozena C. Welborne. 2010. "Piety and Redistributive Preferences in the Muslim World." *Political Research Quarterly* 64(3):491–505.

Pew Survey. 2010. "Public Knows Basic Facts about Politics, Economics, but Struggles with Specifics," http://www.people-press.org/2010/11/18/public-knows-basic-facts-about-politics-economics-but-struggles-with-specifics.

———. 2012. "The World's Muslims: Unity and Diversity," http://www.pewforum.org/2012/08/09/the-worlds-muslims-unity-and-diversity-executive-summary.

Piaget, Jean. 1985. *The Equilibration of Cognitive Structures: The Central Problem of Intellectual Development*. Chicago: University of Chicago Press.

Pierson, Paul. 1993. "When Effect Becomes Cause: Policy Feedback and Political Change." *World Politics* 45(4):595–628.

Pollock, Phillip. 1983. "The Participatory Consequences of Internal and External Efficacy: A Research Note." *Western Political Quarterly* 36:401–409.

Posner, Daniel N. 2004. "Measuring Ethnic Fractionalization in Africa." *American Journal of Political Science* 48(4):849–863.

———. 2005. *Institutions and Ethnic Politics in Africa*. Cambridge: Cambridge University Press.

Prater, David. 2010. "Improving the Position of Women in Malian Political Parties." *Netherlands Institute for Multiparty Democracy*, July 9, http://www.nimd.org/news /2024/improving-the-position-of-women-in-malian-political-parties.

Pringle, Robert. 2005. *Democratization in Mali: Putting History to Work*. Washington, DC: United States Institute of Peace.

Przeworski, Adam. 2008. *Self-Government in Our Times*. Florence, Italy: European University Institute.

Resnick, Danielle. 2010. "Opposition Parties and Populist Strategies: Mobilizing the Urban Poor in African Democracies." PhD diss., Cornell University.

Resnick, Danielle, and Nicolas van de Walle, eds. 2013. *Democratic Trajectories in Africa: Unravelling the Impact of Foreign Aid*. Oxford: Oxford University Press.

Riedl, Rachel Beatty. 2012. "Transforming Politics, Dynamic Religion: Religion's Political Impact in Contemporary Africa." *African Conflict and Peacebuilding Review* 2(2):29–50.

———. 2014. *Authoritarian Origins of Democratic Party Systems in Africa*. Cambridge: Cambridge University Press.

Rose, Pauline. 2006. "Collaborating in Education for All? Experiences of Government Support for Non-State Provision of Basic Education in South Asia and Sub-Saharan Africa." *Public Administration and Development* 26:219–229.

Rose, Pauline, and Kwame Akyeampong. 2005. "The Non-State Sector and Education: Literature Review and Four Country Study." Unpublished paper, Centre for International Education, University of Sussex.

Rose, Richard, Doh C. Shin, and Neil Munro. 1999. "Tensions Between the Democratic Ideal and Reality: South Korea." In *Critical Citizens: Global Support for Democratic Government*, ed. Pippa Norris, 154–164. Oxford: Oxford University Press.

Rosenstone, Steven J., and John Mark Hansen. 1993. *Mobilization, Participation, and Democracy in America*. New York: Macmillan.

Saad, Elias N. 1983. *Social History of Timbuktu: The Role of Muslim Scholars and Notables, 1400–1900*. Cambridge: Cambridge University Press.

Sabatier, Peggy. 1978. "'Elite' Education in French West Africa: The Era of Limits, 1903–1945." *International Journal of African Historical Studies* 11(2):247–266.

Sanankoua, Bintou, and Louis Brenner, eds. 1991. *L'Enseignement Islamique au Mali*. Bamako: Jamana.

Sanankoua, Diarah Bintou. 1985. "Les écoles 'Coraniques' au Mali: Problèmes actuels." *Canadian Journal of African Studies* 19(2):359–367.

Schaffer, Frederic. 2000. *Democracy in Translation: Understanding Politics in an Unfamiliar Culture*. Ithaca, NY: Cornell University Press.

Schlozman, Kay, et al. 1993. "Citizen Activity: Who Participates? What Do They Say?" *American Political Science Review* 87:303–319.

Schulz, Dorothea. 2008. "(Re)Turning to Proper Muslim Practice: Islamic Moral Renewal and Women's Conflicting Assertions of Sunni Identity in Urban Mali." *Africa Today* 54(4):21–43.

Scieszka, Casey, and Steven Weinberg. 2011. "Timbuktu Kidnappings Hurt Mali Tourism." *Global Post*, December 14, n.p.

Scott, James. 1998. *Seeing Like a State: How Certain Schemes to Improve the Human Condition Have Failed*. New Haven, CT: Yale University Press.

Sears, Jonathan. 2007. "Deepening Democracy and Cultural Context in the Republic of Mali, 1992–2002." PhD diss., Queen's University, Department of Political Science.

Sen, Amartya. 1999. *Development as Freedom*. New York: Oxford University Press.

Seymour, Lee. 2008. "Pathways to Secession: Mapping the Institutional Effect of Secessionist Violence." PhD diss., Northwestern University, Department of Political Science.

Shingles, Richard D. 1981. "Black Consciousness and Political Participation: The Missing Link." *American Political Science Review* 75(1):76–91.

Skinner, Ryan. 2012. "Cultural Politics in the Post-Colony: Music, Nationalism and Statism in Mali, 1964–75." *Africa: The Journal of the International African Institute* 82(4):511–534.

Slater, Daniel. 2013. "Democratic Careening." *World Politics* 65(4):729–763.

Smith, Zeric Kay. 1997. " 'From Demons to Democrats': Mali's Student Movement 1991–1996." *Review of African Political Economy* 24(72):249–263.

———. 2001. "Mali's Decade of Democracy." *Journal of Democracy* 12(3):73–79.

Snyder, Richard. 2001. "Scaling Down: The Subnational Comparative Method." *Studies in Comparative International Development* 36(1):93–110.

Soares, Benjamin. 2004. "Islam and Public Piety in Mali." In *Public Islam and the Common Good*, ed. Armando Salvatore and Dale F. Eickelman, 205–226. Leiden: Brill.

———. 2005. *Islam and the Prayer Economy: History and Authority in a Malian Town*. Ann Arbor: University of Michigan Press.

———. 2006. "Islam in Mali in the Neo-Liberal Era." *African Affairs* 105:77–95.

———. 2012. "Islam in Mali since the 2012 Coup." *Cultural Anthropology*, http://www.culanth.org/fieldsights/321-islam-in-mali-since-the-2012-coup.

Somit, Albert, and Stephen Peterson. 1987. "Political Socialization's Primacy Principle: A Biosocial Critique." *International Political Science Review* 8(3):205–213.

Soss, Joseph. 1999. "Lessons of Welfare: Policy Design, Political Learning, and Political Action." *American Political Science Review* 363–380.

———. 2002. *Unwanted Claims: The Politics of Participation in the U.S. Welfare System*. Ann Arbor: University of Michigan Press.

Soss, Joseph, and Sanford F. Schram. 2007. "A Public Transformed? Welfare Reform as Policy Feedback." *American Political Science Review* 101(1):111.

Stasavage, David. 2005. "Democracy and Education Spending in Africa." *American Journal of Political Science* 49(2):343–358.

"Summary of Results: Round 3 Afrobarometer Survey in Mali." 2005. Compiled by Michigan State University, www.afrobarometer.org.

Thachil, Tariq. 2011. "Embedded Mobilization." *World Politics* 63(3):434–469.

Thiongʼo, Ngũgĩ wa. 1985. "The Language of African Literature." *New Left Review* (March–April):150.

Thunnissen, Karolyn. 2009. *Sector Study Support in Practice: Case Study, Mali.* London: Overseas Development Institute and Mokoro.

Tilly, Charles. 2007. *Democracy.* Cambridge: Cambridge University Press.

Tilly, Charles, and Sidney Tarrow. 2006. *Contentious Politics.* Boulder, CO: Paradigm.

Tower, Craig. 2008. "Radio Ways: Society, Locality, and FM Technology in Koutiala, Mali." PhD diss., Northwestern University, Department of Anthropology.

Tripp, Aili Mari. 2001. "The Politics of Autonomy and Cooptation in Africa: The Case of the Ugandan Women's Movement." *Journal of Modern African Studies* 39(1): 101–128.

Uchendo, Victor. 1979. *Education and Politics in Tropical Africa.* London: Conch Magazine.

Umar, M. Sani. 2009. "Islam and the Public Sphere in Africa: Overcoming the Dichotomies." Working Paper 09-00. Evanston, IL: Institute for the Study of Islamic Thought in Africa, Buffet Center, Northwestern University.

UNESCO Institute of Statistics. 2011. *Financing Education in Sub-Saharan Africa: Meeting the Challenges of Expansion, Equity, and Quality.* Montreal: UNESCO Institute of Statistics.

"USAID Meeting EFA Targets: Mali Case Study." 2006. http://www.equip123.net/docs /e2-MaliCaseStudy.pdf.

van de Walle, Nicolas. 2001. *African Economies and the Politics of Permanent Crisis.* Cambridge: Cambridge University Press.

———. 2007. "The Path from Neopatrimonialism: Democracy and Clientelism in Africa Today." Working Paper Series. Ithaca, NY: Mario Einaudi Center for International Studies, Cornell University.

Vasquez, Olga, Lucinda Pease-Alvarez, and Sheila M. Shannon. 1994. *Pushing Boundaries.* New York: Cambridge University Press.

Verba, Sidney, Kay Schlozman, and Henry Brady. 1995. *Voice and Equality: Civic Voluntarism in American Politics.* Cambridge, MA: Harvard University Press.

Vicente, Pedro C. 2013. "Is Vote-Buying Effective? Evidence from a Field Experiment in West Africa." *Economic Journal* 124(574):F356–F387.

Villalón, Leonardo A. 1995. *Islamic Society and State Power in Senegal.* Cambridge: Cambridge University Press.

———. 2010. "From Argument to Negotiation: Constructing Democracy in African Muslim Contexts." *Comparative Politics* 42(4).

———. 2012. "Rethinking Education in the Sahel: Democracy, Religious Change, and the Politics of Reform." In *Societal Transformations and the Challenges of Gov-*

ernance in Africa and the Middle East, ed. Stephen Ndegwa and Ellen-Lust Okar. Boulder, CO: Lynne Rienner.

Villalón, Leonardo, and Abdourahamane Idrissa. 2005. "The Tribulations of a Successful Transition: Institutional Dynamics and Elite Rivalry in Mali." In *The Fate of Africa's Democratic Experiments: Elites and Instituions*, ed. Leonardo A. Villalón and Peter von Doepp. Bloomington: Indiana University Press.

Villalón, L. A., A. Idrissa, and M. Bodian. 2012. *Religion, demande sociale, et reformes éducatifs au Mali: Quand les acteurs sociaux poussent l'état à encadrer la transition des médersas arabo-islamiques au system franco-arabe*. http://www.institutions-africa.org/page/religious-education.

VonDoepp, Peter. 2002. "Malawi's Local Clergy as Civil Society Activists? The Limiting Impact of Creed, Context and Class." *Commonwealth and Comparative Politics* 40(2):21–46.

Warren, Mark. 2006. "Democracy and Deceit: Regulating Appearances of Corruption." *American Journal of Political Science* 50(1):160–174.

Weber, Eugene. 1976. *Peasants into Frenchmen*. Stanford, CA: Stanford University Press.

Weghorst, Keith, and Eric J. Kramon. 2012. "Reducing Response Bias in Developing Countries: Improving List Experiment Performance for Measuring Vote-Buying and Political Violence." Unpublished paper in author's possession.

Weghorst, Keith R., and Staffan I. Lindberg. 2013. "What Drives the Swing Voter in Africa?" *American Journal of Political Science* 57(3):717–734.

Weinstein, Jeremy. 2007. *Inside Rebellion*. Cambridge: Cambridge University Press.

Weisskirch, Robert, and Sylvia Alva. 2002. "Language Brokering and the Acculturation of Latino Children." *Hispanic Journal of Behavioral Sciences* 24(3):369–378.

Whitehouse, Bruce. 2012. "The Force of Action: Legitimizing the Coup in Bamako, Mali." *Africa Spectrum* 47(2–3):93–110.

———. 2013. "'A Festival of Brigands': In Search of Democracy and Political Legitimacy in Mali." *Strategic Review for Southern Africa* 35(2):35–52.

Wickham, Carrie Rosefsky. 2002. *Mobilizing Islam*. New York: Columbia University Press.

Wing, Susanna. 2008. *Constructing Democracy in Transitioning Societies of Africa: Constitution and Deliberation in Mali*. New York: Palgrave Macmillan.

———. 2012. "Women's Rights and Family Law Reform in Francophone Africa." In *Societal Transformations and the Challenges of Governance in Africa and the Middle East*, ed. Stephen Ndegwa and Ellen-Lust Okar. Boulder, CO: Lynne Rienner.

Wolf, Patrick J., and Stephen Macedo, eds. 2004. *Educating Citizens: International Perspectives on Civic Values and School Choice*. Washington, DC: Brookings Institution Press.

World Bank. 2008. *Education Statistics*, http://data.worldbank.org/data-catalog/ed-stats.

Young, Crawford. 1994. *The African Colonial State in Comparative Perspective*. New Haven, CT: Yale University Press.

———. 2012. *The Postcolonial State in Africa*. Madison: University of Wisconsin Press.

Young, Daniel. 2009. "Is Clientelism at Work in African Elections? A Study of Voting Behavior in Kenya and Zambia." Afrobarometer Working Paper 106, www.afro barometer.org.

Zucco, Cesar. 2011. "Conditional Cash Transfers and Voting Behavior: Redistribution and Clientelism in Developing Democracies." Unpublished paper in author's possession.

www.ingramcontent.com/pod-product-compliance
Lightning Source LLC
Chambersburg PA
CBHW050644280326
41932CB00015B/2773